GENTLEMEN AND SCHOLARS

W. Bruce Leslie

GENTLEMEN AND SCHOLARS

College and Community in the "Age of the University," 1865–1917

The Pennsylvania State University Press
University Park, Pennsylvania

Library of Congress Cataloging-in-Publication Data

Leslie, William Bruce.
Gentlemen and scholars : college and community in the "Age of the University," 1865–1917 / W. Bruce Leslie.
p. cm.
Includes bibliographical references (p.) and index.
ISBN 0-271-00829-6 (alk. paper)
1. Private universities and colleges—United States—History—19th century—Case studies. 2. Private universities and colleges—United States—History—20th century—Case studies. 3. Education, Higher—Social aspects—United States—History—19th century—Case studies. 4. Education, Higher—Social aspects—United States—History—20th century—Case studies. I. Title.
LB2329.U6L48 1992
378.73—dc20 91–30514
CIP

Printed in the United States of America

It is the policy of The Pennsylvania State University Press to use acid-free paper for the first printing of all clothbound books. Publications on uncoated stock satisfy the minimum requirements of American National Standard for Information Sciences—Permanence of Paper for Printed Library Materials, ANSI Z39.48–1984.

This is also Nancy Acton Leslie's book.

Contents

List of Illustrations

List of Tables

Preface

With American power in relative decline, debates over the meaning of the American experience assume new urgency. Those looking for "American exceptionalism" can scarcely find a better example than its colleges. They are remarkably visible institutions. Bumper stickers, window decals, and T-shirts proclaim college loyalties. Prominent highway signs directing motorists to campuses are testimony that colleges are places of public interest. Gaining admission to and paying for college is a primary concern of most upper middle-class American families. Colleges are also conspicuous in popular culture. Campuses have been a favorite Hollywood setting since the 1920s. Millions watch college football and basketball teams perform rites complete with popularly recognized anthems and totems. College football bowl games and parades are the center of attention on New Year's Day. Many who have never attended a college feel pride in the athletic, architectural, or academic prowess of "their" college or university.

The cultural prominence of American higher education is unparalleled. By contrast, the British institutions that spawned the first American colleges are relatively invisible to the public. Except for an annual boat race, even Oxford and Cambridge receive little public exposure and remain obscured in mystique. Higher education, remote to most Europeans, feels familiar to most Americans.

The visibility of American colleges reflects the reality that middle-class American youths come of age differently from their counterparts in other industrialized countries. Whereas the average European youth leaves school by the age of seventeen, almost half of American youths go on to higher education, and about one-third of twenty- and twenty-one-year-olds are still enrolled. UNESCO figures show nearly twice as many "college-age" youths attending the "third level of education" in the United States than in any European country.

The visibility and accessibility of American colleges play an important ideological role. Secondary and higher education has been promoted as an antidote to radical reform of the distribution of power and wealth. The myth that accessible education combined with private enterprise guarantees equal opportunity dates back to the writings of Horace Mann. Successive social groups seeking access to the "American dream" have applied Mann's formulation beyond the "common school," leading them either to seek access to existing colleges or to create their own. Visible and accessible colleges have been an important ingredient in the American middle-class consensus that "the system works" for them and will continue to work for their children.

The history of higher education offers particularly fruitful social insights in the United States. In Europe the relatively small number of institutions of higher education were shaped primarily by central governments for national purposes. In contrast there was little federal support for American higher education until the mid-twentieth century. Competition among local, regional, racial, gender, and ethnoreligious groups led to the founding of thousands of colleges across the United States. Americans created a unique institution based on the intellectual tradition of the European university but with a significantly different institutional structure. Within decades of independence, colleges dotted the young republic and attracted children of the elite as well as a surprising number of young Americans from farming and small-business families. Financial sponsorship was inspired primarily by localism or ethnoreligious affinity.

After the Civil War, urbanization and industrialization created forces that challenged the local and denominational groups that had founded the colleges. The late nineteenth century witnessed dramatic changes at all levels of American education that reflected the competing visions and ambitions of many Americans. By World War I a clearly articulated educational system was established in which colleges played a prominent part and research universities were the capstone.

More than two decades ago, when I first became interested in the history of American higher education, the canon of the field told a triumphant story of enlightened educational reformers overcoming entrenched conservatives between the Civil War and World War I. The traditional college was portrayed as an obstacle to progress, and the research university was the jewel in the reformers' crowns. But at a time when the "military-industrial-university complex" was wreaking havoc in Southeast Asia, all powerful institutions seemed suspect; the university had become the locus of powerful forces rather than an island of rationality. I began to question a history that focused upon the university and ignored the "losers" and the roads not taken. If community and small institutions were being lost in modern America, might the triumph of the university have been part of the impersonalization, and the defeat of traditional colleges part of the loss? That story took on immediate significance. While the urgency of twenty years ago has faded, fears about the states of education and community in the United States remain. It is an intriguing American saga.

Acknowledgments

For most college teachers, research and writing occur in stolen moments, and projects stretch out for years. Publication of a work started as a dissertation written in youth too often becomes a middle-age rite of passage. This is no exception. Such long gestation is frustrating and conjures up uncomfortable thoughts of mortality, but it also has benefits. Author and discipline have a chance to mature. Over two decades many of the puzzles that stumped me as a graduate student have been addressed. In particular, the once "new" social history produced methods, information, and conceptual frameworks that unlocked some mysteries and offered plausible answers to others.

This book explores the relationship between American society and its colleges. The medium has been the message. My experience in writing it has been a personal saga of college life. As an undergraduate at Princeton University, I was privileged to experience the intellectual and social community that a college, at its best, can provide. As a doctoral student at Johns Hopkins University, the first American research university, I was exposed to the very different ethos of graduate school and professional training in a discipline. While I tried to develop the historical skills demanded for university research, dormitories and lacrosse fields near the library reminded me of collegiate life. Finally, as a professional, for two decades I have participated in the struggle of a state college to find an identity that is true to the ideals of mass higher education as well as older collegiate traditions.

The origins of this project can be traced back to a swimming pool in the summer of 1964, where I was working as a lifeguard for a former high school social studies teacher, Robert Searles. When I shared with him my lack of a topic for my junior paper at Princeton, he suggested the history of education. Donald G. Mathews kindly directed the paper in a field outside his specialty. That venture led me to Johns Hopkins University, where the late John Walton had the vision to bring graduate students from various disciplines together to apply their tools to the study of education. Timothy L. Smith directed my dissertation, giving me the benefit of his unique view of American history and his pioneering methodological and interpretive achievements.

Working on this project for nearly a quarter of a century, I have compiled numerous debts that I take joy in finally acknowledging. At Johns Hopkins, Charles Biebel contributed personal and intellectual support in difficult times. Two seminar colleagues and friends, Elizabeth Ross and George Woytanowitz, read my initial efforts and shared the anxieties and discoveries that accompany writing a dissertation.

I came to the State University of New York College at Brockport thanks to the faith of George C. Simmons and the late Sig Synnestvedt in interdisciplinary work. George Simmons has inspired me with his love of scholarship and his humanity. I have been lucky to be part of an exceptionally supportive department. John Ingham and Steve Ireland introduced me to the wonders of the "new" social history and gave me faith in the value of my scholarly work at a critical stage. John Ingham, now at the University of Toronto, has uncomplainingly read and reread this work in its various reincarnations. Ken O'Brien has offered support as friend, colleague, and chairman on many occasions, most memorably by doctoring my ailing computer late one hot summer evening. Brenda Peake has spent parts of many summers typing different versions of this work with extraordinary skill and good cheer. I also thank my other departmental colleagues, with whom I have shared the successes and frustrations of mass higher education over two decades. Mark Anderson has frequently crossed the disciplinary divide from English to prod me into reconsidering the canon of my field.

As Harold Wechsler recently commented over Indian food, one advantage of the history of higher education is that people only study it if they are committed to the field and to scholarship as a shared venture. The subspecialty may have a low profile, but the sense of community is high. Harold has generously given his time and thoughts to me. David Potts has encouraged me for twenty years, repeatedly giving me encouragement and insights. Colin Burke, Louise Stevenson, Frank Stricker, and Ira Read have unselfishly shared their work and ideas with me. I also want to thank two anonymous readers for Penn State Press who saw merit in the manuscript and offered ways to improve it. It is conventional to accept the blame for all shortcomings and absolve all others of guilt. But it seems more useful to say that this book profited immensely from the generosity of others, and that it shares the strengths and weaknesses of the way our generation has tried to understand the evolution of American society.

I have accumulated debts to several generations of archivists at a number of institutions. I was assisted in the Bucknell University Archives by Ann Mumper and Doris Dysinger. Dorothy Neprash and Charlotte B. Brown led me to materials in the Franklin and Marshall College Archives. At Princeton the late Halsey Thomas, Alexander Clark, Francis J. Dallett, Earle E. Coleman, and Nanci A. Young have guided me through the Princeton University Archives and Manuscript Collection. At the Friends Historical Library at Swarthmore I was helped by the late Frederick Tolles, Robert W. Fowler, and Mary Ellen Chijioke. Former Swarthmore President Robert Cross offered assistance to a fellow historian at a difficult moment.

I am also indebted to the staffs of the American Baptist Historical Society (Rochester), the Colindale Newspaper Library (London), the Enoch Pratt Free Library (Baltimore), the Historical Society of the United Church of Christ (Lancaster), the Lancaster County Historical Society, the Library of Congress, the Milton S. Eisenhower Library of Johns Hopkins University, the New College Library (Edinburgh), the Presbyterian Historical Society (Philadelphia), the Public Records Office (London), and the Rush Rhees Library at the University of Rochester.

A National Defense Education Act Fellowship financed the first year of work on the dissertation, and a Johns Hopkins University Fellowship underwrote the second. A State University of New York Research Foundation grant helped finance my research on James McCosh. The State University of New York College at Brockport has provided a number of valuable resources. In particular, Robert Gilliam has performed interlibrary miracles, bringing rare sources to a small upstate New York college. My appreciation also goes to the outstanding staff of the Drake Memorial Library, who have provided exceptional service over many years.

Harold Wechsler, editor of the *History of Higher Education Annual*, has graciously given permission to use material from my 1990 article, "When Professors Had Servants: Prestige, Pay, and Professionalization, 1860–1917." Some of the material in this work has appeared in the *History of Education Quarterly, Pennsylvania History, Liberal Education*, and the *Journal of Sport History*.

Sanford G. Thatcher and Peter J. Potter, and other members of Penn State Press, have been models of the integrity and scholarly support that make university presses such an important part of the academic world.

My only regrets about this book are personal. I wish that my parents, William and Annette R. Leslie, had lived to see this product of the education for which they sacrificed so much. I do hope, however, that my stepmother, Dorothy K. Leslie, enjoys this as part of her voracious reading program. I also regret the amount of time my work stole from family life. An earlier draft was completed in an office cum nursery shared with my son Andrew. The final project took long enough for him to help me compile the statistics in Chapters 3 and 7. My daughter Sarah was born as I started reshaping the work into its next phase. In that time she has grown up into a young woman with her own interest in history. Finally, Nancy A. Leslie shared this project with me for nearly a quarter-century. Her belief in scholarship and her contributions to the life of a college have inspired me. I thank her for her sacrifices and dedicate this book to her.

Introduction

"It is, Sir, as I have said, a small College. And yet, *there are those who love it*."[1] Daniel Webster's sentimental defense of Dartmouth College before the Supreme Court contained an essential truth. Nineteenth-century American colleges were valued vehicles of prestige for many communities, and of identity for ethnoreligious groups, classes, and the genders. Struggles to control the destinies of colleges reflected important social and cultural divides. Americans increasingly turned to colleges to perpetuate their cultural values and social position in the next generation.

The social role of the American college has received relatively little attention from historians, especially for the period between the Civil War and World War I. This book argues that colleges of the period were at the intersection of powerful social forces and emerged as one of the winners in the resulting changes. Colleges began the period as agents of ethnoreligious subcultures and local boosterism. The rapid growth of industrial wealth and the white-collar professional and business class, however, produced students and donors with different worldviews. The resulting conflicts challenged the traditions of many colleges while fueling their ambitions.

By World War I the most materially successful colleges catered to the urban Protestant upper and upper-middle classes, drawing on their new wealth to build their institutions. These colleges successfully positioned themselves on the path to the most desirable professional positions; gentlemen had to be scholars too. Urban wealth, Protestant

1. Richard Hofstadter and Wilson Smith, *American Higher Education: A Documentary History* (Chicago: University of Chicago Press, 1961), 1:212.

culture, and collegiate ambitions combined to create institutions indebted to colonial traditions and university innovations, but with a unique role shaped by dramatic social, economic, cultural, and educational changes under way at the turn of the century. By 1917 a small number of private colleges had forged a model that continues to influence American higher education and society.

Scholarship on higher education between the Civil War and World War I emphasizes newly founded universities and the few colleges that added large professional and graduate schools and became universities. But the overwhelming majority of institutions remained colleges, and even the lives of most undergraduates in universities remained "collegiate" in many senses of the word. Disproportionate attention to a few institutions has distorted our understanding of the forces that shaped American higher education.

For several decades most historians depicted colleges of the period as sectarian institutions that obstructed progress until being swept away by the refreshing winds of the "academic revolution." Quite the reverse of Webster's loving imagery, colleges were portrayed as isolated and unpopular institutions. This version of history portrayed post–Civil War benefactors and reformers meeting a pent-up demand for practical, democratic institutions capable of responding to the economic needs of a modernizing society. Only racial, ethnoreligious, and gender discrimination flawed the triumph.

The fate of colleges during this "age of the university" was left in a historical vacuum. Even Laurence Veysey's masterful work, *The Emergence of the American University*, maintains that "the only course of action which these men could urge was to hold on, perhaps making minor concessions, and hope that their institutions would be able to survive."[2] The lack of explicit coverage left the impression that most colleges continued in the path of their antebellum predecessors, slowly surrendering to university reforms and barely surviving into the twentieth century. Colleges were not given a distinct role again until histories reached the 1920s.

This interpretation developed in the 1950s and early 1960s, a time of severe criticism of higher education. Conservative critics like Wil-

2. Laurence R. Veysey, *The Emergence of the American University* (Chicago: University of Chicago Press, 1965), 9.

liam Buckley defended traditional colleges and attacked the academic revolution for supposedly undermining religion, patriotism, and laissez-faire.[3] To academics defending their professional world against McCarthyism and other enemies of academia, the image of the "old-time college" became a negative backdrop against which "progress" could be measured. In this atmosphere a history that promoted the modern academic profession and the research university was articulately crafted by historians, particularly Richard Hofstadter, who molded it into an attractive paradigm of the history of American higher education.[4]

In addition to defending mainstream academia, Hofstadter and others raised the history of higher education to academic respectability. They chronicled the meteoric success of research universities, detailing the rise of academic freedom, Germanic scholarship, curricular reforms, academic disciplines, professional organizations, and the new student culture in highly literate, professional works. The history of higher education was transformed from an arcane avocation of elderly faculty into a professional inquiry. Unlike the traditional antiquarian college "house histories,"[5] the new works fit the history of higher education into the dominant theoretical model of 1950s history: functionalist modernization. The academic revolution was explained in terms of differentiation of function, specialization, and bureaucratization. The university's role in promoting intellectual progress and social change without major conflict placed higher education neatly within the dominant "consensus history" that functionalism encouraged. Publication of Veysey's *Emergence of the Amer-*

3. William Buckley, *God and Man at Yale* (Chicago: Henry Regner, 1951).

4. Hofstadter's approach was disseminated in three jointly written books: Richard Hofstadter and C. DeWitt Hardy, *The Development and Scope of Higher Education in the United States* (New York: Columbia University Press, 1952); Hofstadter and Walter Metzger, *The Development of Academic Freedom in the United States* (New York: Columbia University Press, 1955); and Hofstadter and Smith, *American Higher Education: A Documentary History*. The two main surveys of the history of American higher education share this perspective: Frederick Rudolph, *The American College and University* (New York: Vintage Books, 1962); and John S. Brubacher and Willis Rudy, *Higher Education in Transition*, 2d ed. (New York: Harper & Row, 1968).

5. However, the "house histories" can be valuable. For insights into their utility, see Richard Angelo, "A House Is Not a Home," *History of Education Quarterly* 24 (Winter 1984); and John Goodchild and Irene Huk, "The American College History," in John Smart, ed., *Higher Education: Handbook of Theory and Research*, vol. 6 (New York: Agathon Press, 1990).

ican University in 1965 raised "the age of the university" literature to a new level and showed how far the history of higher education had come since Buckley wrote *God and Man at Yale*.[6]

Over two decades later the interpretive framework perfected by Veysey still dominates the vision of historians and academic policymakers. Its persistence in nonspecialist historical literature is illustrated by Lewis Perry's depiction of late nineteenth-century colleges in his highly respected survey of American intellectual history: "While most of the old religiously oriented colleges and seminaries endured in increasing isolation and obscurity, a few raised new funds, discarded the traditional lockstep curriculum, created new departments and specialized schools, and attracted larger faculties and student bodies."[7] The best-selling American history textbook, *The American Nation*, depicts colleges as irrelevant institutions teaching little but classical languages.[8]

The paradigm also continues to dominate the historical understanding of policymakers in American higher education. A poll of leaders in American higher education by *Change* magazine in the mid-1980s asked them to name the "best book [they] ever read about higher education." The result was a tie between Veysey's *Emergence of the American University* and Christopher Jencks and David Reisman's *Academic Revolution*, a sociological analysis of American higher education crafted within the same historical framework. Both chronicle the academic revolution brilliantly and deserve the plaudit, but they

6. Veysey's use of irony and conflict posed implicit criticisms of the academic order that tested the outer limits of consensus. His work continues to give insightful and innovative direction to the field, but his *Emergence of the American University* is so dominant that it has inhibited exploration of some of the intriguing themes he introduced as they relate to colleges. As he later pointed out, he was writing before the "new" social history and wrote essentially an intellectual history. Laurence R. Veysey, "The History of Higher Education," *Reviews in American History* 10 (December 1982): 288.

7. Lewis Perry, *Intellectual Life in America: A History* (New York: Franklin Watts, 1984), 281. Perry provides important new insights into the role of academics in intellectual life but adopts the conventional interpretation of collegiate institutions.

8. John A. Garraty and Robert A. McCaughey, *The American Nation*, 6th ed. (New York: Harper & Row, 1987), 340–41. Some other popular texts are more sensitive to the shortcomings of the dominant interpretation. They avoid discussion of colleges per se and briefly discuss the ethos of growth and provisions for women and minorities. See Mary Norton et al., *A People and a Nation*, 2d ed. (Boston: Houghton Mifflin, 1986), 2:597–99; and Richard N. Current et al., *American History*, 7th ed. (New York: Knopf, 1987), 2:542–43.

stereotype and virtually ignore colleges between the Civil War and World War I. When the Carnegie Council on Policy Studies began its influential study of curricula, it commissioned Frederick Rudolph, author of the standard survey of the history of American higher education, to write its historical volume. The result was an often-quoted book written wholly within the dominant interpretation. Even comparative works are shaped by it. Fritz Ringer's widely praised *Education and Society in Modern Europe* draws almost entirely on the above mentioned books for its comparison of American and European higher education.[9]

The continuing influence of these works testifies to the quality of their scholarship and writing. However, an interpretive tradition that initially provides insight eventually becomes heuristically restrictive. Since the early 1970s, specialists in the history of higher education have been trying to break out of the limitations of the tradition. Much of the resulting research on colleges has focused on antebellum higher education, thoroughly revising our understanding of that period. Most recent scholarship agrees that antebellum colleges were accessible and flexible institutions with a viable intellectual life despite financial limitations. Hofstadter's depiction of "the great retrogression" has been largely discredited among specialists.

Revision of the history of post–Civil War colleges is less advanced. It started in an interpretive vacuum. A few pioneer universities still dominate histories of Gilded Age and Progressive Era higher education. The lack of attention given to colleges leaves the impression that they remained wedded to antebellum traditions. In Veysey's words, they could only "hold on" until finally converted to university values in the twentieth century. Even two recent outstanding books on higher education invoke this one-dimensional image of late nineteenth- and early twentieth-century colleges.[10] Historians have been trapped by the dichotomous assumption that the "old-time college"

9. The poll appeared in *Change* 17 (July–August 1985): 23. Christopher Jencks and David Riesman, *The Academic Revolution* (Chicago: University of Chicago Press, 1968); Fritz K. Ringer, *Education and Society in Modern Europe* (Bloomington: Indiana University Press, 1979).

10. Roger L. Geiger, *To Advance Knowledge: The Growth of American Research Universities, 1900–1940* (New York: Oxford University Press, 1986), 3–20. David O. Levine, *The American College and the Culture of Aspiration, 1915–1940* (Ithaca: Cornell University Press, 1986), chaps. 1 and 2.

and the research university were the only alternatives for nineteenth-century higher education.[11] Instead of confronting an explicit interpretation clearly rooted in time, historians of the post–Civil War college have to deal with implicit, elusive images.

The work of revising the history of colleges began in the early 1970s.[12] The dominant theme was that colleges had to be understood in their social context rather than judged in terms of the rhetoric of university founders and the assumed demands of modernization. The "new" social history provided ways to explore the intersection of social change, beliefs, and the institutional ambitions of American colleges. By the 1980s, new scholarship on the history of American colleges in the Gilded Age and the Progressive Era started to appear. Pioneering books by Colin Burke and Louise Stevenson showed that colleges were neither as socially marginal nor as intellectually barren as previously depicted.[13] Other books and articles contributed new insights, especially on women's higher education, academic professionalization, and student life.[14]

There is still no comprehensive interpretation of post–Civil War American colleges. Constructing one requires combining the insights of recent scholarship with institutional studies. Toward that end, this

11. Compounding the conceptual vagueness has been sloppy vocabulary. Prevalent terms such as "old-time college" and "denominational college" defy clear periodization and analysis. Too often a conservative/reformer dichotomy has been employed, usually assumed to be synonymous with the college/university distinction. Thus, such clearly "collegiate" developments as the rise of intercollegiate athletics are awkwardly stuffed into the "age of the university." Rudolph writes vividly about "the collegiate way" and Veysey provides insightful images of collegiate and university values in conflict, but they subsume them within the "university" catchall.

12. The debate began with a panel at the History of Education Society annual meeting in 1971, later published in *History of Education Quarterly* 11 (Winter 1972): 339–89. A series of historiographic articles developed the critique. See esp. James McLachlan, "The American Colleges in the Nineteenth Century: Toward a Reappraisal," *Teachers College Record* 80 (December 1978): 287–306; David Potts, "Curriculum and Enrollments: Some Thoughts on Assessing the Popularity of Antebellum Colleges," *History of Higher Education Annual* 1 (1981), 88–109; and Veysey, "The History of Higher Education," 281–91.

13. Colin Burke, *American Collegiate Populations: A Test of the Traditional View* (New York: New York University Press, 1982); Louise L. Stevenson, *Scholarly Means to Evangelical Ends: The New Haven Scholars and the Transformation of Higher Learning in America, 1830–1890* (Baltimore: Johns Hopkins University Press, 1986).

14. Among the most significant books on women's colleges have been Barbara M. Solomon, *In the Company of Educated Women* (New Haven: Yale University Press, 1985); and Lynn D. Gordon, *Gender and Higher Education in the Progressive Era* (New Haven:

book is based upon a multiple case study of four colleges within a region. This methodology provides a perspective that is lost in single case studies. As Laurence Veysey pointed out about a book published for the 350th anniversary of Harvard, "Any history of an individual institution, no matter how well done, is by its nature provincial and limited. What we need above all are comparative studies, or at least studies of several institutions side by side, so that the single campus, such as Harvard's, automatically reveals its peculiarities when juxtaposed against the record of others."[15] In addition, national syntheses tend to obscure the fundamentally local and regional nature of nineteenth- and early twentieth-century higher education.

I selected institutions attended by the dominant social groups of late nineteenth-century America: private colleges controlled by white, male Protestants. I limited the study to one economically mature area to eliminate frontier development as a variable. New England was excluded because it has excessively influenced interpretations of the history of higher education.[16] The postbellum South lay in ruins and faced unique problems. I chose the Middle Atlantic states, which were rapidly industrializing and urbanizing but whose colleges have rarely been studied. For convenience, I limited my search to eastern Pennsylvania and New Jersey.

There are fifteen private, white, Protestant, male or coeducational

---

Yale University Press, 1990). On professionalization, see Burton J. Bledstein, *The Culture of Professionalism* (New York: W. W. Norton, 1976); William R. Johnson, *Schooled Lawyers: A Study in the Clash of Professional Cultures* (New York: New York University Press, 1987); Paul Starr, *The Social Transformation of American Medicine* (New York: Basic Books, 1987); Edward T. Silva and Sheila A. Slaughter, *Serving Power: The Making of the Academic Social Science Expert* (Westport, Conn.: Greenwood Press, 1984); and Nathan O. Hatch, ed., *The Professions in American History* (Notre Dame, Ind.: University of Notre Dame Press, 1988). On student life, see Helen L. Horowitz, *Campus Life: Undergraduate Cultures from the End of the Eighteenth Century to the Present* (New York: Knopf, 1987); and Ronald A. Smith, *Sports and Freedom: The Rise of Big-Time College Athletics* (New York: Oxford University Press, 1988).

15. Laurence Veysey, review of *Glimpses of the Harvard Past, History of Education Quarterly* 27 (Summer 1987): 274–75. For other multiple collegiate case studies, see George E. Peterson, *The New England College in the Age of the University* (Amherst, Mass.: Amherst College Press, 1964); Timothy L. Smith, "The Religious Foundations of Higher Education in Illinois" (unpublished manuscript); Joan G. Zimmerman, "College Culture in the Midwest, 1890–1930" (Ph.D. diss., University of Virginia, 1978); and Ira Read, "Church and College in the South" (paper presented at the annual meeting of the History of Education Society, Atlanta, Ga., November 1990).

16. Burke, chap. 2, critiques the historiographic damage done by excessive generalizing from the New England experience.

institutions that conducted baccalaureate programs in 1870 in eastern Pennsylvania and New Jersey and continue to operate today. I chose four on the basis of denominational variety and archival resources: Bucknell University, Franklin and Marshall College, Princeton University, and Swarthmore College.[17]

The institutional titles raise an obvious question. Why do two of the colleges bear the name "university"? Bucknell's use of the term dates back to the founders' unfulfilled dream of adding law and medical schools to the undergraduate college. The result was "a college miscalled a university."[18]

Princeton's inclusion raises larger questions. The College of New Jersey was renamed Princeton University in 1896, anticipating creation of a graduate school that did not mature until the 1910s. Pre–World War I Princeton remained "an institution very similar to the New England College."[19] In spite of that, studies of "the age of the university" often include Princeton, an anachronism based on the university structure that later evolved there. At the beginning of the period, Princeton was the largest of the four colleges but had many similarities to the other three. Ascertaining what eventually enabled Princeton to take a different institutional form than the others highlights some of the forces that shaped American higher education. Nineteenth-century "Colleges" were multilevel, multipurpose institutions that often included preparatory schools, normal schools, and graduate programs. The institutional changes that led to precise, nationally accepted labels are part of the phenomena examined in this study.

I chose a conventional periodization of history, from the Civil War to World War I. These wars remain useful demarcations in American higher education. The Civil War disrupted all four colleges, spurring drastic changes in the 1860s. American involvement in World War I was shorter, but it also had a traumatic impact on the colleges. The 1920s saw major changes at Bucknell and Swarthmore and significant

17. The other eleven colleges were Dickinson College, Gettysburg College, Haverford College, Lafayette College, Lebanon Valley College, Lehigh University, Lycoming College, Moravian College, Muhlenberg College, Rutgers University, and Ursinus College. In the pursuit of denominational variety, several colleges were mutually exclusive (e.g., Lafayette and Princeton).

18. J. Orin Oliphant, *The Rise of Bucknell University* (New York: Appleton-Century-Crofts, 1965), xi.

19. Peterson, 201.

innovations at Franklin and Marshall and Princeton, all of which set that decade apart.

The book weaves together events on individual campuses, comparisons among the four, and broader social forces, looking for both uniqueness and commonality. Chapter 1 examines the traditions and forces that defined each college in the late 1860s. The events of the following half-century are divided by the 1890s, a watershed decade that serves as the break between Part One and Part Two. Both parts examine the relationships between the colleges and their communities and their impact on faculty, curriculum, and student life. Part Three examines the broader implications of these case studies for understanding American educational and social development between the Civil War and World War I.

Most students, faculty, administrators, and trustees of these Middle Atlantic colleges were from the dominant social group of the period: male "WASPs," in modern parlance. But the study's importance extends well beyond those demographic boundaries. This group shaped a model of higher education that influenced leading women's colleges. The newly affluent from other ethnic, religious, and racial groups also adapted the model to their purposes. The study of these four colleges not only illuminates an important educational institution, but also sheds light on cultural identity and class formation in late nineteenth- and early twentieth-century America.

1

Four Colleges and Their Communities

Founding a college in nineteenth-century America required courage and vision, if not foolhardiness. There was no European precedent for creating numerous small institutions of higher education; this was truly an American enterprise. Many colleges were doomed to fail or become secondary schools; a surprising number succeeded. Survival depended on attracting varied sources of support: local, denominational, ethnic, and governmental. The emotions that inspired support also produced conflict: those who cared enough to pay expected colleges to conform to their vision. These extraordinary ventures reflected the aspirations of many different Americans.

A variety of forces shaped the four colleges in this study after the Civil War. To understand the constraints and opportunities they faced after 1865, we must analyze the groups that founded the colleges, the clientele that supported them, and the structures and practices already in place.

One of the nine colonial colleges, Princeton had a long history and national reputation that gave it potential support unavailable to the other three colleges. But by the 1860s, sectional and denominational schism eroded these advantages.

Princeton was the first college of the Great Awakening, born of the Old Side and New Light controversy that split Presbyterianism in 1736. Unwelcome at Old Side Yale and out of place at Harvard and at William and Mary, New Light ministers from the Synod of New York and New Jersey established the College of New Jersey, conventionally called Princeton College, in Newark.

Founded to train Calvinist ministers, its mission and clientele soon broadened. Scotch-Irish New Light Presbyterians in Pennsylvania attached themselves to the new college. The royal governor of New Jersey offered support in exchange for places on the board of trustees for himself and four members of his council. Both groups insisted on a more central site than Newark. Princeton outbid New Brunswick and, in 1756, opened Nassau Hall, the largest building in colonial America.

This impressive edifice reflected Princeton's expanded base. In religiously heterogeneous New Jersey, sectarianism would have been suicidal. Although Presbyterians dominated the board of trustees, it included Anglicans, Quakers, and non-Presbyterian Calvinists. Princeton was not legally tied to the synod, which, in turn, contributed little financially. Most donations came from individuals and were earmarked for liberal rather than ministerial education. New Jersey contributed occasional grants. Thus Princeton had neither formal governmental nor denominational ties; it was a spiritually denominational college with a public purpose. Most faculty were Presbyterian; students and supporters belonged to various Protestant denominations.

Fig. 1. Nassau Hall, the College of New Jersey, ca. 1860.

Princeton had a broad geographic base. Almost half of Princeton's eighteenth-century students came from New England and the South; only about one-quarter came from New Jersey. Financial support came from all sections of the country and even from overseas; contributions for Nassau Hall came from England, Ulster, and Scotland.[1]

The cosmopolitan contacts of the struggling college were enhanced by recruiting the Rev. John Witherspoon from Scotland as president. He became the only Scottish signer of the Declaration of Independence. During Witherspoon's presidency (1768–95), the institution produced many political leaders; its alumni constituted 16 percent of the Constitutional Convention, including James Madison. Later in Witherspoon's tenure and under his successor, Samuel Stanhope Smith, the production of ministerial candidates dropped precipitously. Smith's theological and disciplinary liberalism made enemies for him in the denomination. When students torched Nassau Hall in 1802, the trustees stepped in.[2]

Over the next sixty years denominational influence grew. After another campus riot in 1807, the Presbyterian General Assembly decided that contact with undergraduates contaminated ministerial candidates and built a separate seminary nearby. Although legally discrete, the seminary strongly influenced the wayward college. Of sixty-four trustees elected to the board at Princeton College between 1812 and 1868, thirty-six were also connected to Princeton Theological Seminary.[3]

The college's fortunes sank in the 1810s and 1820s. Presbyterian philanthrophy was diverted toward the seminary. Smith's successor showed that the iron hand did not stop student disruptions—but it did effectively reduce enrollment. By the late 1820s there were only

1. Thomas J. Wertenbaker, *Princeton, 1746–1846* (Princeton: Princeton University Press, 1946), 1–47; Howard Miller, *The Revolutionary College: American Presbyterian Higher Education, 1707–1837* (New York: New York University Press, 1976), 60–75.

2. In the classes of 1753, 1763, and 1773, 49.2 percent of the graduates became ministers; in the classes of 1783, 1793, and 1803, only 8.9 percent entered the ministry. Princeton University, *General Catalogue, 1746–1896* (Princeton: Princeton University Press, 1896), 42–151; Miller, 68; Wertenbaker, 116. For excellent intellectual histories of the Witherspoon-Smith years, see Douglas Sloan, *The Scottish Enlightenment and the American College Ideal* (New York: Teachers College Press, 1971), chaps. 3 and 4; and Mark A. Noll, *Princeton and the Republic, 1768–1822* (Princeton: Princeton University Press, 1989).

3. Varnum L. Collins, *Princeton*, American College and University Series (New York: Oxford University Press, 1914), 119–27; Wertenbaker, 118–52, 238–39.

seventy students, and the president considered closing the institution. But Professor (later President) John Maclean repaired the financial base by organizing the alumni association as a new source of revenue and reformed the curriculum. The result was a financial and intellectual renaissance. Enrollment more than tripled between 1829 and 1839, and talented new faculty were hired. The departure of three of the ablest in the mid-1840s, including physicist Joseph Henry, who went to Washington to become the first director of the Smithsonian Institution, ended the intellectual revival. As Maclean aged, he became increasingly concerned with the faculty's piety and bequeathed his successor an undistinguished, solidly Calvinist faculty.[4]

By the late 1860s Princeton was drawing its students from the narrowest geographic range in its history. Princeton had lost its appeal in New England with the reconciliation of the New Light and the Old Side a century earlier. For almost a century Princeton drew primarily on the Middle Atlantic states and the South. Many border-state Scotch-Irish were disaffected when the Presbyterian schism of 1837 left the college in the anti-evangelical Old School camp. Then the sectionalism of the 1850s evaporated the southern student pool. After the Civil War about two-thirds of the students came from the Middle Atlantic states, and most of the remainder from the border states. Its clientele had become regional rather than national.[5]

While its geographic base and academic reputation were shrinking, Princeton's potential for raising money grew. The spectacular growth of New York City was particularly helpful. A railroad connected the college to both New York and Philadelphia in the early 1840s, making it accessible to two sources of urban wealth. In the 1850s Princeton raised $60,000 for scholarships and quickly got the funds to repair Nassau Hall after a fire. In the midst of the Civil War the college raised $100,000, primarily from New York businessmen.

The long and sometimes distinguished history of the college gave it credibility with the wealthy of New York and Philadelphia, particularly among Scottish and Scotch-Irish Presbyterians. The central

4. Collins, 127–64; Wertenbaker, 153–289; Princeton College, *Plan for a Partial Endowment of the College of New Jersey* (1853); Stephen Alexander, *Address at the Laying of the Cornerstone of the Astronomical Observatory* (Newark, N.J., 1867); Princeton College, *Catalogue of the College of New Jersey* (1866/67).

5. Proportions were calculated from the catalogs and class publications. Wertenbaker, 175–81; Patricia Graham, *Community and Class in American Education, 1865–1918* (New York: John Wiley & Sons, 1974), 183–84.

New Jersey corridor was the center of early Scottish settlement and culture in North America. A number of Presbyterians involved in the founding of Princeton were Scots or Scotch-Irish. Scottish trading houses in New York, Perth Amboy, and Philadelphia linked with Scotland and Ulster to create a transatlantic Scottish culture. Although initially many Scots and Scotch-Irish were not Presbyterians, and many Presbyterians were English, Scottishness and Presbyterianism became increasingly synonymous in America. With that convergence, in Thomas Wertenbaker's words, "Nassau Hall became the religious and educational capital of all Scotch-Irish America."[6] For all of its problems, Princeton retained the loyalty of many wealthy Presbyterians in the Middle Atlantic states. The growing prosperity of Scots and Scotch-Irish in New York and Philadelphia gave Princeton considerable potential for the future.

Franklin and Marshall College also enjoyed a period of internationally recognized intellectual achievement. But it served a small ethnoreligious group with a much more limited social and financial potential than Princeton. Franklin and Marshall was formed in 1853 by a merger of two institutions. Franklin College predated the Constitution, and its founders included several of the framers. Marshall College was one of the most remarkable intellectual successes among the "hilltop colleges" of the early republic.

Franklin College was founded in 1787 by Benjamin Rush and several other prominent Philadelphians to assimilate the heavily Germanic population of southeastern Pennsylvania into the republican values and English-speaking culture dominant in the eastern end of the state. The new college in Lancaster, then the largest inland town in the United States, promoted Americanization with the country's first collegiate bilingual program.

The college's orientation soon changed. Its charter established a board of trustees composed of fifteen Lutherans, fifteen German Reformed, and fifteen without denominational restriction, the first legally stipulated church-college relationship. But the real divisions followed geographic lines. The Philadelphians lost interest, thereby allowing Reformed and Lutheran Lancasterians to gain control and reorient the college toward promoting German culture and language.

6. Wertenbaker, 113; Ned C. Landsman, *Scotland and Its First American Colony, 1683–1765* (Princeton: Princeton University Press, 1985), 3–13, 175–79.

Few students appeared, and the college closed without conferring degrees, later operating fitfully as a secondary school.[7]

Higher education did not return to Lancaster until the town lured a college that successfully combined German ethnicity with the denominationalism of the Calvinist German Reformed church. A product of the Reformation, the Reformed church thrived in the Palatinate until the Thirty Years' War and succeeding conflicts ravaged the area, driving Mennonites, Lutherans, and Quakers as well as Reformed north to Holland and England. From there many were drawn by the religious tolerance and fertile lands of southeastern Pennsylvania. German Calvinists initially were affiliated with the Dutch Reformed church before establishing the German Reformed church in 1793.[8]

German immigration following the abortive revolutions of 1830 and 1848 increased church membership from about 20,000 in the 1820s to over 100,000 by the Civil War. In the late 1830s, the church began to develop the denominational apparatus of Sunday schools, missionary societies, journals, and colleges. The fivefold increase in pastorates and the denomination's belief in highly educated clergy compelled it to make formal provisions for higher education.[9]

Given the Lancasterians' failure to sustain Franklin College, the initiative for German Reformed education fell to a small group that moved from one southern Pennsylvania town to another like medieval scholars for twenty-five years. In 1825 Dr. Lewis Mayer opened a seminary to train German Reformed ministers in Carlisle, attached

7. David W. Robson, *Educating Republicans: The College in the Era of the American Revolution* (Westport, Conn.: Greenwood Press, 1985), 196–205; Jurgen Herbst, *From Crisis to Crisis: American College Government, 1636–1819* (Cambridge: Harvard University Press, 1982), 200–201; Miller, 136; Owen S. Ireland, "The Crux of Politics: Religion and Party in Pennsylvania, 1778–1789," *William and Mary Quarterly* 42 (October 1985), 453–75.

8. The name was changed to "Reformed Church in the United States" (not to be confused with the Dutch Reformed church, which became the "Reformed Church in America"). The German Reformed church merged with the Evangelical church in 1934 and the Congregational church in 1957, creating the United Church of Christ. Winthrop S. Hudson, *American Protestantism* (Chicago: Chicago University Press, 1961), 158–59; Robert T. Handy, *A History of the Churches in the United States and Canada* (New York: Oxford University Press, 1977), 98, 151; James I. Good, *History of the Reformed Church in the United States in the Nineteenth Century* (New York: Board of Publications of the Reformed Church of America, 1911).

9. Glenn Weaver, "The German Reformed Church and the Home Missionary Movement Before 1863: A Study in Cultural and Religious Isolation," *Church History* 22 (December 1953): 298–313.

to the Presbyterians' Dickinson College and funded by European contributions. Friction with Dickinson authorities soon led Mayer to York. Since many students did not intend to enter the ministry, a "High School of the Reformed Church" was attached to the seminary in 1832. Financial troubles forced another move, this time to Mercersburg, a small mountain town in southern Pennsylvania.

Spurred by the Lutheran's recent founding of Gettysburg College, the synod decided to add a collegiate branch to the Mercersburg institutions. The Pennsylvania legislature responded by incorporating Marshall College and granting it twelve thousand dollars. The Mercersburg community raised another ten thousand dollars. The name "college" was quickly translated into reality by a talented faculty shared with the theological seminary.[10]

Marshall College evolved from European forms toward an ethnically distinct American denominationalism. While there were classes in German language and literature, most instruction was in English. The German-speaking sections of the literary societies ceased functioning in the 1840s. The contact with German universities was crucial to the remarkable intellectual success of this small institution in an unlikely American setting. Former Heidelberg professor and later Marshall College President Frederick A. Rauch wrote *Psychology* (1841), one of the first works to bring the new German psychology to America. Professors John W. Nevin and Phillip Schaff epitomized the Anglo-German atmosphere. Schaff was brought from Germany to teach at the theological seminary. Nevin, Scotch-Irish and originally a Presbyterian, trained at Princeton Theological Seminary before being hired by Marshall College and converting to the Reformed church. They published two of the most influential theological journals of the period, the *Mercersburg Review* and *Die Kirchenfreund.*

Despite the intellectual achievements and fruitful blending of two cultures, the Mercersburg institutions did not have unified Reformed support. Schaff and Nevin's "Mercersburg Theology" was an internationally respected defense of high church practices, but it split the German Reformed church. The controversy flared up in 1843 when

10. Ibid., 307–11: Joseph Henry Dubbs, *History of Franklin and Marshall College* (Lancaster, Pa.: Franklin and Marshall Alumni Association, 1903), 151–78. An indication of Mercersburg's extraordinary intellectual achievement is that three of the faculty of this tiny college (Rauch, Nevin, and Schaff) are noted in a major survey of American intellectual history: Lewis Perry, *Intellectual Life in America: A History* (New York: Franklin Watts, 1984), chap. 5.

Dr. Nevin attacked revivalism in "The Anxious Bench." A year later Schaff's inaugural address portrayed Protestantism as an outgrowth of, rather than a departure from, Catholicism. At a time of fervent revivalism and anti-Catholicism, the Mercersburg Theology divided the denomination and drove some members toward more evangelical sects.[11]

By the late 1840s the Mercersburg institutions were financially troubled. Reformed congregations in Ohio and North Carolina created separate colleges, and many Pennsylvania congregations refused to contribute to the college or the seminary. The German Reformed church had created the typical institutions of American denominationalism but lacked the wealth or unity to support them comfortably. Marshall College was having difficulty maintaining its high standards; events in Lancaster offered a solution.

In the 1840s Lancaster enjoyed an economic boom. A mercantile city in a fertile agricultural area, Lancaster was the fifteenth largest city in the United States in 1800. Its economy stagnated with the decline of artisanal crafts, but Lancaster became an industrial center after the arrival of the railroad. Most of the successful industrialists were of German extraction; many were German Reformed. Most leading non-Germans were also Calvinists, Scotch-Irish Presbyterians.[12] Lancaster was a booming small city that lacked an important civic institution: a college.

The vestige of Franklin College, operating as a secondary school, offered a solution. Its officers proposed a merger with financially troubled Marshall College, whose trustees accepted despite a sense of betrayal among Mercersburg residents. The German Reformed synod approved the merger in January 1850. The Lutherans, who already controlled Gettysburg College, agreed to sell their one-third share of Franklin College.

The Pennsylvania legislature granted a charter uniting Franklin

11. James H. Nichols, *Romanticism in American Theology: Nevin and Schaff at Mercersburg* (Chicago: University of Chicago Press, 1961), 1–4, 192–235, 281–311; George W. Richards, "The Mercersburg Theology—Its Purpose and Principles," *Church History* 20 (September 1951): 42–55; Handy, 206–7; Dubbs, 179–202; *Dictionary of American Biography* (New York: Scribners' Bros., 1934), 13:442–43, 16:417–18; Perry, 212–23, 249–52.

12. John W. Loose, *Heritage of Lancaster* (Woodland Hills, Calif.: Windsor Publications, 1978), 1–49; Thomas R. Winpenny, *Industrial Progress and Human Welfare: The Rise of the Factory System in Nineteenth-Century Lancaster* (Washington, D.C.: University Press of America, 1982), 1–19, 41–44.

Fig. 2. Old Main and the Diagnothian and Goethean Literary Societies, Franklin and Marshall College, 1860.

College and Marshall College in 1850. For three years the German Reformed church raised the seven thousand dollars owed to the Lutherans, while the citizens of Lancaster raised twenty-five thousand dollars for the endowment that Marshall College demanded before moving. That done, Marshall College combined its students, faculty, and scholarly reputation with the resources of Lancaster in 1853.[13]

In the next few years an impressive neo-Gothic main building was constructed, along with matching side buildings for the literary societies. But the new college could not escape the Mercersburg Theology controversy. The trustees selected a president who had not been involved in the recent conflicts, but he soon proved to be a Mercersburg Theology partisan. Former Marshall College faculty and their Mercersburg Theology controlled the college, the seminary, and the denominational publications but alienated many in the small denomination.[14] The Civil War aggravated the crisis; the class of 1866 numbered only six. The financial condition of the school was desperate. In addition, opponents of the Mercersburg Theology founded

13. Dubbs, 141–47, 237–47; H.M.J. Klein, *History of Franklin and Marshall College, 1787–1948* (Lancaster, Pa., 1952), 61–63.

14. Nichols, 221–35; Dubbs, 255–81, 302–14; Good, 298.

a rival college (ironically called Mercersburg College) that further divided Reformed support.[15] Franklin and Marshall College entered the post–Civil War era tied to a small, divided ethnic denomination with a tradition of highly educated clergy. Despite its earlier international prestige, its survival now depended on students and money from south-central Pennsylvania, and especially Lancaster.

Like Franklin and Marshall, Bucknell University owes its existence to the unique American combination of denominationalism and boomtown boosterism. But while it seemed strange for a city of Lancaster's size not to have a college, founding Pennsylvania's first Baptist college in Lewisburg, a small town far up the Susquehanna River, was brashly optimistic.

As evangelicals, Baptists accepted the concept of a highly educated clergy more slowly than the high church Presbyterians and German Reformed. But by the 1820s Baptists, particularly in the North, were attracting a wealthier clientele and developing denominational organizations and a professionalized clergy. The rapidly growing demand for ministers led Baptists in many states to found colleges in the 1820s and 1830s. However, the New Jersey and Pennsylvania Baptist organizations, including the influential Philadelphia Baptist Association, failed in their attempts to create a college. In the early 1840s, the New Jersey and Pennsylvania Baptist education societies still sent their ministerial candidates to colleges in New York state.[16]

The opportunity to build an institution commanding the loyalty of New Jersey and Pennsylvania Baptists was seized by a small group in Lewisburg, a town of two thousand on the Susquehanna River in north-central Pennsylvania. In 1840 the Northumberland Baptist Association, composed of Lewisburg area congregations, had only 267 members, and there was no Baptist church in Lewisburg. A revival bolstered membership, and in late 1843 Baptists in Lewisburg began planning for a church and, improbably, a university. Two years later the Northumberland Baptist Association endorsed the audacious

15. Dubbs, 302–14; Klein, 93–101; Franklin and Marshall College, Board of Trustees, Minutes (Franklin and Marshall Archives), 7 and 8 July, 1868.

16. J. Orin Oliphant, *Beginnings of Bucknell University: A Sampling of the Documents* (Lewisburg, Pa.: Bucknell University Press, 1954), 11; Robert G. Torbet, *A Social History of the Philadelphia Baptist Association, 1707–1740* (Philadelphia, 1944), 72–76. There is an outstanding account of antebellum Baptist ventures in higher education, including Bucknell: David B. Potts, *Baptist Colleges in the Development of American Society, 1812–1861* (New York: Garland Press, 1988).

project and formally proposed to Pennsylvania's Baptists "that a Literary Institution should be established in Central Pennsylvania, embracing a high school for male pupils, another for females, a college, and also a theological Institution, to be under the influence of the Baptist denomination."[17]

A committee drew up plans, purchased land, and hired an agent, Stephen Taylor, who had recently resigned from Madison (now Colgate) University. He secured legislative approval of the charter creating the University of Lewisburg, which was to be governed by a board of trustees with general powers and a board of curators to oversee academic affairs. All of the trustees and a majority of the curators were to be Baptists.

The charter placed the institution under the "patronage, supervision and direction" of Baptists but also stipulated that "no religious sentiments are to be accounted a disability" in the selection of faculty or students. The charter also required the backers to raise $100,000. The *Lewisburg Chronicle* supported the venture, and residents from various denominations quickly raised $12,000. The demand for Baptist ministers had created an extraordinary opportunity for a small town.

This interdenominational support reflected the economic base of Lewisburg. The construction of the eastern branch of the Pennsylvania Canal in the late 1820s spurred a commercial boom. The two canal builders, a Presbyterian and a Baptist, were founders of the college. The leading merchant was a Lutheran and a prominent college supporter. Lewisburg was the market town for the fertile Buffalo Valley, and by the 1840s it had foundries, gristmills, tanneries, and other industries. Members of its elite were willing to back any institution that would advance their civic ambitions. But a population of less than two thousand was a modest base for an institution of higher learning.[18]

17. Oliphant, *Beginnings*, 24. For the history of Lewisburg, see Lois Kalp, *A Town on the Susquehanna, 1769–1975* (Lewisburg, Pa.: Colonial Printing Co., 1980), which integrates town and gown particularly well. There is also a county history that sheds light on the origins: Charles M. Snyder, *Union County, Pennsylvania: A Bicentennial History* (Lewisburg, Pa.: Colonial Printing House, 1976), 90–94, 106–9.

18. Bucknell is blessed with two excellent institutional histories that describe the founding very well. J. Orin Oliphant, *The Rise of Bucknell University* (New York: Appleton-Century-Crofts, 1965), 3–35; and Lewis Edwin Theiss, *Centennial History of Bucknell University, 1846–1946* (Williamsport, Pa.: Grit Publishing Co., 1946), 11–55.

The Lewisburg community and the Northumberland Baptist Association pledged about one-third of the requisite $100,000. Taylor then approached the Philadelphia Baptists. He convinced the pastors and congregations to support this unlikely venture, then a three-day journey from the metropolis. They pledged another third of the required sum. Among the leading contributors were two men whose names grace the two institutions later spawned by the University of Lewisburg: John P. Crozer and William Bucknell.

Classes started in Lewisburg while two Baptist ministers canvassed Baptist congregations in the rest of Pennsylvania, Delaware, and New Jersey for financial support. It took them three years to collect the remainder of the $100,000; the University of Lewisburg was then offically incorporated in 1849. Three wealthy Philadelphians (William Bucknell, John P. Crozer, and Dr. David Jayne) had donated a total of $25,000, while 4,481 others contributed the other $75,000.

From its inception, the university was a multipurpose institution. Since only one of the twenty-two original students knew Latin and Greek, the studies were necessarily preparatory. In the second year, a few students began collegiate work. When this group became the first graduating class in 1851, enrollment in the four college classes numbered sixty-one, a figure that remained relatively stable for forty years. This first collegiate section was dwarfed by the 186 students in other sections of the university: the academic department (i.e.,

Fig. 3. Old Main, the University of Lewisburg.

college preparatory), the English division, the female division, and the primary department. The last was soon handed over to a local schoolmaster, but the other three divisions remained part of the university for over sixty years, and a theological seminary was soon added.

Taylor became professor of mathematics and natural philosophy and built a solidly Baptist faculty for the collegiate department. For reasons that remain unclear, Taylor was passed over for the presidency in favor of the Rev. Howard Malcom, a Baptist educator whose antislavery stance had recently cost him a college presidency in Kentucky. Malcom's tenure in Lewisburg was also stormy. His combination of liberal curricular ideas and stiff pietism discomforted some trustees and led to his resignation in 1857.

The university was soon torn by the tension of being situated in Lewisburg while drawing on Philadelphia for a major share of its students and funds. In 1856 John P. Crozer offered fifty thousand dollars if the institution moved to Chester, twenty miles south of Philadelphia. The trustees declined the offer by a 10–4 vote, with Crozer and William Bucknell in the minority. The division resurfaced in the search for a new president. The nominating committee proposed a prominent Philadelphia pastor, but a Lewisburg resident and son of one of the founders nominated University of Lewisburg professor Justin Loomis. After fourteen ballots Loomis became the president, at the cost of alienating some Philadelphia trustees.[19]

The geographic schism and other problems plagued the university during Loomis's presidency. Minor disputes angered important supporters, including several of the founders, and weakened the university's appeal in some Baptist congregations. Financial limitations put faculty pay in arrears and delayed dormitory improvements, leading to the death of three students from tuberculosis. These problems and the disruption caused by the Civil War reduced the enrollment to thirty-five in 1862. President Loomis averted disaster by raising $100,000 in the last years of the war. The major contribution, $20,000, came from John P. Crozer. Conspicuous by his absence from the list of major donors was William Bucknell.

The University of Lewisburg entered the postwar years renewed.

19. Potts, 134–61; Oliphant, *Rise*, 29–87; Theiss, 39–89, 142–43; Sanford Fleming, "American Baptists and Higher Education" (Unpublished manuscript, American Baptist Historical Association, Rochester, N.Y., 1965), 184–85.

Collegiate enrollment in 1865–66 reached a record eight-six, and the academy was booming. Local Baptists had to be gratified to be running a large institution that served local needs for secondary education as well as offering baccalaureate degrees and graduate theological studies for Baptists in Pennsylvania and New Jersey. By 1865 the institution could also claim the loyalty of many Philadelphia clergy who were alumni or trustees. On the other hand, some former supporters, including William Bucknell, had been alienated by the factional disputes. Localism, denominationalism, and chance had conspired to bring a large educational institution to an unlikely spot on the banks of the Susquehanna.[20]

The evolution of Swarthmore College is one of the more unusual sagas in the history of American higher education. Swarthmore is a nationally prestigious college that Burton Clark labeled a "model of undergraduate education."[21] But Swarthmore developed along a unique path that contradicts most assumptions about nineteenth-century denominational colleges. Many of its Quaker founders were uncomfortable with intellectual endeavors and ambivalent about education beyond the secondary school. Swarthmore was rooted in traditional piety, yet it was a curricular innovator and one of the first coeducational colleges in the Northeast. Its curriculum emphasized science, downplayed the classics, and had an elective system before Charles Eliot's famous speech at Harvard.

For five decades after it opened in 1869, Swarthmore College was torn between its distinctive Quaker tradition and more worldly pressures. The demanding Quaker life-style and beliefs originated in the religious turmoil of seventeenth-century England. Discomforted by Stuart elegance and Cromwellian authoritarianism, Quakers challenged both with a "plain" life-style and pacifism. The resulting persecution drove many members of the Religious Society of Friends to William Penn's colony. After actively participating in Pennsylvania affairs into the 1750s, most Quakers withdrew into "Quietism."

Friends exhibited as much nonconformity in education as in politics. Their aversion to legal, political, and clerical professions made

20. Theiss, 67–68, 114, 136–41, 154–75; Bucknell University, *Quinquennial Catalogue* (Lewisburg, Pa., 1900).

21. Burton R. Clark, *The Distinctive College: Antioch, Reed, and Swarthmore* (Chicago: Adams Publishing Co., 1970), 172.

much of traditional education irrelevant or repugnant to them. The clerical faculty and denominationalism of most colleges alienated Quakers. They valued training for teaching, commerce, and agriculture, subjects that were not taught in most colleges.

Quaker emphasis upon practical knowledge dictated a utilitarian education. George Fox, founder of the movement, wanted schooling restricted to the "civil and useful," a view shared by most Friends. To provide vocational training within the context of "guarded education" and prevent common schools from luring away young Friends, a number of Yearly Meetings established boarding schools in the early 1800s.[22]

Dissatisfaction with Quietism led to denominational schism in 1827. A restive group desiring a more activist approach gained control of the Philadelphia Meeting. A dominantly Quietistic group seceded to form a separate meeting, dubbed "Hicksite." Similar splits occurred in the New York, Baltimore, Ohio, and Indiana meetings. The ideological split partially followed urban/rural lines. This was particularly pronounced in the Philadelphia Meeting, where the Orthodox outnumbered Hicksites in the city by 3,000 to 1,500 but had a mere 5,000 followers in the surrounding environs, where there were 14,500 Hicksites.[23]

The Orthodox included most wealthy urban Friends who could finance denominational activities. They started a journal seventeen years before the Hicksites created their *Friends Intelligencer*. The Orthodox also seized the initiative in education. Having retained control of most Quaker schools, they added new academies and founded Haverford College and Earlham College in the 1850s.[24]

Hicksites were composed of three main groups. The largest was

22. A standard history of Quakerism is Sydney V. James, *A People Among Peoples* (Cambridge: Harvard University Press, 1963). John M. Moore, ed., *Friends in the Delaware Valley: Philadelphia Yearly Meeting, 1681–1981* (Haverford, Pa.: Friends Historical Association, 1981) has important essays; those by J. William Frost and Edwin B. Bronner are particularly relevant to this study. See also Homer D. Babbidge, Jr., "Swarthmore College in the Nineteenth Century: A Quaker Experience in Education" (Ph.D. diss., Yale University, 1953), 18–30.

23. Robert W. Doherty, *The Hicksite Separation* (New Brunswick, N.J.: Rutgers University Press, 1967), 67–89, provides a sociological analysis of the schism.

24. On the first two Orthodox colleges, see Opal Thornburg, *Earlham: The Story of the College, 1847–1962* (Richmond, Ind.: Earlham College Press, 1963); and Gregory Kannerstein, ed., *The Spirit and the Intellect: Haverford College, 1833–1983* (Haverford, Pa.: Haverford College, 1983).

made up of rural Friends who resented the wealthy urban Orthodox leaders. A second group consisted of urban artisans who were threatened by the Industrial Revolution and wanted to cling to traditional ideas. The third group, and the one that later financed much of Swarthmore's work, represented established wealth that viewed the Orthodox leaders as nouveau riche. Hicksite Quietism discouraged denominational activism and stunted educational progress. But a non-Quietist minority who valued the Hicksite movement more for its tolerance than for its Quietism and traditional life-styles became increasingly anxious to have a college under Hicksite auspices.[25]

In 1860 several members of the Hicksite Baltimore Yearly Meeting proposed establishing a boarding school and a teacher training institute to provide "additional facilities for the guarded education of Friends' Children, and especially for the supply of suitable teachers in membership with us to whom to entrust our children in our neighborhood Schools."[26] The Baltimore Yearly Meeting approved the proposal and soon procured assistance from the Philadelphia and New York meetings. The three Yearly Meetings published a joint appeal for financial support in early 1861, but national events intervened.

The contributors elected sixteen male and sixteen female Hicksite Friends to a board of managers and authorized it to start classes when fifty thousand dollars had been subscribed. In 1864, the Pennsylvania legislature chartered Swarthmore College, named for George Fox's home. The following year land was purchased outside Philadelphia, and a president selected. Four years of fund-raising lay ahead before Swarthmore could open its doors.[27] The Hicksites developed their denominational mechanisms, including their college, late and ambivalently. But their purpose was clear: to defend a distinctive denominational life-style.

When the Civil War ended, these four institutions were very different from what they would be when the United States entered World War I. Each could depend on denominationalism and localism for modest

25. Doherty, 67–89; Babbidge, 33–41; Moore, 59–102.

26. "Proceedings in Baltimore," Edward Parrish, Presidential Papers (Friends Historical Library), 2 October 1860; Babbidge, 42–53.

27. Babbidge, 50–68; Swarthmore College, Board of Managers, Minutes (Friends Historical Library), 2 December 1862–5 December 1865.

Fig. 4. Main Building (later Parrish Hall) under construction, Swarthmore College, 1869.

support. But each suffered from divisions within those groups. All four were constricted by limited resources, albeit the financial potential of their supporters differed considerably.

Although their existence was modest, the mere survival of these institutions and hundreds like them showed a remarkable commitment to advanced education, though the four-year college was just one part of a broader commitment. Only the College of New Jersey stood alone. At Bucknell and at Franklin and Marshall, secondary education appeared first and continued to be a major part of the institution, and the founders of Swarthmore were more interested in secondary and normal education than higher studies. These were multifunctional institutions rather than the freestanding colleges of the twentieth century. They were also surprisingly popular institutions that were not isolated from antebellum American society.

Denominational ambitions were essential to the creation of each college, and most faculty and trustees were members of the sponsoring denomination. But the phrase "denominational college" obscures the complex nature of support. In two cases denominationalism also conveyed ethnicity, and in a third a unique life-style. Only Bucknell was the product of a relatively undifferentiated American Protestant denominationalism. In all cases the colleges depended on local boosterism for financial support as well as for students, regardless of denomination. State and local public funds mixed with private. Formal denominational fund-raising brought in only modest sums; the largest donations came from wealthy New Yorkers, Philadelphians, and Lancasterians, most of whose donations were induced by denominational loyalty.

In 1865 higher education was not yet a national enterprise. Historians have wondered why a modernized academia with a professionalized professoriate based on national organizations and shared values did not emerge more quickly. But as Bucknell, Franklin and Marshall, and Princeton emerged from the Civil War and Swarthmore planned to open its doors, none faced a strong demand to heed reformers' calls to promote research and stop giving moral guidance. Indeed, it would have been strange for these schools to have done so—strange and disloyal to their roots. These four colleges were staffed by, and served, members of communities to whom university reform had little relevance. The colleges shared an intellectual tradition but developed within the context of local, regional, and denominational communities whose values would be challenged by rapid social change after Appomattox.

Part One

COLLEGES AND COMMUNITIES, 1865–1890

2

Rural Piety and Urban Wealth

A British invasion, a recent merger, a takeover, and stockholders quarreling with management: these late twentieth-century news items could also describe the four colleges in the twenty-five years after Appomattox. The denominational and local groups that controlled the colleges in 1865 could not provide sufficient revenue to satisfy the colleges' postbellum ambitions. The rapid industrialization of the mid-nineteenth century created new potential donors. Most shared the colleges' traditional denominational and ethnic affiliations, but some were young urbanites for whom the affiliation had a different meaning. In the next quarter-century, each college was shaken by conflict between the denominationalism and localism that shaped the antebellum institutions and new versions of those traditions.

These side currents of industrialization and urbanization affected each college differently. Each was at the intersection of a unique convergence of forces. It is therefore necessary to examine the particular dynamics within each college community separately in this chapter before examining common patterns in Chapters 3, 4, and 5.

Of the four institutions, the College of New Jersey was in the best position to tap the new sources of wealth. In the 1850s and 1860s, Princeton College had lost its intellectual edge and national clientele, but it retained some prestige in the Middle Atlantic states, especially among Scottish and Scottish-Irish Presbyterians. Princeton needed to capitalize on their loyalty if it was to regain its former eminence and keep pace with colonial rivals like Harvard and Yale.

The selection of a new president in 1868 to replace the aged John Maclean exposed the denominational forces contesting the college's future. The college had to choose between continuing as the bastion of Old School "high church" Presbyterianism or adopting a Presbyterianism more compatible with mainstream evangelical Protestantism. The strongest support for continuity came from local ministers, especially several who taught at Princeton Theological Seminary while sitting on the college's board of trustees. The Presbyterian church exercised no official control, but Presbyterians dominated college governance. Until 1901 one-half of the trustees had to be clergymen; no denominational affiliation was specified, but the self-perpetuating board normally appointed Presbyterians.[1] The leading Old School Presbyterian theologian, the Rev. Charles Hodge, presided over the trustees. The board's first choice for president was a leading opponent of the new biblical criticism on the theological seminary faculty. One alumnus expressed the progressives' dismay that the trustees had "cut a plug out of the prow to stop a leak in the stern of the old ship."[2]

When the candidate declined, the board made a more daring choice. Princeton's enrollments and reputation had been sinking for two decades, and while the dominant faction of the trustees wanted loyalty to Old School Presbyterianism, they also sought educational respectability. Lacking another candidate with all of the desired qualifications, the board went outside American Old School Presbyterianism. Echoing John Witherspoon's appointment a century earlier, they turned to the home of Presbyterianism, Scotland, to recruit someone who had been outside the Old School/New School schism and who would bestow the aura of European academic respectability on Princeton.

The Rev. James McCosh, a Scot teaching at the Scotch-Irish Queens University in Belfast, was well known to American Presbyterians. His philosophical and religious writings were more popular in the United States than in Great Britain, where Scottish philosophy was out of fashion. Assisted by his American publisher, Robert Carter, a New York–based Scottish immigrant, McCosh toured American colleges in 1866. Fortuitously, both the New and Old School Presbyterians were meeting simultaneously in St. Louis, seeking to end their schism.

1. Princeton University, *General Catalogue, 1746–1906* (Princeton: Princeton University Press, 1908), 20–24; Princeton University, *Charters and By-Laws of the Trustees* (Princeton: Princeton University Press, 1883).

2. F.B.H. to Kittie, 10 April 1868, McCosh Papers (Princeton University Manuscript Collection).

Both sides accorded McCosh a place of honor. McCosh briefly visited Princeton on his trip east. He returned to Belfast after attacking Mill, Comte, Spencer, and the pantheists before an appreciative audience of New York Presbyterians.

Two years later he was offered Princeton's presidency. The *New York Observer*, the leading Presbyterian newspaper, had reported McCosh's trip very approvingly. Its editor, Irenaeus Prime, was a Princeton trustee who may have nominated McCosh. His involvement in the evangelical alliance must have worried the Old School faithful like Hodge. But the chance to recruit an internationally known Presbyterian educator on the centennial of John Witherspoon's migration to Princeton apparently overcame the trustee's misgivings about McCosh's evangelicalism.[3]

Although historians have usually labeled McCosh an educational conservative, he dramatically reformed Princeton. At the inaugural, Charles Hodge's welcoming address pointedly warned against major departures. McCosh reassuringly couched his proposals in language reminiscent of the Yale Report of 1828, but they were a departure for Princeton. He believed religion and science were easily reconciled and was even willing to expose students to agnostic scientists. Modern languages and literature would receive more attention. Scholarship should be promoted, albeit with more attention to teaching and spiritual oversight than occurred in the German universities.[4]

McCosh quickly implemented many of his designs. In twenty years McCosh renovated the curriculum and faculty, transformed the campus, and increased the student body from 264 to 604. By the time of his departure in 1888, Princeton had a considerably strengthened faculty and a rising reputation within and beyond academia.

How did McCosh achieve these reforms in the face of opposition from influential members of the board of trustees? Some credit surely goes to the president's remarkable energy, despite beginning his twenty-year term at the age of fifty-seven. He astutely played the trustees and faculty against each other. In addition, McCosh's timing was

3. J. David Hoeveler, *James McCosh and the Scottish Intellectual Tradition: From Glasgow to Princeton* (Princeton: Princeton University Press, 1981), 3–229. This is an outstanding biography. For a brief overview of McCosh's early years, see W. Bruce Leslie, "James McCosh in Scotland," *Princeton University Library Chronicle* 36 (Autumn 1974): 47–60.

4. Princeton College, *Inauguration of James McCosh* (New York: Carter & Bros., 1868); 87–92: Hoeveler, 229–33.

good; the recent healing of the Presbyterian church schism made his brand of evangelicalism more acceptable. But personal energy, educational reforms, and denominational peace alone cannot explain this remarkable growth.

The educational reputation of Princeton may have sunk in the two decades before McCosh's appointment, but it could still draw upon a valuable social reputation. Princeton had been reduced to a regional institution by the 1860s, but since its region included New York and Philadelphia, parochialism did not mean pauperism. McCosh, an experienced fund-raiser for the Scottish Free church, quickly exploited the opportunity. In his first fifteen months, donations of over $150,000 endowed two professorships, financed a gymnasium and a classroom building, and increased the endowment.[5]

In twenty years McCosh raised almost $3 million. Some funds came from alumni, but most came from businessmen with an ethnoreligious affinity for the college. McCosh was particularly well suited to exploit Princeton's historic connections with Presbyterianism and Scottishness. The largest contributor was John C. Green, a Presbyterian who built a fortune on the China trade. Green was not college-educated but was devoted to Presbyterian causes. The new gymnasium was donated by Robert Bonner, a Scotch-Irish immigrant who became the publisher of the *New York Ledger* and president of the Scotch-Irish Society of New York City. Robert Stuart, a first-generation Scottish-American sugar magnate from New York, contributed $100,000. John A. Stewart, an associate of John Jacob Astor and Peter Cooper, was also drawn to Princeton by its Scottish Presbyterianism. So too were many smaller donors and many of the contacts McCosh made in the Midwest. Princeton received particularly strong support from the Scotch-Irish Pittsburgh elite, including the steel duo of Jones and Laughlin.[6] McCosh had a genius for promoting Princeton in a way that provided a sense of community and respectability to a group not yet fully accepted or at home in America.

Official denominational contributions were minimal. The only of-

5. Thomas J. Wertenbaker, *Princeton, 1746–1896* (Princeton: Princeton University Press, 1946), 294–315, 335–43; Hoeveler, 272–300; Princeton College, *Opening Exercises of the Gymnasium* (Princeton, 1870), 11–17.

6. Hoeveler, 279–84. Although essentially an intellectual biography of McCosh, Hoeveler very insightfully analyzes Princeton's ethnoreligious network. See also John N. Ingham, "Masters of the Mill: Innovation and Social Class in the Nineteenth-Century Iron and Steel Industry" (unpublished manuscript, 1986), 190–209.

ficial support was the New Brunswick Presbytery's annual donation of several prizes and scholarships for six to eight Princeton undergraduates who planned to enter the ministry. Except for an 1887 admonition urging "the Churches of Princeton and the Faculty of the College to use their influence in closing the saloons in the place," the presbytery's reports on college activities were perfunctory and approving. McCosh reduced Princeton Theological Seminary's influence on the college.[7] The financial payoff of Princeton's denominational connection came from individual rather than official sources.

McCosh also promoted a sense of community among alumni. He encouraged the development of local alumni clubs, traveling often to speak at their meetings. He also championed alumni representation on the board of trustees. The trustees rejected this innovation, crimping McCosh's solicitation of funds. Although gifts prompted by ethnoreligious loyalty funded most of McCosh's projects, he perceived the value of the new relationship. It could, however, be a two-edged sword. Many younger alumni embraced the new collegiate life-style, centered on athletics and fraternities, that McCosh found repugnant. His abolition of fraternities in the early 1870s pitted him against many younger New York alumni, some of whom were related to benefactors and trustees. The college's rising reputation also attracted wealthy Episcopalians, whose conspicuous consumption offended the president. By successfully tapping funds to build an attractive campus, McCosh unintentionally promoted a life-style he detested.[8]

McCosh's influence declined in the late 1870s. The board's opposition to alumni representation as well as McCosh's discomfort with the new student life-style alienated some affluent alumni. Traditional Presbyterian trustees who disapproved of McCosh's liberal Presbyterianism and educational innovations regained the initiative and blocked McCosh's desire to start a graduate school. When McCosh retired in 1888, they rejected his choice of a successor, a young genteel scholar with liberal Presbyterian leanings, and replaced him with an ardent conservative.[9]

7. Presbytery of New Brunswick, Minutes, 1876–1902 (Presbyterian Historical Society). Passage quoted is from 4 October 1887.

8. Hoeveler, 295–300; Princeton University, Trustees, Minutes (Princeton University Archives), 1875, 444–63; Wertenbaker, 322–23, 331.

9. Hoeveler, 322–40.

Fig. 5. James McCosh looks back, cà. 1890.

McCosh has often been cited as the archdefender of the old-time denominational college. The rhetoric of his late-career battles with Harvard's President Eliot has obscured his innovations. His broadly evangelical Victorian piety placed him in the Protestant mainstream. When McCosh left, the trustees tried to reestablish Princeton's close ties to the traditionalist minority in Presbyterianism. To be sure, Princeton would not long retain McCosh's evangelical Protestantism, but neither would it reclaim the traditional piety of Old School Presbyterianism nor sustain its Scotch-Irish identity. McCosh's success in attracting the scions of the new industrial wealth would draw Princeton toward an affluent gentlemanliness that shunned evangelicalism, piety, and ethnicity.

In Lancaster, Pennsylvania, another Calvinist college stayed even closer to its traditional base. The aftermath of the Civil War, which had come within a few miles of Lancaster, brought Franklin and Marshall College under the formal control of the German Reformed church. When the class of 1866 numbered only six and finances were desperate, the trustees acted. They removed the president as well as James Buchanan, the president of the board of trustees, and coaxed noted theologian John W. Nevin out of retirement to be president. The trustees legally bound the college to the German Reformed church with a new charter granting the synod the right to name all trustees in exchange for its promise to raise $100,000 and move the theological seminary from Mercersburg to join the college in Lancaster.[10]

Lancaster was the economic hub of south-central Pennsylvania. The market town for agriculturally rich Lancaster County, the city also had an industrial base, especially in pig iron and cotton textiles. Between 1850 and 1880, the number of people employed in manufacturing plants in Lancaster grew from 1,688 to 4,252, and the capital invested in manufacturing grew from $895,285 to $3,795,740. Despite the city's growth, its economy was increasingly controlled by Philadelphians. By 1890 the boom was over, and textiles, iron, and cigar-making were declining. Other industries replaced them, but Lancaster was clearly a secondary city.[11]

In 1890 Lancaster remained a heavily Germanic city. The Lutheran, German Catholic, and Reformed churches accounted for a majority of Lancaster's church membership. Anglo denominations (Methodist, Episcopal, Presbyterian, Irish Catholic) accounted for about one-third.[12] Thus Franklin and Marshall's overlapping German, Reformed, high church, and Calvinist traditions potentially ap-

10. Franklin and Marshall College, Board of Trustees, Minutes (Franklin and Marshall Archives), 1865–1868; H.M.J. Klein, *History of Franklin and Marshall College, 1787–1948* (Lancaster, Pa., 1952), 93–101.

11. Thomas R. Winpenny, *Industrial Progress and Human Welfare: The Rise of the Factory System in Nineteenth-Century Lancaster* (Washington, D.C.: University Press of America, 1982), 34–49; John W. Loose, *Heritage of Lancaster* (Woodland Hills, Calif.: Windsor Publications, 1978), 105–14.

12. Winpenny, 107–8.

pealed to much of Lancaster's population. But German Reformed leaders were ambivalent about appeals outside the denomination.

Unfortunately for Franklin and Marshall, the denomination was also unwilling to give the college a monopoly in Reformed education. It was the most prestigious Reformed institution, but not the only one. The lingering traditionalist/evangelical battles engendered by the Mercersburg Theology further undercut any hopes of monopoly. By the time peace between the factions was finally made at the General Synod of 1873, there were already several rival colleges competing for the limited denominational funds.[13]

The Pennsylvania congregations of the Reformed church were the logical source of funds for a formally denominational college. The synod approved a plan to solicit at least one dollar from every adult member of the Reformed church in Pennsylvania. Although the synod directed the pastors to implement the Dollar Plan, it slipped quietly into oblivion. The college's hired agent, a retired Reformed minister, obtained thirty-five thousand dollars to endow a professorship of history from an elderly eccentric who had once been impressed by one of the agent's sermons. But among the congregations, the agent encountered rival claims from other Reformed institutions and dissatisfaction with Franklin and Marshall Academy.[14] The college had created a secondary program immediately after the 1853 merger, but it was run poorly for several decades.[15] Since an academy was more attractive to most farmers than a college, its weakness limited the appeal of Franklin and Marshall as well as depriving the college of a dependable source of Reformed students.

In 1872 the church reiterated its determination to control the college. A synod committee complained to the board of trustees about a plan that granted scholarships to any Lancaster County school district whose inhabitants contributed one thousand dollars because the scholarship plan increased the belief "among a large part of our

13. Franklin and Marshall, Trustees, 7 and 8 July 1868; George W. Richards, "The Mercersburg Theology—Its Purpose and Principles," *Church History* 20 (September 1951): 42–55; James H. Nichols, *Romanticism in American Theology: Nevin and Schaff at Mercersburg* (Chicago: University of Chicago Press, 1961), 194–217, 308–11.

14. Franklin and Marshall, Trustees, 28 January 1869, 26 June 1871, 16 February 1875, and June 1875; Reformed Church in the United States, *Acts and Proceedings of the Synod* (Philadelphia, 1869), 75; Theodore Appel, *The Life and Work of John Williamson Nevin* (Philadelphia: Reformed Church Publication House, 1889), 255–66.

15. Klein, 104; Charles Stahr Hartman, "Franklin and Marshall Academy, 1872–1943" (Master's essay, Johns Hopkins University, 1948), 13–21.

people that the College was no longer an Institution of the Church, but belonged to the world, and their particular interest for it, in distinction to the many other institutions would be lost."[16] Although local residents responded favorably to the plan, the trustees withdrew it in the face of synodical criticism. A further comment by the synod's committee illuminated another dimension of the college's financial problem. It suggested that the trustees lower the goal of a $500,000 fund-raising campaign because "our people are mostly engaged in agriculture and not in commercial pursuits."[17]

The theological seminary, raising money to build its own campus, was a formidable rival for congregational contributions. In addition, several other Reformed church institutions had sprouted in Pennsylvania: Ursinus College, Palatinate College, Clarion Collegiate Institute, and Mercersburg College. The principal of Franklin and Marshall Academy attacked the splintering effect of these rivalries in the *Mercersburg Review* and recommended channeling all Reformed church energy into creating denominational feeders for Franklin and Marshall College. But the editors disagreed, telling Franklin and Marshall to accept its denominational rivals.[18]

The alumni association dated from the Marshall College days, but its loyalty was not matched by financial ability; it was dominated by professors at the college and ministers until the late 1880s.[19] Its campaign to establish an alumni professorship of English literature and belles lettres dragged on for decades.

As the only officially denominational college in this study, Franklin and Marshall demonstrates the advantages and disadvantages of that status. The college retained a definite mission and the loyalty of a faction in the denomination. But the financial rewards were limited. The denomination encouraged congregational giving, but it had few funds of its own. Congregations had many demands on their beneficence, and higher education was a low priority to most members of this heavily rural denomination. The limited funds committed to collegiate work were scattered among several institutions. The principal denominational contributions came from a few individuals.

16. Franklin and Marshall, Trustees, June 1872, 414–45.

17. Ibid., 416–47; Klein, 102.

18. Cyrus Mays, "A Gymnasium or a University?" *Mercersburg Review* 19 (January 1872): 32–49. The editorial response is on 153–57.

19. Franklin and Marshall College, *Catalogue of Officers and Students, 1787–1903* (Lancaster, Pa., 1903), 133–53.

Lancaster offered alternative sources, but German and Anglo non-Reformed citizens were not regularly solicited. As German ethnicity weakened, it became an identity that Franklin and Marshall's authorities only promoted when it coincided with denominationalism. They had sufficient denominational and local support to maintain a modest college but not to provide the expensive new facilities demanded by the growth of science and more gentlemanly student life-styles.

While Lancaster could support a modest college, Lewisburg could not. Philadelphians finally engineered a dramatic takeover. But when the Civil War ended, there were few indications of the tumultuous events to come. The reverse of Franklin and Marshall, the University of Lewisburg entered the postwar years in good health and with weakened denominational ties.

A backhanded contribution removed a burden from the institution. Since 1855 the university had operated a theological seminary. When John P. Crozer died in 1866, his estate offered to finance relocating the seminary in Chester. The university agreed and relinquished control of the renamed Crozer Theological Seminary to the Philadelphia Baptist Association. Although Crozer's attempt to move the whole university ten years earlier had precipitated dissension, this offer did not. The seminary was an albatross that employed two Lewisburg professors and tied up forty thousand dollars of endowment but produced no revenue, since ministerial candidates paid no tuition. The seminary's removal effectively increased the endowment while reducing expenses. Although the removal reduced the University of Lewisburg's claims on the largesse of Pennsylvania and New Jersey Baptists, it initially strengthened the university, now left with its collegiate department, academy, and female institute.

At the same time the Baptists of Lewisburg had grown to sufficient numbers and wealth to erect an impressive stone Gothic church to replace the modest structure in which the first university classes had been held. The sight of President Justin Loomis personally shingling the 175-foot steeple seemed to symbolize the strength of the university and its ties to the local community. So too did the occupation of the pastorate by the Rev. Robert Lowry, a nationally known Baptist hymn writer and a professor of literature at the university.

The apparent stability proved illusory. Ironically, construction of the church was one reason, leaving the local Baptists twenty thousand dollars in debt. The panic of 1873, floods, and fires undercut the town's and the university's finances. Even the Chicago fire was felt in Lewisburg because the university had invested some of its endowment in Chicago real estate destroyed by Mrs. O'Leary's cow.

Loomis's attempt to duplicate his successful fund drive of 1864–65 in the early 1870s failed. While local funds were dissipating, President Loomis and the board of trustees angered alternative sources in Philadelphia. Loomis and some local trustees banned fraternities and curbed athletics in the early 1870s, despite protests from the Philadelphia Alumni Club. Several fraternities operated secretly with alumni support, until Loomis ended Sigma Chi's sub-rosa existence and expelled a member of the class of 1875 shortly before his graduation. In response the alumni demanded the unprecedented priv-

Fig. 6. President Loomis (seated, right), Professor James (standing behind him), and the rest of the University of Lewisburg faculty, 1874.

ilege of nominating every third trustee. The board promised to select more alumni but kept selection in its own hands.[20]

Loomis aggravated the situation by attacking Charles James, a popular professor of classical languages at the university since 1851. At Loomis's insistence the board of trustees fired James by a 9–3 vote on questionable charges. The decision aroused bitter opposition, especially among some of James's former students. When the trustees met in June 1878, they were greeted with demands for Loomis's removal from the Philadelphia Alumni Club and the board of curators, the weaker half of Bucknell's two-headed governance structure. They requested reconsideration of the cases of Professor James and the expelled student. Loomis resigned, but the trustees loyally urged him to remain another year, against the wishes of the curators and the alumni.[21]

The demise of President Loomis was symptomatic of a deeper crisis. The continual strife within the college alienated the alumni, many of whom were the very Baptist clergy the college relied on for students and funds. In the late 1870s enrollment dropped sharply, with disastrous financial results. There were only forty-four college students left when Loomis resigned in 1878, and the class of 1879 numbered only seven. Enrollments in the academy and the female institute also dropped dramatically, reducing total enrollment to 135, only half the normal number.

The younger alumni and the trustees pinned their competing hopes on the new president. After a prominent Philadelphia Baptist minister declined the job, the trustees turned to a young faculty member, David Jayne Hill. Only twenty-eight years old, he had published highly successful books on rhetoric and American literature. As the son of a Baptist minister and part of the University of Lewisburg "family," he was acceptable to the trustees. He went through a perfunctory ordination as a minister to satisfy the trustees, but he shared the

20. Bucknell University, Board of Trustees, Minutes (Bucknell University Archives), 25 June 1872, 25 June 1873, and 29 June 1875; Lewis Edwin Theiss, *Centennial History of Bucknell University, 1846–1946* (Williamsport, Pa.: Grit Publishing Co., 1946), 161–75; Lois Kalp, *A Town on the Susquehanna, 1769–1975* (Lewisburg, Pa.: Colonial Printing Co., 1980), 82–85.

21. University of Lewisburg, Trustees, 29 June 1875 and 24–25 June 1878. The trustees claimed they received the requests too late, but the minutes show that the curator and alumni notes were tabled until Loomis could be asked to remain for another year.

curators' views. He reinstated fraternities, added electives to the curriculum, and consulted with alumni and students. Enrollments immediately increased.

Hill's administration also faced financial problems. In the first year of his presidency he used over 10 percent of the endowment to finance his reforms. He sought a rich savior and virtually put the institution's name up for sale. He targeted William Bucknell, who had tried to move the institution to Philadelphia twenty-five years earlier, as the most likely candidate. Bucknell was a rags-to-riches real estate and utilities magnate who had given over half a million dollars to Baptist causes but was disenchanted with the University of Lewisburg. Hill eventually got a sympathetic hearing; Bucknell renewed his offer of fifty thousand dollars to move the university to Philadelphia. Eventually Hill convinced Bucknell to offer the sum without removal if the university raised a matching amount and transferred governance to a single body whose membership would be chosen by Bucknell. The financially desperate board of trustees capitulated. The matching fifty thousand dollars was raised, and on 7 March 1882 William Bucknell's handpicked board of trustees took office. With Bucknell calling the tune and the Crozer family as the leading contributor of the matching funds, the battle of the 1850s had come full circle.[22]

At the 7 March meeting the trustees obediently resigned. The new charter eliminated the board of curators and vested sole authority in the board of trustees, four-fifths of whom were to be Baptists. Bucknell retained eight of the old trustees and replaced twelve incumbents. William Bucknell, not surprisingly, was elected chairman of the board, and the Rev. Judson Rowland, the leader of the old board of curators, was named treasurer. Baptist pastors played prominent parts on both sides of the struggle, and the same number were on the old and new boards. Some non-Baptists were on the old board of curators as well as the newly constituted board of trustees.The change was geographic and generational; the new trustees were younger, and most were Philadelphians. This was not a revolt against

22. University of Lewisburg, Trustees, 24 June 1879 and 21 April 1881; University of Lewisburg, Board of Curators, Minutes (Bucknell University Archives), 24 June 1879; Aubrey Parkman, *David Jayne Hill and the Problem of World Peace* (Lewisburg, Pa.: Bucknell University Press, 1975), 15–26; J. Orin Oliphant, *The Rise of Bucknell University* (New York: Appleton-Century-Crofts, 1965), 144–46.

the "denominational college"; it was a modernization and urbanization of it.[23]

The old board of trustees had been dominated by Baptists from the Lewisburg area, many of whom had been governing the university since the 1850s. The economic reverses of the early 1870s that temporarily reduced local sources of funding had precipitated the crisis, but Lewisburg soon started to grow again. In the 1880s the Reading Railroad extended its line to Lewisburg and built an impressive station. New mills and furniture factories were established. Lewisburg could support a few stately churches and some elegant Victorian homes, but it could only have sustained a college by extraordinary sacrifices. Lewisburg's temporary reverses had only hurried the inevitable.[24] Even a prosperous Lewisburg was not in the same league as Philadelphia. Keeping control in Lewisburg would have meant forgoing the expensive new facilities parents and students were beginning to expect—or even bankruptcy. A united and heroic effort by local wealth might have prevented the urban takeover, but the internal dissension and competing claims on local Baptist largesse made that unlikely.

William Bucknell contributed handsomely, personally donating a chapel, a chemistry building, and an observatory for the college as well as underwriting improvements in the academy and the female institute. In addition, sports-crazed alumni donated a gymnasium. The campus was modernized by 1890. The ailing endowment, which almost dropped below $100,000 in 1881, was over $350,000 in 1890, primarily due to William Bucknell. The University of Lewisburg was renamed Bucknell University in 1886, accurately reflecting the donor's importance. President Hill had astutely cultivated this philanthropy. Bucknell expressed his personal esteem for Hill in an invitation for Christmas dinner, when "we will talk about University [and] all my relatives will be glad to meet the Great President of LU [University of Lewisburg] and their Father's prince."[25]

Hill avoided alienating Bucknell through radical departures or expensive expansion. Although retaining "university" in the new name,

23. Bucknell University, *Alumni Catalogue* (Lewisburg, Pa., 1915), 6–7; Oliphant, 146–47.

24. Kalp, 85–115.

25. William Bucknell to David Jayne Hill, 21 December 1885, Hill Papers (University of Rochester Library Special Collections); Bucknell University, *Catalogue, 1889–90*.

Hill created a modernized multipurpose institution with a modest collegiate section and no graduate students. He rebuilt enrollments to Civil War levels, but eschewed expansion. When he left there were 71 college students in a total institution of 286. He relied on Bucknell's generosity rather than growth to finance projects. Hill's addition of electives to the curriculum and acceptance of fraternities and intercollegiate athletics met students' expectations for collegiate life in the 1880s. Yet he retained a relatively traditional curriculum and grading system, strict social rules, required chapel, and the annual day of prayer for colleges.[26]

Although he made no attempt to turn Bucknell into a true university, he personally thirsted for the intellectual life and social freedom of a university. He was corresponding with Daniel Gilman about studying psychology under G. Stanley Hall at Johns Hopkins University when the Baptist-sponsored University of Rochester offered him its presidency. William Bucknell and the board begged Hill to decline and countered with the offer of a new house, a raise, and a year of study leave with pay. However, Gilman and others easily persuaded Hill to take the new position.[27] He left behind a modest, prosperous college that was part of a multipurpose "university" controlled and supported by Philadelphia Baptists in a small central Pennsylvania town.

As at Bucknell, control of Swarthmore shifted toward wealthy urbanites, especially Philadelphians. The Baltimore Quakers who initiated the idea of founding the college envisioned a rural institution financed by a large number of stockholders with equal votes. They soon lost on both issues to wealthier Philadelphia and New York Quakers. A campus site was purchased within ten miles of Philadelphia in 1865, and after bitter debate the stockholder system was revised to favor wealthier contributors.

The Baltimoreans demonstrated their dissatisfaction through reduced contributions. Of the $93,000 pledged at the time of incorporation, Philadelphians promised $55,000 and New Yorkers $32,000, while the Baltimore Meeting subscribed only $6,000. Their share

26. Bucknell, Trustees, 27 June 1882–1 January 1889; Oliphant, 161–63.

27. David Jayne Hill to Daniel C. Gilman, 26 March, 20 June, and 10 July 1888, Gilman Collection (Johns Hopkins University Manuscript Collection); Gilman to Hill, 20 June 1888, Hill Papers; David Jayne Hill, As It Seemed to Me (ca. 1930, University of Rochester Library Special Collections, typescript), 474–76; Parkman, 32–35.

later declined even further, shrinking to only $250 of the $30,000 collected in 1867. When Benjamin Hallowell, one of the founders, resigned from the board in 1868, his seat, previously reserved for a Baltimorean, was given to a New Yorker. Before the college had even opened its doors, control had moved to the north.[28]

The geographic shift reflected growing dependence upon wealthy contributors. By 1866 there were sufficient funds to begin constructing the main building. But contributions lagged, and in spring 1869 the enterprise was still in doubt. Then Samuel Willetts, a New Yorker and chairman of the board of managers, pledged one-half of the necessary fifty thousand dollars if that amount was matched by Philadelphians. They did so, and on 21 October 1869 classes began with 173 students in the preparatory department and 26 qualified to begin at the collegiate level.[29]

The managers of Swarthmore insisted that classes not begin until dormitory rooms were ready for all students—an indication of their cultural defensiveness. Although of English ancestry, nineteenth-century members of the Religious Society of Friends resembled an embattled ethnic minority. Following the doctrine of simplicity, Quakers continued their distinctive "plain speech." Many also adhered to "plain dress"; some Quaker men still wore brimmed hats and gray coats without lapels. The faithful avoided holiday celebrations and distrusted music, art, and modern literature. Remaining culturally distinctive was especially demanding for a group that, unlike the Mennonites, did not retreat to rural isolation. The main hope for passing the life-style and values to their children lay in providing a "guarded education."[30]

Swarthmore College was founded when Quaker education, particularly for Hicksites, was in decline. Hicksites were united in their determination to stem the drain on Hicksite membership, but they

28. Swarthmore College, Board of Managers, Minutes (Friends Historical Library), 1 December 1863, 2 December 1867, and 1 December 1868; Homer D. Babbidge, "Swarthmore College in the Nineteenth Century: A Quaker Experience in Education (Ph.D. diss., Yale University, 1953), 54–68.

29. Swarthmore, Managers, 4 December 1865–5 August 1869; *Friends Intelligencer* 26 (13 March, 17 April, and 26 June 1869); Babbidge, 226.

30. Philip S. Benjamin, *The Philadelphia Quakers in the Industrial Age, 1865–1920* (Philadelphia: Temple University Press, 1976), 3–48; Edwin Bronner, "A Time of Change: Philadelphia Yearly Meeting, 1861–1914," in John M. Moore, ed., *Friends in the Delaware Valley: Philadelphia Yearly Meeting, 1681–1981* (Haverford, Pa.: Friends Historical Association, 1981), 103–37.

disagreed on the nature of "guarded education." Liberals such as Lucretia Mott and John Hicks demanded only commitment to Quaker beliefs, whereas traditionalists demanded zealous protection of their life-style and customs. Swarthmore's first president, Edward Parrish, was in the liberal camp and felt that if students were given considerable autonomy they would be guided by their intuitive sense of right and wrong. Traditionalists, however, gained control of the board of managers and forced Parrish to resign. His successor, Edward Magill, had taught at Boston Latin School and was more willing to impose the discipline and traditional Quaker values demanded by the board. The managers' reports to the stockholders stressed their assiduous efforts to keep campus life consistent with the Hicksite ideals on dress, plain speech, entertainment, and religious services. One manager even sought to ban Orthodox Quaker writings from the campus. Another provided funds for an on-campus meeting-house, which liberals had previously blocked. The traditionalists dominated until the late 1880s. However, Hicksites did not argue over one subject that was deeply divisive elsewhere—coeducation of the sexes—reflecting the Hicksite belief in the intellectual equality of the sexes.[31]

Control of the board of managers by the traditionalists exacerbated a deeper problem. Swarthmore could not attract enough Friends to get more than a small coterie of college-level students and, even by filling the "college" with preparatory students, could not get more than about half the desired number of Friends children. Although the traditionalist managers resisted admitting outsiders, Swarthmore's financial structure necessitated it. Stockholders had agreed to invest the initial sum for constructing the college; it was supposed to run at cost thereafter. Gifts from managers or other wealthy Hicksites financed some capital expenditures, but all current expenses were to come from tuition, making it suicidal to reject applicants from other denominations.

With only half the college's students being Friends, the managers

31. Edward Parrish, *An Essay on Education in the Society of Friends* (Philadelphia: J. B. Lippincott & Co., 1866), 89–90; Richard J. Walton, *Swarthmore College: An Informal History* (Swarthmore, Pa.: Swarthmore College, 1986), 5–6; Swarthmore College, Stockholders, *Minutes of the Annual Meeting of the Stockholders*, 1870–84; Babbidge, 109–18. For examples of the liberal and traditionalist philosophies of education, see the speeches by John Hicks and William Dorsey in Swarthmore College, *Proceedings of the Inauguration of Swarthmore College* (Philadelphia, 1869).

Fig. 7. Swarthmore students passing the science building on the way to the meetinghouse.

constantly felt that guarded education was threatened. In response they increased the worship requirements, applied them to all students, and rejected a student request to bring ministers of other faiths onto the campus. In 1880 they instructed Magill to reject all further non-Quaker applications, but it was a pipe dream. Their subsequent $100 reduction of the college's $350 fee for Friends was insufficient to entice many more of the faithful.[32]

The failure to attract more Hicksite students stemmed from the social composition and educational attitudes of the denomination. In the schism Hicksites had done considerably better than the Orthodox in the countryside; a large proportion of their members were farmers, few of whose children desired higher education. For secondary education, a majority of Hicksites entrusted their offspring to the public schools rather than face the daunting costs of preparatory classes at

32. Swarthmore, Stockholders, 1880, p. 58. The Edward Magill Papers (Friends Historical Library), box 1, contain a letter from the managers directing Magill to decline applications from non-Friends. Babbidge, 109–18.

Swarthmore. A guarded education was particularly expensive since everyone (except a few day students) had to live at the college.[33]

Even among Hicksites able to pay for a Swarthmore education, few were particularly interested in collegiate work. Although the faculty and presidents Parrish and Magill wanted to emphasize the collegiate program, a majority of the managers shared the rank-and-file priority on preparatory and teacher training programs. Most students entered those programs with no intention of continuing on to the college. Of those students who did begin the collegiate program in the 1870s and early 1880s, only about one-third graduated. President Parrish perceived this danger from the start and warned that only unceasing vigilance would keep the institution aimed at a collegiate ideal. Magill urged the managers to raise the minimum age for admission and eliminate the preparatory classes; instead the managers added a younger class in 1877.[34]

The desire to provide teachers for Friends schools led to the opening of a normal department in 1878. The program included special courses and practice teaching for four-year college students as well as a shorter certificate program. The preparatory department served as a model school. In 1884 the managers increased the program's size by encouraging students to abandon the baccalaureate program in favor of one or two years of normal courses. This directly threatened the collegiate work, especially since normal program students paid a considerably reduced fee that drained funds from the college. In addition, preparatory students, who had always exceeded the collegians, outnumbered them by nearly three to one by 1883–84. Magill corresponded with numerous other college presidents, including David Jayne Hill at Bucknell, and received an almost unanimous response: a normal department did not belong in a collegiate institution. In a report to the managers the faculty asserted that the best training for future teachers was instruction by proficient professors in a regular college curriculum supplemented by lectures on pedagogy. The faculty also recommended dropping all preparatory classes.[35]

33. Parrish, 36–43; Benjamin, 33–34, 221–22.

34. Edward Magill, *Sixty-Five Years in the Life of a Teacher, 1841–1906* (Boston: Houghton Mifflin, 1907), 149–50, 187–90; Swarthmore, Stockholders, 1873, p. 48; 1878, pp. 48–50. Edward Parrish published his warning in the *Friends Intelligencer* 26 (10 July 1869): 291–95; Babbidge, 227.

35. The faculty report and Magill's correspondence with other college presidents are in box 8 of the Magill Papers. Swarthmore College, *Annual Catalogue*, 1884/85 and 1885/86. Hill's letter to Magill was dated 7 April 1885.

The faculty recommendations were eventually accepted after a change in the board's composition. Clement Biddle and M. Fisher Longstreth led the fight to save the preparatory classes and support the normal school. But when Eli Lamb, headmaster of a Friends school in Baltimore, succeeded Biddle as chairman of the managers' Committee on Instruction in 1884, the tide turned. Lamb shared the faculty's belief in collegiate standards and disliked the normal program, preferring a replica of G. Stanley Hall's pedagogical lectures that Lamb had attended at Johns Hopkins University. Lamb kept Magill informed of the board's feelings, and they plotted to elect like-minded managers. They met stiff opposition, and at the height of the battle over the normal department, Lamb warned Magill that they "must step very cautiously or there will be trouble. CMB [Clement M. Biddle] must have a hearing."[36] Magill and Lamb prevailed; the normal program was abolished, and the preparatory classes were phased out.[37] Lamb represented a new generation of Hicksites who were challenging the control of the traditionalists.

It was a dangerous victory for Magill and the faculty. Phasing out the preparatory and normal programs eliminated more students than could be attracted by collegiate studies. Although the number of collegians increased from 83 to 123, total enrollment declined from 304 to 240 between 1883–84 and 1886–87 as younger students were eliminated. Since the managers remained wedded to the principle that tuition should meet current expenses, the college's revenue declined. It took many years to replace all of the preparatory students. When the preparatory program was phased out completely in 1894, the college enrolled a near-record 187 students; but even that was smaller than the total enrollment had been in 1869.[38]

Eliminating the subcollegiate programs reduced Swarthmore's potential Quaker clientele. The president and faculty had won over enough managers to the idea of emulating more prestigious colleges that were eliminating noncollegiate programs. But the stockholder system and the refusal to solicit non-Quaker donors added to the sacrifice. Some wealthy, urban managers apparently shared the col-

36. Eli Lamb to Magill, 9 April 1885, Magill Papers.

37. There are several valuable letters between Lamb and Magill in box 8 of the Magill Papers (Friends Historical Library). Magill, 195–201; Swarthmore College, *Annual Catalogue*, 1880/81–1889/90; Swarthmore College, Committee on Instruction, Minutes, 15 June 1885.

38. Swarthmore, Managers, 20 June 1887; Babbidge, 226, 230.

Table 1. Undergraduate and Total Enrollments, 1869–1890

	Princeton	F&M	Bucknell	Swarthmore
1869–70	328	72	64	26
		(155)	(215)	(199)
1879–80	425	90	51	128
	(473)	(156)	(171)	(290)
1889–90	556	136	71	163
	(771)	(273)	(285)	(273)

NOTE: Numbers without parentheses indicate the number of regularly enrolled undergraduates. The numbers in parentheses indicate the total institutional enrollment.

SOURCE: The figures were compiled from catalogs and college histories. The methods of counting differ slightly depending on which branches of the institution were included and how part-time students were counted.

legiate vision. They backed a more casual student life as well as the abolition of the preparatory and normal programs. They also offered the additional financing that the college badly needed to compete with similar institutions. A campaign to create Swarthmore's first endowed professorship dragged on for years until three urban managers offered to endow matching chairs. In 1887 Swarthmore suddenly had four endowed chairs.

These decisions had deeper ramifications for the Hicksite community. The editors of the *Friends Intelligencer* supported collegiate standards and more relaxed rules for students at Swarthmore. But for many Hicksites the doctrines of plainness and simplicity defined their distinctiveness. Adopting the mainstream model of collegiate life endangered denominational identity, especially for rural Hicksites. Philip Benjamin found that 13.5 percent of the influential Philadelphia Race Street Monthly Meeting had some college education. This showed considerable interest in higher education among urban Hicksites; but the base was small, and over half the college graduates had attended non-Quaker institutions.[39] Whether to compromise with "the world" posed a ideological and practical dilemma for Swarthmore.

Collegiate enrollments at these four institutions were small by modern standards. The colleges, however, were part of larger multifunctional institutions (see Table 1). Only the College of New Jersey ever stood

39. *Friends Intelligencer*, for instance 18 December 1875 and 26 September 1885. In the 1880s it began a regular column on Swarthmore. Benjamin, 217–22.

alone in this period, and even it ran a preparatory school for six years and admitted students to subfreshman classes. The other three colleges included educational ventures running the gamut from elementary school to theological seminary.

A surprising number of colleges survived; but why were they not supported more fully in this period? Their failure to undertake major curricular innovation has been offered as an explanation. But this does not seem to have been the case. Swarthmore, which had the most innovative curriculum, attracted relatively few applicants and was pressed by supporters to shift resources to noncollegiate programs. The experiences of these colleges suggest that there was broader public interest in denominationally sponsored secondary and normal schools than in higher education. These colleges could not have prospered merely through curricular reform; three of the four only survived as part of multifunctional ventures. The ideal of a freestanding college existed in the minds of faculty, but it was unrealistic for most institutions. These case studies offer no evidence that curricular reforms would have unleashed an untapped demand for higher education.

The denominational connections, official and unofficial, provided little systematic financial assistance. The denominations were insufficiently hierarchical to command large sums of money, and few congregations were willing to make deep sacrifices for colleges, which had to compete with academies, theological seminaries, and foreign and home missionary societies for denominational solicitations. The small share of denominational funds given to colleges was increasingly targeted to future ministers.

The financial significance of denominationalism was its ability to generate individual benevolence. Denominational colleges were essentially voluntary associations that depended upon the generosity of those who felt loyalty to them. Most contributions between 1865 and 1890 came from a few individuals whose sense of connection with the college came from ethnoreligious affiliation. Even for Franklin and Marshall, with a legal denominational connection, denominationalism was a surrogate for a complicated nexus of influences controlling and financing the institution. Denominationally inspired funds, combined with those stimulated by local boosterism, were sufficient to maintain a modest college comfortably. Franklin and Marshall demonstrates the limitations of formal denominational control, and the University of Lewisburg demonstrates the limitations of small-town support. But when the local community was replaced by two metropolises, as for Princeton, significant sums of money could be raised.

Access to urban industrial wealth best explains the differences in institutional facilities and size. Princeton's 1869 endowment ($522,000) was larger than that reached by any of the other three colleges until the 1890s.[40] By 1890 its endowment was $1,524,000 when endowments at each of the other colleges were under $300,000. Princeton was a denominational college with a traditional curriculum, but it was able to use its ethnoreligious connections to draw upon the wealth of two metropolises. The other three colleges lacked the same access to wealth. Franklin and Marshall College and Bucknell University served social groups that were less urban and less wealthy, while Swarthmore owed its existence to a group that had severe reservations about higher education. Even at Princeton the existing sources were insufficient to finance all of the academic, social, and athletic facilities that had become fashionable by 1890. Meeting both these demands and the colleges' ambitions required new approaches. Another identity, alumni status, started to be cultivated by 1890, especially at Princeton.

The courting of alumni revealed deeper generational tensions within Protestant society. For college authorities in the 1870s and 1880s, denominationalism encompassed ethnicity at Franklin and Marshall and at Princeton, and a distinct life-style at Swarthmore. In addition, most donors and faculty expected the four colleges to promote the sober ascetic piety of Victorian Protestantism. But the students showed increasing discomfort with these values and later, as alumni, promoted a less denominationally centered and more indulgent genteel Protestantism. In each college generational tensions grew between older ethnoreligious and life-style traditions and the vanguard of muscular Christianity. The former were stronger in rural areas and small towns, while the latter was gaining favor among the urban industrial elites. By 1890 financial growth depended upon a college's ability to tap the wealth of the latter. The more colleges wanted to

40. Varnum L. Collins, *Princeton*, American College and University Series (New York: Oxford University Press, 1914), 410. The largest endowment in 1869 was Harvard's $2.4 million; Yale had $1.5 million. Peter D. Hall, *The Organization of American Culture, 1700–1900* (New York: New York University Press, 1984), 262.

build laboratories, dormitories, and gymnasiums, the more they needed to satisfy the desire of the new upper and upper-middle classes for institutions that could provide them with a sense of community without the restrictions of Victorian piety and denominationalism. Truly distinctive colleges risked marginality after 1890.

3

When Professors Had Servants

As the census taker for the south ward of Lewisburg interviewed families on wide tree-lined streets in the summer of 1860, he visited the homes of the five members of the Bucknell faculty. The Rev. Justin Loomis lived in a house worth five thousand dollars with his wife Mary, three children, and a servant. His colleagues, the Revs. George Bliss, Charles James, and Thomas Curtis, lived in similarly substantial homes on the same street. The newly appointed Rev. Francis Tustin rented nearby, where he lived with his wife and a servant. In addition to their houses, the five faculty listed personal estates averaging one thousand dollars. All had servants except James, whose household included two young women who probably served a similar function. Some of the most affluent and powerful citizens in Lewisburg were their neighbors.[1]

The census and other sources show that faculty at these four colleges were generally affluent and lived among the local elite.[2] For instance, in 1870 professors Bliss, James, and Loomis still lived next to each other in Lewisburg. Their close neighbors included Thomas Frey, a flour manufacturer living in an $18,000 house, and Daniel Kreamer, a reaper manufacturer listing a personal wealth of $10,000

1. Bureau of the Census, Decennial Census, 1860, reel 1188, Lewisburg South Ward, visits 1084, 1166, 1167, 1168, and 1169.

2. Historians have relied on rhetorical evidence due to their inability to examine faculty in the context of local communities. The manuscript census, which has rarely been used by historians of higher education, facilitates reconstruction of faculty families and their social milieu. I accidentally discovered this while checking Colin Burke's assertion that the census is not very useful for studying students. Burke proved to be correct, but in the process I kept stumbling across faculty families.

and a house worth $5,000. Professionals and skilled craftsmen headed most of the other neighboring households.[3]

Princeton faculty had even more affluent neighbors. An extreme case was Lyman Atwater, who lived next to a wealthy widow whose house was valued at $100,000 and personal wealth at $50,000. Professor Stillwell Schanck's more typical neighborhood included a banker, a dry goods merchant, and a tailor.[4]

Fig. 8. House built by Professor (later President) Loomis in Lewisburg in the 1850s. Later purchased by the university and still used as the president's house.

3. The censuses used were 1860 (reels 697, 1125, 1126, 1188), 1870 (871, 1337, 1356, 1458), and 1880 (788, 1125, 1142, 1143, 1197). Although 1860 predates the period covered in this chapter and the founding of Swarthmore, the fire that consumed the 1890 census necessitated including 1860 to provide a twenty-year period. In selecting the "neighbors" and "community" I created random samples of about fifty cases for each college. The sample ratios ranged from one in ten for Lewisburg in 1860 to one in seventy-five for Lancaster in 1880. The colleges' political units (my definition of "community") were Lancaster City, Lewisburg Borough, Princeton Borough and Township, and Springfield Township (Swarthmore).

4. In the 1860, 1870, and 1880 manuscript censuses for the four college towns, I located faculty and presidents eighty-eight times, over three-quarters of the possible total. In addition, I sampled 262 of the faculty members' "neighbors," defined as the five households listed immediately before and after the faculty member on the census roll. For another comparison I sampled the whole "community," defined as the college's political unit, coding 470 households. The findings are explained more fully in W. Bruce Leslie, "When Professors Had Servants: Prestige, Pay, and Professionalization, 1860–1917," *History of Higher Education Annual* 10 (1990): 19–30.

Faculty reported much higher personal estates in the 1860 and 1870 censuses than those of their neighbors, who in turn were considerably more affluent than the general community. Of faculty reporting personal estate, 74 percent listed over one thousand dollars as opposed to only 12 percent of their neighbors and 4 percent of the general community. No faculty member reported less than one hundred dollars, whereas a majority of their neighbors and the community reported such a nominal sum (Table 2).

Faculty also owned considerable real estate (Table 3). Thirty-two percent of faculty were not homeowners, as opposed to 42 percent of their neighbors and 52 percent of the community. Among those who owned homes, faculty had slightly higher home values than their neighbors, and considerably higher home values than the rest of the community. For instance, 79 percent of faculty homes were valued at two thousand dollars or more, as opposed to 72 percent of their neighbors' houses and 53 percent of those in the community.[5]

Table 2. Personal Estate, 1860 and 1870

	Faculty		Neighbors		Community	
None listed	9%	—	15%	—	25%	—
Under $100	0	0%	54	64%	59	79%
$100–999	18	19	21	25	13	17
$1,000–4,999	53	58	8	9	3	4
$5,000–49,999	12	13	2	3	0	0
$50,000+	9	10	0	0	0	0
	N=34		N=188		N=320	

SOURCE: United States Census, 1860 and 1870; see notes 3–5.

NOTE: Some families listed no property. Because the meaning of these omissions is ambiguous, two sets of statistics have been calculated. In Tables 2 and 3 the left-hand columns in each category include all heads of households. The right-hand columns calculate only those who listed Personal or Real Estate. Percentages may not equal 100% due to rounding.

5. These figures probably underestimate the neighbors' wealth. The 1860 and 1870 censuses did not record addresses in small towns, forcing me to sample from the ten nearest census visits. Some of these "neighbors" probably lived down alleys and around corners. This bias and impressionistic evidence suggest that faculty and their "real" neighbors were more similar than the figures indicate. If so, it bolsters my conclusion that faculty were living among the local elite.

Table 3. Real Estate, 1860 and 1870

	Faculty		Neighbors		Community	
None listed	32%	—	42%	—	52%	—
Under $500	2	4%	6	10%	2	3%
$500–1,999	12	17	11	19	21	44
$2,000–9,999	29	44	26	45	20	41
$10,000–99,999	24	35	15	26	6	12
$100,000+	0	0	1	1	0	0
	N=34		N=188		N=320	

SOURCE: United States Census, 1860 and 1870; see notes 3–6.

Lee Soltow's *Men and Wealth in the United States, 1850–1870* provides comparative national figures. Soltow calculated that only 3 to 4 percent of white adult males had real estate valued at more than ten thousand dollars. In my sample 24 percent of faculty, 16 percent of their neighbors, and 6 percent of the community listed such plush dwellings. The mean value of real estate in his sample is $1,492 in 1860 and $1,782 in 1870. My figures for faculty are about two and one-half times higher, $4,146 and $4,000. Soltow created another measure that he labeled "total estate" by averaging real estate (double weighted) and personal estate; his figure for white adult males in 1870 is $2,691. My calculation for faculty is $5,898, a little more than double his national average.[6] Thus, the faculty were privileged members of relatively affluent towns.

Unfortunately for understanding class, wealth questions were dropped from the census after 1870, making assumptions about wealth from later censuses inferential. The number of servants living in the household, which continued to be recorded after 1870, is a possible surrogate. Comparing the number of servants and the personal estates in 1860 and 1870 shows the former to be a very useful surrogate for wealth. In those censuses 77 percent of faculty households included servants, as opposed to 28 percent of their neighbors and 10 percent of the community at large. The percentages of those listing one hundred dollars or more in their personal estates are: faculty, 91 percent; neighbors, 31 percent; and community, 16 percent. These two sets of figures are strikingly parallel.

6. Lee Soltow, *Men and Wealth in the United States, 1850–1870* (New Haven: Yale University Press, 1975), 53–77. Note that Swarthmore is omitted from the 1870 figures because faculty lived on campus and no wealth was listed for them.

If servants continued to bear the same relation to wealth, faculty were still very affluent in 1880. In that census 79 percent of faculty households included servants, as opposed to 31 percent of their neighbors and 13 percent of the whole community. Thirty-seven percent of faculty households included more than one servant, as opposed to 8 percent of their neighbors and 1 percent in the community sample.

For the combined 1860, 1870, and 1880 censuses, 79 percent of faculty households included servants, as opposed to only 30 percent of their neighbors and 11 percent of the community (Table 4). Even the households of young married faculty members usually included a servant, such as those of two Bucknell professors in their twenties living on Lewisburg's "faculty row," William Grier and George Phillips. The most pampered was a young Princeton historian, William Sloane, whose household of seven included four servants. Stereotypically, most faculty servants were Irish or black.[7]

By the time most faculty reached middle age, their households were large. Franklin and Marshall professor William Nevin's household of seven, including two servants, was typical of the older generation. The average faculty household had six members; in addition to a spouse, children, and servants, many of these households included relatives from outside the nuclear family.

The census yields similar evidence for three colleges. However, Swarthmore's faculty lived in the main college building and did not head households as defined by the census. Since the census taker

Table 4. Servants Living in Households, 1860–1880

No. of Servants	Faculty	Neighbors	Community
None	20.7%	71.4%	88.7%
1	34.5	20.2	9.1
2	24.1	7.3	1.3
3+	20.6	1.2	0.8
	N=58	N=262	N=470

SOURCE: United States Census, 1860, 1870, and 1880; see notes 3–7.

7. I included those labeled "domestics," "companions," "nurses," and "housekeepers" as "servants." Since the other labels occurred more frequently in nonfaculty households than in faculty households, their inclusion biased the data against my conclusion.

recorded only minimal information for those in institutions, there is no way to ascertain the wealth of the Swarthmore faculty.

Comparing the professions of "heads of household" of neighbors and the entire community provides another indicator of faculty status (Table 5). Throughout these decades, faculty neighborhoods were about twice as likely to contain professionals or proprietors of large enterprises (15 percent) as the rest of the community (7 percent). Fewer faculty neighbors were manual workers and small businessmen (53 percent) than was typical in the community (66 percent). The elusive category "none" (in which I included the retired) probably hides a greater disparity between neighbors and community. Impressionistically, it appears that many reporting "none" who lived near faculty were independently wealthy, a status sometimes indicated by phrases like "living on own income." "None" in other parts of town often seemed to be linked with poverty. The census establishes that the faculty at Bucknell, Franklin and Marshall, and Princeton lived in affluent neighborhoods, headed privileged households, and possessed considerable personal wealth.

The source of faculty affluence is less clear. Some brought family wealth to the job; a striking number of faculty wives recorded personal wealth in the 1860 and 1870 censuses. Many families maintained a higher standard of living than their salaries could have provided. No doubt teaching was a calling for some who gave up better-paying alternatives, but historians have been too ready to accept contemporary complaints about faculty pay.[8]

Table 5. Occupations in the Neighborhood and Community, 1860–1880

	Neighborhood	Community
Professional	7.3%	3.8%
Large Proprietor	7.3	3.0
Small Business/Craftsmen	33.6	42.0
Semi- and Skilled Manual	4.6	3.2
Unskilled Manual	14.9	21.1
Keeping House	15.6	15.3
None	11.1	6.8
Other	5.7	4.9
	N=262	N=470

SOURCE: United States Census, 1860, 1870, and 1880; see notes 3–7.

8. See, e.g., Rossiter Johnson, "College Endowments," *North American Review* 136

Fig. 9. A student view of the Franklin and Marshall faculty in the *Oriflame*, 1888.

Faculty salaries were considerably above those of most Americans. Thomas Winpenny's study of Lancaster permits a direct comparison between the salaries at Franklin and Marshall College and those of local industrial workers. The average annual wage in Lancaster's fifteen leading industries ranged from $168 to $290 in 1850 and from $204 to $461 in 1880. Professors at Franklin and Marshall earned an average of $1,200, and the president's salary ranged from $1,500 to $1,800 in these decades. Thus, Franklin and Marshall salaries were three to four times the average wage in the highest paid local industry and six to nine times the average in the fifteenth-ranked industry.[9]

(May 1883): 490–96. Johnson claimed that only Columbia and Johns Hopkins paid decent wages. He sampled eleven colleges and found salaries ranging from $850 to $3,000. Bucknell and Franklin and Marshall fall in the middle of his range, and Princeton and Swarthmore were at the top end.

9. Thomas R. Winpenny, *Industrial Progress and Human Welfare: The Rise of the Factory System in Nineteenth-Century Lancaster* (Washington, D.C.: University Press of America, 1982), 92–93.

Lancaster's manufacturing wages were typical of those in the Middle Atlantic states, which averaged about $350 in 1880. From the 1860s through the 1880s, salaries at the four colleges ranged from about $1,000 to $3,400, averaging about $2,000. Swarthmore and Princeton faculty averaged $2,500, about $1,000 above Bucknell and Franklin and Marshall. Presidential salaries ranged from $1,200 at Bucknell in the 1860s to $4,000 and a house at Princeton and Swarthmore in the 1880s.[10] Thus, faculty made more than five times the average industrial wage in the region, and presidents received as much as twelve times that figure.[11]

Olivier Zunz's study of the Chicago, Burlington and Quincy Railroad provides another comparison. Of its more than 10,000 employees in 1880, 191 were executives. The twenty-three top-level executives made over $4,000, more than all college employees except the Princeton and Swarthmore presidents. Salaries of the 168 middle-level managers ranged from $1,500 to $4,000.[12] The faculty at the four colleges were in the lower end of this range. Faculty made less than the few top executives, but their salaries were similar to those of middle management, equating them with the top 2 percent of Chicago, Burlington and Quincy employees. The cries of poverty must be put into perspective; if faculty were poor, it was only in comparison with their wealthiest neighbors.

Faculty affluence and social status were not accompanied by modern professional prerogatives. Faculty had little influence over selecting their colleagues. Appointments were made by presidents and governing boards that, in the absence of strong professional expertise, felt competent to make the decisions. The procedures were similar at the four colleges, although the balance of power between the president and trustees differed.

Franklin and Marshall trustees filled vacancies at their annual June meeting; but if the candidate declined or if a vacancy occurred during

10. Clarence D. Long, *Wages and Earnings in the United States, 1860–1890* (Princeton: Princeton University Press, 1960), 42, 68, 150. I found salary figures in board minutes and other scattered sources.

11. These estimates are in line with Colin Burke's estimate that faculty salaries were 7.5 times those of unskilled workers in 1850, 5.2 in 1890, and 4.0 in 1910. Colin Burke, *American Collegiate Populations* (New York: New York University Press, 1982), 233; see also Charles Bishop, "Teaching at Johns Hopkins," *History of Education Quarterly* 27 (Winter 1987): 138–47.

12. Olivier Zunz, *Making America Corporate, 1870–1920* (Chicago: University of Chicago Press, 1990), 40–46.

the summer, the appointment was left in the president's hands, limited only by a stipulated salary. The faculty and president were formally deferential, as in 1880 when they told the board that "we have no request to make of the Board, but we express our desire that a good and competent man be appointed to the position."[13] Records do not indicate whether such formal deference hid a stronger role.

At Princeton, better records and a forceful president, James McCosh, reveal occasional confrontations. To fill important positions, such as the new professorship of civil engineering and applied mathematics in 1875, the board of trustees appointed a committee to make suitable inquiries and to present a candidate; the committee's charge provided no role for the president and faculty. But surviving correspondence indicates that McCosh investigated the candidates and undoubtedly influenced the final decisions. President McCosh had considerable authority to make minor appointments. He presented the candidate's credentials to the trustees along with a faculty recommendation that usually was accepted.[14]

Through formal and informal power, McCosh was able to shape a new faculty in his twenty-year tenure. Although McCosh discomfited some trustees by reaching beyond the ministry and even beyond Presbyterianism for many of his appointments, he often prevailed. Only where McCosh did not exercise his influence did the board seem to determine appointments, and in doing this it committed at least one extraordinary gaffe. In 1883 John Bach McMaster, a young engineering instructor, surprised all but his closest friends by publishing the highly successful *History of the People of the United States.* The faculty recommendation that a chair in American history be established for him was serenely brushed away by the trustees, with the sentiment that McMaster should stick to engineering. McCosh stayed on the sidelines, miffed that McMaster had not acknowledged Princeton in his volume. McMaster soon accepted a chair at the University of Pennsylvania, where he became an eminent historian.[15]

13. Franklin and Marshall College, Board of Trustees, Minutes (Franklin and Marshall Archives), 15 June 1880.

14. James McCosh to President Caffree, 1875, McCosh Papers (Princeton University Manuscript Collection); Princeton University, Trustees, Minutes (Princeton University Manuscript Collection), 26 and 28 June 1876, 29 June, 25 August, and 27 October 1875.

15. William B. Scott, Some Memoirs of a Paleontologist (ca. 1930, Princeton University Manuscript Collection, typescript), 586; Eric F. Goldman, *John Bach McMaster*

At Swarthmore the governing board played a stronger role, particularly in the early years. President Magill formed careful alliances with several sympathetic managers and gradually increased his role. It was a touchy process, as indicated in an 1885 search for science and Latin professors. Some candidacies began with personal letters to Magill or the board, while others stemmed from direct intervention by interested managers and Quaker educators. Magill apparently took the initiative in seeking out candidates' views and qualifications and checked carefully with Eli Lamb, chairman of the Committee on Instruction. Lamb secretly advised Magill on how to maneuver past some managers: "I think thee managed the Dr. Leidy business admirably. It was entirely proper to write Dr. Dolley. Thee could do no less. Dr. B. Sharp though will try for the place with a pretty good backing. Emmor Roberts is decidedly [for] him, so do one or two others from our Com. [on Instruction]. Thee would do well to see Emmor."[16] Dr. Dolley was appointed.

Such conflicts usually resulted from different attitudes toward professional qualifications. The governing boards and presidents shared many values, but the latter were more sensitive to the claims of expertise and the former to the claims of piety. The disagreements were never a clear-cut dichotomy between piety and expertise. Rather, they disagreed over how to blend the competing demands of denominationalism, institutional mission, and scholarship.

In the 1870s and 1880s, the expansion of knowledge, the prestige of European universities, and the new opportunities for nontheological graduate work slowly changed the accepted standards of scholarly competence. The colleges sought to combine their traditional demand for proper religious qualifications and willingness to provide personal, even pastoral, service to students with the growing demand for specialized scholarship. The choice of a new mathematics professor at Franklin and Marshall in 1880 exemplifies the desired amalgam. The trustees' Committee on Instruction considered five acceptable candidates before selecting Jefferson Kershner. He filled every qualification: Kershner was German Reformed, had done grad-

---

(Philadelphia: University of Pennsylvania Press, 1943), 50–51; J. David Hoeveler, *James McCosh and the Scottish Intellectual Tradition: From Glasgow to Princeton* (Princeton: Princeton University Press, 1981), 242.

16. Eli Lamb to Edward Magill, 9 April 1885, Magill Papers (Friends Historical Library).

uate work at Yale, and was the only Franklin and Marshall alumnus among the candidates. The committee's recommendation emphasized the latter qualification. A member of the board, writing in the leading Reformed journal, acknowledged that faculty members must increasingly be specialists, yet he maintained that even in a world of specialists the colleges should seek out clergymen first, and if none were available with a special fitness for teaching then "let other men of sound Christian faith . . . be employed."[17]

At Princeton, McCosh similarly broadened the criteria. Six of the ten faculty he inherited had graduated from the college or Princeton Theological Seminary or both, and all were Calvinists. McCosh aggressively recruited candidates from outside Princeton, Presbyterianism, and even the country. He came to Princeton both as an outsider determined to build Princeton's academic reputation and as an evangelical who chafed at Old School Presbyterian sectarianism. Thirteen of the seventeen appointments made between 1868 and 1880 had no previous affiliation with the two Princeton institutions, and several were not Presbyterian. McCosh recommended that the board of trustees "should take at times an instructor belonging to another evangelical denomination, provided he is very eminent in his department. This will not impair but rather strengthen our Presbyterianism. Of the 30 officers of the College, 28 are at the present time Presbyterians, and a good number, perhaps too many, are Presbyterian ministers."[18] The trustees did not like hearing this, even from a Presbyterian minister. They countered with a preference for alumni, for teaching ability, and, as far as possible, for "members of the Presbyterian Church, or of those denominations closely allied to it, the Reformed Dutch and the Congregational."[19]

Although McCosh accepted non-Presbyterians he wanted formally religious faculty who would act as moral guardians. Inquiring about a candidate, McCosh explained to another president that "we do not expect any religious pledge. We do not require candidates to belong to any particular denomination. But as we are professedly a religious College we should like our instructors to be people showing respect to religion and attending on its public ordinances. Can you say any-

17. Lewis Steiner, "American College on the Defensive," *Mercersburg Review* 18 (April 1871): 195. On Kershner's appointment, see Franklin and Marshall, Trustees, 15 June 1880.

18. Princeton, Trustees, 26 June 1876; see also Hoeveler, 238–45.

19. Princeton, Trustees, 8 February 1877.

thing on this point? Did Professor Kerr wait on your religious services—Episcopal I believe[?]"[20]

A similar concern pervaded McCosh's correspondence with William Scott, a recent graduate. The president encouraged Scott's graduate work at Heidelberg but, before offering him a job, broached his concern. "You are aware that the Trustees and all your friends here are resolute in keeping the College a religious one. You have passed through various scenes since you left us. . . . If a man has the root in him he will only be strengthened in the faith by such an experience. It will be profitable to me to find how you have stood all this."[21] McCosh even tolerated a few skeptics and hired two talented young scientists who made little pretension of theism. They were neighbors on what was branded "atheists' corner."

In his last report to the board of trustees McCosh described his recruiting policy as looking for the best man available and then inquiring about his probable influence on the college's religious and moral life. But his definition of the best man changed during his presidency. To build a respected faculty quickly, McCosh recruited from other colleges at first. Then in the 1880s he sought out "me bright young men" like Scott. McCosh encouraged talented undergraduates to pursue graduate work, usually in Europe. He often chose the sons of wealthy Princeton backers who could afford the project. If their work was successful and their faith unshaken, a Princeton position beckoned. Fifteen of his last twenty-three appointments were alumni. This may have been McCosh's response to the trustees' opposition to his academic ambitions for Princeton. With these appointments he still gained faculty with European training and personal loyalty to him, while soothing trustee fears of outsiders.[22]

Although McCosh respected scholarly research, teaching ability also weighed heavily. His letters to Scott were filled with advice on teaching. In a letter to Daniel Gilman at Johns Hopkins University, McCosh reported that although he was convinced of a candidate's

20. McCosh to Caffree, 1875, McCosh Papers (Princeton University Manuscript Collection).

21. McCosh to William Scott, 15 March 1880, McCosh Papers (Princeton University Manuscript Collection).

22. Princeton, Trustees, 9 February 1888; Scott, 456; Princeton University, *General Catalogue 1746–1896* (Princeton: Princeton University Press, 1896), 33–37; Hoeveler, 284–95.

scholarly ability he was "anxious to know whether he is *also a lively teacher*."[23]

At Swarthmore the managers constantly pressed for more Quakers on the staff. Traditional Quaker antipathy to higher education, the absence of professional clergy, and the college's recent founding limited the normal sources of faculty, and many non-Friends had to be hired. Magill had to defend his staff publicly in the *Friends Intelligencer*, pointing out that twelve of the twenty-one faculty were Friends and that four others had Quaker lineage. Furthermore, he maintained that "in the appointments of professors and instructors at Swarthmore, other things being equal, a member of our Religious Society is always preferred."[24] At another time he pointed out to traditionalist manager Clement Biddle that the number of Friends employed had risen in the thirteen years of operation. Magill questioned prospective faculty members on their religious affiliation, apparently to be sure that their beliefs would not prevent them from participating in the campus meetings rather than to require adherence to Quakerism.[25] Magill also questioned applicants on their ability to maintain discipline. His concern with this quality overshadows any interest in scholarly attainment in his correspondence.[26]

The autonomy of faculty members increasingly became an issue as they began to resist overseeing student life. The extent of their autonomy depended on the circumstances at individual institutions, especially on the president and his relationship to the board of trustees. Presidents then were not primarily administrators. They were the heads of the faculty, carrying a heavy teaching load and chairing weekly faculty meetings. Sometimes they were far more. Some, such as Nevin and McCosh, brought significant academic reputations to the job. Others, like Hill and Magill, were relatively unknown. But presidential reputation and personality intersected with denomina-

23. McCosh to Daniel C. Gilman, 11 December 1876, Gilman Collection (Johns Hopkins University Manuscript Collection); McCosh to Scott, 15 March and 14 May 1880, McCosh Papers (Princeton University Manuscript Collection); Scott, 451–52.

24. Letter to the Editor, *Friends Intelligencer* 27 (21 February 1880): 6–7.

25. Magill to Biddle, 24 June 1882, Magill Papers. See letters to Magill from Thomas Stein (3 April 1883), Edward White (4 April 1885), and H. I. Riley (5 April 1885), Magill Papers. Poor records and little hiring prevent getting a clear picture of the process at Bucknell.

26. Letters from W. C. Collar and F. A. Christie to Magill, 3 April 1885, Magill Papers, indicate Magill's persistence on this question.

tional traditions, institutional finances, and the composition of the board to create widely divergent conditions for faculty at different colleges.

At Franklin and Marshall, fiscal crisis and the ouster of the president in 1866 led the trustees to increase their campus oversight. A new trustee committee observed final exams, while another frequently visited to oversee religious and moral life. Although the new president, John W. Nevin, was a prestigious theologian, his advanced age prevented him from being a strong administrator. The board was delighted to have Nevin's prestige but unwilling to give him much autonomy.[27] Nevin even had difficulty defending faculty control of honorary degrees. He complained that since the public held the faculty responsible for the quality of academic degrees, earned or honorary, could "it be right then to allow the faculty no voice whatever in the conferring of them?"[28] The board refused to change the procedure, although it began to screen candidates more carefully. The faculty did not receive an effective veto over honorary degree candidates until 1884.[29] While this change reflected a growing national concern about cheap degrees, it also resulted from the election of a less prestigious, but younger and more vigorous, president.

During the Rev. Thomas G. Apple's tenure, the trustees became less intrusive. They elected Apple with a keen sense of the need to strengthen the faculty after Professor Nathan C. Schaeffer wrote a scathing letter of resignation, calling for an infusion of new talent. Enough dissatisfaction existed to prompt the unusual step of reading the letter into the minutes of the board of trustees. The board, increasingly occupied with operating the academy and raising money for new facilities, allowed Apple and the faculty more discretion in educational matters. Apple received broad powers to deal with problems arising between the board's annual meetings. The trustees, intimately involved in campus affairs after the crisis of 1866, retreated to a more distant role enforced primarily by controlling the purse strings in the 1880s.[30]

At Bucknell the trustees also backed away after a period of intense involvement. Both of its governing boards were intensely involved

27. Franklin and Marshall, Trustees, 7 and 8 July 1868.
28. Ibid., June 1870.
29. Ibid., 27 June 1871 and 17 June 1884.
30. Ibid., 1877–88. Schaeffer's letter was recorded in the June 1877 minutes.

in the firing of Professor James, the forced retirement of President Loomis, and the William Bucknell "coup." With the defeat of the Lewisburg elements and their replacement by William Bucknell's Philadelphia coterie, the board of trustees became literally more distant. Most lived at least a day's journey from the campus. By gaining William Bucknell's confidence and avoiding controversy, President Hill gained a free hand.

At Princeton, President McCosh dominated events in his early years, but in the 1880s traditional trustees began to reassert their influence. McCosh played faculty and trustees against each other. One example was his campaign against fraternities in the early 1870s, in which he marshaled faculty support to convince trustees to eliminate the Greeks. But at the same meeting he showed no compunction about asking the board to remind the faculty of his right to be informed whenever they sought to leave the campus. The trustees accepted many of McCosh's ideas for modernizing the campus, but they continued to be regularly involved. Young Professor Scott complained: "The Board had gained a most inflated conception of its authority and importance. When I came home [from Heidelberg University in 1880], the Trustees were a first-class nuisance, meddling with every petty detail of administration and demanding that they be consulted before anything whatever could be done."[31] He soon found himself in a trustee's law office in New York, apologizing for an outburst during a joint trustee-faculty committee meeting. Young faculty recruited by McCosh to bring scholarly distinction to Princeton chafed under continuing demands from both the president and the board to act in loco parentis. The conflict between two ideals was heightened by the selection, over the objections of the faculty and the retiring president, of a very conservative Presbyterian minister to succeed McCosh in 1888.

The other three campuses were models of academic autonomy compared with Swarthmore, where the board of managers zealously enforced the ideal of a guarded education. The tone was set early: President Parrish did not survive Swarthmore's second year, after conflicts with the managers.[32] Edward Magill, principal of the pre-

31. W. Scott, 454. His visit to the trustee is described on 455. Princeton, Trustees, 22 December 1875.

32. The executive board minutes record only the appointment of a committee to deal with trouble in the faculty. A month later Parrish's resignation was recorded without comment. Swarthmore College, Executive Board, Minutes (Friends Historical

paratory school, was elevated to the presidency in 1871. Magill was more malleable, catering to the board to an extent that even he later regretted. Despite his deference, the managers considered reducing Magill's salary near the end of his term.[33]

The board of managers was organized to give close scrutiny to the campus. Its four-member visiting committee made weekly inspections. At monthly meetings its executive board dealt with everything from admissions and faculty appointments to outbreaks of measles and the use of tobacco. The board defended the faculty from external attack on occasion but barred even Magill from its meetings.[34] Although the visiting committee reports were verbal, and thus inaccessible to the historian, the committee's vigorous oversight surely restricted faculty prerogatives.

Trustees' expectations that faculty would continue to provide moral stewardship were generally accepted by older faculty. But the younger generation, trained in doctoral programs, were more resistant. Across the four campuses, nonacademic duties were reduced slightly during the 1870s and 1880s but remained onerous by today's standards. Although specialized expertise was slowly becoming more valued, faculty were still multifunctional professionals, in the mold of ministers. Faculty had numerous nonacademic tasks; acting in loco parentis was hard work. Professor Ferris Price found himself overseeing lunch six days a week at Swarthmore, as well as proctoring study halls and taking attendance at Bible classes and Sunday meeting. Other professors doubled as librarians, museum curators, and registrars. The president and trustees took the nonacademic tasks as seriously as the academic ones. President McCosh sternly held the faculty to their chapel duties. At Bucknell one of President Loomis's charges against Professor James was that he refused to spend evenings keeping order in the college dormitory. Professor Maria San-

---

Library), 8 December 1869–14 March 1871. Parrish blamed Magill in his diary, though his overreaction to Magill may have triggered the managers' action. Homer D. Babbidge, Jr., "Swarthmore College in the Nineteenth Century: A Quaker Experience in Education" (Ph.D. diss., Yale University, 1953), 86–100. Magill told a different version, saying the managers feared Parrish. Edward H. Magill, *Sixty-Five Years in the Life of a Teacher* (Boston: Houghton Mifflin, 1907), 152–53.

33. Magill, 152–53, 191–92; Swarthmore College, Board of Managers, Minutes (Friends Historical Library), 20 June 1887.

34. Magill, 191–92; Swarthmore, Executive Board, 8 December 1869–26 June 1872; Swarthmore College, *Annual Catalogue*, 1871/72, p. 35–36.

ford was fired from Swarthmore for failing to inform the managers' Committee on Instruction when she left campus for speaking engagements.[35]

Professional duties were not standardized. Faculty were expected to be willing to vary their work to serve the institution. A death in the faculty, new courses, or financial retrenchment meant increased teaching loads. When President McCosh called on the Princeton trustees to reduce the size of freshman classes by creating extra sections, the trustees responded by adding an hour to each tutor's daily work load. Although in this case there was extra pay, the board reiterated the principle that "the Trustees do not by such act admit that the Trustees are not entitled to all of the time of each tutor."[36] Such bonuses rarely rewarded extra work; the faculty had to wait for relief until the board chose to augment the staff.[37]

The positive side of the lack of specialization was the potential for a sense of academic community. Before 1890 all four colleges were small enough to hold weekly meetings to deal with discipline, scheduling, grading, and student activities. The largest, Princeton, had ten regular faculty and nine junior and part-time members when McCosh arrived. By 1890 there were forty-five faculty, many in junior positions. The complement of each of the other three faculties never exceeded a dozen in these decades. In a day when professors frequently spent an entire career in one institution, close ties no doubt developed. The absence of departmental barriers and the presence of common religious commitments provided a basis for social and intellectual community.

Although the college community probably offered psychic comfort, faculty lacked formal security. Faculty salaries could be reduced in times of financial distress. The payroll was sometimes in arrears, especially at Franklin and Marshall. One year at Swarthmore, salaries were attached to a sliding scale based on enrollment. The lack of a tenure system made it possible for a professor with years of service to be dropped suddenly, as happened to Professor James at Bucknell.

35. See, for instance, "General Organization 1890–91," a notebook in the Appleton Presidential papers (Friends Historical Library), or McCosh's reports to the board of trustees on 22 December 1875 and 9 February 1888.

36. Princeton, Trustees, 27 October 1875.

37. Trustee minutes at the four colleges give similar pictures of working conditions, job security, and nonacademic tasks in the 1870s and 1880s.

But arbitrary dismissal was rare; despite the lack of procedural protection, faculty enjoyed considerable de facto security.

The absence of guaranteed pensions was a more serious source of insecurity. When a professor died in office, trustees apparently had clear consciences as long as the survivors received the remainder of the year's pay. A few venerable professors were lucky enough that, when they could no longer teach, the trustees arranged a pension. When William Nevin (brother of the famous theologian and former Franklin and Marshall president) could no longer carry a full teaching load, he received a pension and continued to teach a few classes. By setting the pension at eight hundred dollars annually and hiring a young replacement at seven hundred dollars, the pension involved no additional initial expenditure.[38] Like other Americans, aging faculty had to depend on family, personal fortune, and good health.

While institutionalized pensions were decades away, working conditions improved in the 1880s. Most notably, boards began to support leaves of absence for graduate study in European universities or American graduate schools. More money was also appropriated for scientific research, field trips, and libraries.[39]

Despite the limited institutional provisions for support, formal security, and career "ladders," college teaching was a long-term commitment for most faculty, one usually tied to a single institution. The average career of a faculty member in 1870 ranged between twenty-three and thirty years. For a faculty member in the mid-1880s, the average length of service at Princeton declined slightly to twenty-seven, while it jumped to thirty-three at Bucknell and at Franklin and Marshall. Swarthmore went against the trend, declining to an average of eighteen years due to rapid turnover among assistant professors. The managers considered this to be unhealthy and took steps to increase stability. The mean for full professors at Swarthmore was twenty-four years, and two-thirds of them remained at Swarthmore for over a quarter of a century. William Owens, professor of physics and chemistry at Bucknell for fifty years, served the longest. While most faculty spent their entire teaching careers at one institution, some taught at other colleges, making the total professorial careers longer than the figures shown in Table 6.

38. Franklin and Marshall, Trustees, 15 June 1886. Some expense ensued later as the replacement's salary rose.

39. See, e.g., Bucknell University, Board of Trustees, Minutes (Bucknell University Archives), 23 June 1885 and 12 January 1888.

Table 6. Length of Faculty Service at the Colleges, 1869–1885

Bucknell	1869–70	23	1885–86	33
F&M	1873–74	24	1883–84	33
Princeton	1867–68	30	1884–85	27+
Swarthmore	1872–73	25	1884–85	18

SOURCE: The figures were calculated from college directories and include assistant, associate, and full professors. Tutors and lecturers were not included. The years served by faculty as emeriti were not included.

NOTE: This table measures the average length of service (past and future) to that college of all faculty employed in the specified year. The Princeton 1884–85 figure is a minimum, as some had not completed their service when the directory was published in 1906. Swarthmore's proximity to Philadelphia enabled it to use more part-time and short-term staff than the other three colleges, but the rapid turnover of assistant professors concerned the instruction committee, which recommended granting more professional autonomy to retain faculty (Swarthmore College, Committee on Instruction, Minutes [Friends Historical Library], 6 February 1885). Marilyn Tobias, *Old Dartmouth on Trial: The Transformation of the Academic Community in Nineteenth-Century America* (New York: New York University Press, 1982), 35, found similar longevity at Dartmouth (almost 75 percent worked at least twenty-five years) as at the three colleges in this study outside metropolitan areas.

The prevalence of clerically trained faculty has often been cited as a congenital weakness of the "old-time college." Appointment of nonclerical faculty became historians' litmus test for the victory of professional standards over narrow piety. Most faculty at Franklin and Marshall, Princeton, and Bucknell in 1865 had been trained in theological seminaries. In the next quarter-century the proportion at the latter two declined, with few clerical faculty appointed after 1870. But the significance of this change has been exaggerated. This can be demonstrated by juxtaposing Franklin and Marshall with Swarthmore. The former maintained the most clerical faculty in 1890, whereas Swarthmore, due to the absence of ministers in Quakerism, had none. Swarthmore led in science, but overall Franklin and Marshall probably had a stronger faculty; clerical faculty did not yet necessarily obstruct intellectual life.

Faculty trained in theological seminaries were not simply ministers exiled to academia. In Donald Scott's terms, the clergy moved "from office to profession" in the mid-nineteenth century, becoming a profession that encompassed far more than the ministry. The seminary became the major outlet for those desiring an intellectual profession. The growth of denominational and interdenominational organizations, churches, academies, and colleges offered hope that one's religious and intellectual calling could lead to a profession. College teaching was one of several potential careers for theological seminary graduates.

To criticize colleges for the high proportion of clerical faculty before 1890 anachronistically ignores the realities of intellectual life in the period. Rather than the clergy restricting progress in higher education, the opposite may be closer to the truth. The proliferation of colleges after 1800 created a demand for academics that could only be filled by drawing on the main supply of trained intellectuals: the clergy. The use of clergy, therefore, permitted a remarkable expansion of higher education.

Much of the advanced scholarship of the time was produced under theological auspices. Seminaries had higher standards of admission than other professional schools and provided training in the most advanced intellectual areas, especially linguistics and philosophy. Predating disciplinary barriers, moral and natural philosophy ranged across what today is called the arts and sciences. Only with the founding of Johns Hopkins in 1876 did a more advanced rival appear, and few other graduate schools appeared before 1890. Denominational quarterlies such as the *Reformed Church Review* and *New Princeton Review* were among the most important scholarly outlets of the time. They were sponsored by denominations but published articles on a wide range of intellectual and social issues as well as on specifically theological topics. They were not surpassed until the new disciplinary organizations began publishing their own journals near the end of the century. Theology provided an umbrella for scholarly activities that later divided into the various humanities and social sciences, a transition exemplified by the merger of the *New Princeton Review* and *Political Science Quarterly* in 1888.[40]

Burton Bledstein has written that "above all, what had been missing

40. Lewis Perry, *Intellectual Life in America: A History* (New York: Franklin Watts, 1984), 248–57; Donald M. Scott, *From Office to Profession: The New England Ministry, 1750–1850* (Philadelphia: University of Pennsylvania Press, 1978), 148–55; Natalie A. Naylor, "The Theological Seminary in the Configuration of American Higher Education," *History of Education Quarterly* 17 (Spring 1977): 17–30; Frederick Rudolph, *Curriculum: A History of the American Undergraduate Course of Study Since 1636* (San Francisco: Jossey-Bass, 1977), 179; Hoeveler, 310–11; Stanley M. Guralnick, *Science and the Ante-Bellum American College* (Philadelphia: American Philosophical Society, 1975), 152.

in the old-time college was an academic culture."[41] Such an observation may be accurate, but it misses the point. College faculty in the mid- to late nineteenth century were part of a larger intellectual life that centered around scientific organizations, the lyceum movement, professionalized clergy, and journalism. Clergy, men of letters, and lecturers were cultural heroes within polite circles. Their pictures were available, their works were recited in schools, and their images were even used in the popular parlor game of Authors. They formed the intellectual and cultural leadership that Lewis Perry calls "the inner circle of respectability" within the "larger circle of sentimental culture."[42]

Other faculty moved between scientific and literary circles and the colleges. The lines between genteel culture and academia hardened slowly, first in science. Increasingly, acceptance as a scientist required individuals to join certain scientific organizations, subscribe to certain journals, and be either a doctor, a college-educated lawyer, or a scientist in a college or the government. While many were not full-time scientists, science was becoming more exclusive, and by the 1880s the practice of hiring doctors to teach college science was being replaced by attempts to hire those with Ph.D.'s. The development of an academic culture occurred slowly, and at different speeds in different areas of knowledge.

The older professors who dominated the faculties in the 1870s and 1880s were products of the denominational theological seminaries and the broader literary and scientific world. They were moderately wealthy men who lived alongside the town's elite. They sacrificed potential income in order to teach and had little of the formal security accorded modern academics, but they were much better paid and more secure than most Americans. Most faculty made long-term commitments to college teaching and to a single college. Most were in touch with the intellectual leaders of their local community and denomination. While their intellectual accomplishments would soon be overshadowed by those from research universities, these faculty made possible an extraordinary experiment in higher education.

Faculty life at these four colleges contradicts depressing images of an impoverished, socially isolated college professoriate before what

41. Burton J. Bledstein, *The Culture of Professionalism* (New York: W. W. Norton, 1976), 269.

42. Perry, 185–95, 248–76. The phrases are on 254.

Christopher Jencks and David Reisman dubbed the "academic revolution." Frederick Rudolph, in his classic *American College and University*, concluded that "everyone knew that faculty salaries were distressingly low," which "helped to alienate a large body of American intellectuals from the mainstream of American life."[43] Many other works, documented with pithy quotes from early university reformers, have echoed this theme.[44]

Convincing as the scenario appears, some scholars have challenged it recently. Colin Burke questioned whether late nineteenth-century professionalization brought higher salaries or security. Lewis Perry placed college faculty within the small-town and urban cultural elites. Louise Stevenson found that Yale faculty blended evangelical Protestantism with a lively interest in the most pressing literary, social, and scientific problems.[45]

Modern academic culture was in its infancy in 1890 and beginning to be represented by the junior faculty members, especially at Princeton. As Louise Stevenson has shown for Yale, the generation in power in the 1870s and 1880s at these four colleges acted initially as reformers. These presidents sought to blend antebellum criteria for faculty with new epistemological developments as they recruited the next generation.[46] But one generation's reformers become the next period's conservatives. Those like McCosh's "bright young men" were affiliated with the new disciplinary organizations and had a different vision of academia. Most accepted genteel Protestantism but were committed neither to pious evangelicalism nor to denominational organizations; their world was more exclusive and specialized. After experiences in European or American graduate schools, they chafed at nonacademic chores and sought to invoke university values.

The younger faculty, especially those trained in graduate schools or European universities, changed academia and pioneered academic

43. Frederick Rudolph, *The American College and University* (New York: Vintage Books, 1962), 197, 200.

44. See, e.g., Laurence R. Veysey, *The Emergence of the American University* (Chicago: University of Chicago Press, 1965), 7; Bledstein, 269; Merle Curti, *American Scholarship in the Twentieth Century* (Cambridge: Harvard University Press, 1953).

45. Burke, 232–33; Perry, chaps. 4–6; Louise L. Stevenson, "Between the Old-Time College and the Modern University: Noah Porter and the New Haven Scholars," *History of Higher Education Annual* 3 (1983): 39–57.

46. Louis L. Stevenson, *Scholarly Means to Evangelical Ends: The New Haven Scholars and the Transformation of Higher Learning in America, 1830–1890* (Baltimore: Johns Hopkins University Press, 1986), 14–29, 138–47.

culture after 1890. But the academics they succeeded bore little resemblance to the descriptions of Rudolph and others. They were not just antebellum holdovers, resisting change; the postbellum generation forged its own model. As Louise Stevenson has observed, we must not overlook stages of academic professionalization merely because they were not the final form.

4

"What Knowledge Is of Most Worth?"

In the late nineteenth century, Herbert Spencer's famous question had particular poignance for higher education. A veritable explosion of knowledge challenged the concept that all students could share the same curriculum; depth and breadth were in tension. The ideal of producing, if not Renaissance men, at least graduates familiar with all branches of knowledge was increasingly threatened by the growth of information, a trend that demanded specialization.

The bachelor of arts curriculum at most colleges was based on a philosophy of higher education drawn from classical and medieval traditions. Princeton, Franklin and Marshall, and Bucknell based their bachelor of arts programs on the twin tenets of liberal education: that all students should be introduced to a common body of knowledge, and that these studies should establish a base of information and mental discipline that prepared students for career, culture, and piety.[1]

In the antebellum United States these tenets of liberal education were expressed in wholly prescribed curricula dominated by classical language, philosophy, science, and mathematics. Rapid expansion of scientific knowledge, development of the social sciences, and the growing popularity of modern languages stretched the prescribed curriculum to the breaking point. Franklin and Marshall gave students no choice of course work until the 1890s. Bucknell and Princeton granted a limited number of electives in the upper-class years,

1. For an excellent explanation of the traditions of mental discipline and liberal culture, see Laurence R. Veysey, *The Emergence of the American University* (Chicago: University of Chicago Press, 1965), 21–56, 180–251.

while retaining prescriptions for the first two years to guarantee a secure foundation of liberal studies and mental discipline before catering to student interests. Spokesmen for these three colleges universally condemned the free use of electives at Harvard, which, according to President David Jayne Hill of Bucknell, ignored "the skill and experience embodied in the established curriculum, by entrusting the choice of studies to the crude, the indolent and the inexperienced."[2]

The elective "system"—really a nonsystem—was taken to its most extreme form at Harvard, where President Eilot abolished virtually all requirements. At Princeton, Franklin and Marshall, Bucknell, and Swarthmore, electives were incorporated within a more modest reform of liberal education. A central core of subjects continued to embody the belief that liberal education should impart a unified intellectual experience, with every subject integrated into an overarching worldview. Physics and metaphysics, for instance, were both expected to explain existence within the bounds of conventional Protestant thought. Combining this curriculum with a closely monitored campus life was designed to breed Christian scholars, or at least high-minded Christians.

Shortsighted materialism, rather than electives, was seen as the greatest obstacle to cultivating intellect and virtue. Material success was presumed to follow automatically in business and public service or, after further study, in law, medicine, and the ministry. Scientific studies were justified by their contribution to mental discipline and philosophical wholeness, rather than for production of chemists and engineers.[3] Graduate schools and technical institutes were to fulfill that function. Since the study of any subject in the absence of liberal education could produce a narrow and perhaps irreligious mindset, liberal education had to remain separate from vocational study.[4]

2. Aubrey Parkman, "David Jayne Hill" (Ph.D. diss., University of Rochester, 1961), 41. Quote was in an article by Hill in the *University Mirror* in June 1888.

3. See, e.g., the remarks of Professor John Stahr in Franklin and Marshall College, Board of Trustees, Minutes (Franklin and Marshall Archives), 15 June 1886.

4. Among many expressions of this view are Lyman H. Atwater, "Proposed Reforms in Collegiate Education," *New Princeton Review*, n.s., 10 (July 1882): 100–120; Princeton College, *Inauguration of James McCosh* (New York: Carter & Bros., 1868); Andrew F. West, "Must the Classics Go?" *North American Review* 138 (February 1884): 151–62; Theodore Appel, *The Life and Work of John Williamson Nevin* (Philadelphia: Reformed Church Publication House, 1889), 654; Lewis Steiner, "The American

Advocates of liberal education believed they were holding off the rampant materialism and utilitarianism that threatened religion and scholarship. This feeling, perhaps a constant in higher education, was especially strong in the rapidly changing economic and intellectual climate after the Civil War. In this period Franklin and Marshall's catalog defensively asserted that, despite popular clamor for more practical education, "no experiment of this sort is felt to be the mission of Franklin and Marshall College," and that by no such compromise would it seek "public attention or favor."[5] A few years later, after modest reforms, a college publication more confidently defended liberal education. "Now that the grand mistake of all this has come to be recognized it is pardonable to note how Franklin and Marshall never gave away to this pressure, nor receded an inch from her position of general culture and the true idea of liberal education."[6] Liberal educators slowly added electives and new subjects, making these adjustments within the spirit of mental discipline, liberal culture, and religious stewardship.

The bachelor of arts requirements at Bucknell, Franklin and Marshall, and Princeton were variations on a common theme. Franklin and Marshall, the most traditional, offered a completely prescribed curriculum dominated by the classics; the names Livy, Xenophon, Horace, Cicero, Homer, and Plato dot the course titles. Students completed mathematics as far as integral calculus and took rhetoric, ancient and medieval history, and philosophy. Due to its Germanic heritage, Franklin and Marshall had always offered a modern language. Courses in English literature and art history recognized the humanities in modern form. Science commanded a major portion of the upper-class years, while a senior course in the "connection between Natural Science and Revealed Religion" sought to mitigate the possible inroads of naturalism and empiricism. The social sciences were represented by a course on political economy. Lectures on ethics

College on the Defensive," *Mercersburg Review* 18 (April 1871): 182–95; unsigned [probably Theodore Appel], "The Vocation and Responsibilities of the American College," *Mercersburg Review* 24 (October 1877): 614–38; and Thomas G. Apple, "The Idea of a Liberal Education," *Proceedings of the College Association of Pennsylvania*, 1887–88.

5. Franklin and Marshall College, *Catalogue*, 1873–74, p. 13. For an insightful discussion of post–Civil War intellectuals and intellectual life, see Lewis Perry, *Intellectual Life in America: A History* (New York: Franklin Watts, 1984), chap. 6.

6. *College Days* 5 (February 1879): 5.

and social sciences replaced the antebellum moral philosophy course as the culmination of the educational experience.

Franklin and Marshall students still took a totally prescribed curriculum in 1890. Electives were avoided by increasing the course load to nine per term in the 1870s and ten in the 1880s. Since most sciences were covered in one term, in-depth study was impossible. When students requested the introduction of French in 1889 the faculty agreed, but as an optional course beyond the required ten. The faculty preserved the principle of a unified curriculum while adding new branches of knowledge, but the model was stretched to the breaking point.[7]

Bucknell and Princeton reformed their curricula slightly to incorporate the expansion of knowledge more fully. Bucknell's curriculum in the 1870s resembled Franklin and Marshall's, except students only took five or six courses, supplemented by weekly lectures on other branches of knowledge. In the 1880s, students were permitted to select one-third of their junior and senior courses from within a limited range of choices: for instance, seniors chose among French, Italian, and Juvenal. The classics, mathematics, and philosophy continued to dominate their first two years, and the president still taught "keystone" courses to the senior class.[8]

Shortly after his inaugural in 1868, McCosh brought French and German into the underclass schedule and permitted some choice in the upper-class years at Princeton. Like Hill, he retained much of the older curriculum by restricting most electives to choices among traditional subjects such as Greek, Latin, mathematics, and modern foreign languages. He strengthened the science faculty, adding advanced laboratory work in chemistry and museum work in biology and paleontology. When McCosh retired in 1888, the bachelor of arts curriculum remained a modified form of the traditional practices.[9] Thus Princeton and Bucknell ended the 1880s with workable curricular models, while Franklin and Marshall followed similar principles but awkwardly held onto a wholly prescribed curriculum.

There was an impressive breadth of science offerings at the three colleges. It is often forgotten that the classical curriculum was descended from the ancient Greek trivium and quadrivium, which in-

7. Franklin and Marshall College, *Catalogue*, 1869–70 to 1889–90.

8. Bucknell University, *Catalogue*, 1869–70 to 1889–90; J. Orin Oliphant, *The Rise of Bucknell University* (New York: Appleton-Century-Crofts, 1965), 141, 149–50.

9. Princeton University, *Catalogue*, 1867–68 to 1887–88.

cluded science and mathematics and not merely classical languages and literature. Scientific progress in the early 1800s led most antebellum colleges to add mineralogy, geology, zoology, and biology. After Halley's comet appeared in 1844, observatories became common on campuses. Although the government funded work in astronomy, collegiate enthusiasm was so great that most significant research in this period was performed on campuses. After the Civil War, science courses proliferated. For instance, in the early 1870s Franklin and Marshall students studied zoology, botany, inorganic and organic chemistry, physics, acoustics and optics, astronomy, geology, anatomy, and physiology and attended "Lectures on the connection between Natural Science and Revealed Religion." Few students today, other than science majors, spend as much time on science.[10]

Although the three colleges defended the traditional form of the B.A. degree, they created parallel degrees that substituted science and modern languages for some of the Latin and Greek. Colleges had experimented with parallel programs since the 1820s, but only a few scientific and engineering schools (e.g., Lawrence at Harvard, Sheffield at Yale, West Point) consistently awarded degrees other than the B.A. before 1870. In the following decade the colleges unveiled programs that lacked the prestige of the B.A. but provided alternatives for students wishing to substitute other courses for classical languages and literature.

Princeton established the Green School of Science in 1873. Its three-year bachelor of science was dominated by science and mathematics; the curriculum also included English, history, French, and German. For years the school suffered the stigmas of vocationalism and lower standards. Its admission requirements were lower than those for the B.A., and its students were initially barred from the campus literary societies. Extending the program to four years and instituting a graduate electrical engineering program in the 1880s reduced the invidious distinctions.[11]

10. For a careful revisionist study of antebellum collegiate science, see Stanley M. Guralnick, *Science and the Ante-Bellum American College* (Philadelphia: American Philosophical Society, 1975). Franklin and Marshall College, *Catalogue*, 1873–74.

11. Ibid., 1873–74 to 1888–89; Kenneth W. Condit, *History of the Engineering School of Princeton University, 1875–1955* (Princeton: Princeton University Press, 1962), 1–53; Eric F. Goldman, "The Princeton Period of John Bach McMaster," *Proceedings of the New Jersey Historical Society* 57 (January 1939): 214–30; Wallace J. Williamson, *The Halls* (Princeton, 1947), 37; Herbert Malick, "An Historical Study of Admission Prac-

Bucknell also established a parallel scientific course of study that, like the Green School of Science, began as a weak sister to the B.A. First offered in 1853, the scientific curriculum replaced most of the classics with additional science and mathematics courses. The program languished for decades due to the lack of qualified students and faculty. Finally, a new professor of natural science breathed life into the program, and about 25 percent of Bucknell graduates in the 1880s received Sc.B. or B.L. degrees.[12]

Franklin and Marshall put off parallel curricula until the turn of the century. The delay appears to have been caused by financial limitations rather than hostility toward science. In 1866 a trustee committee recommended creating a parallel scientific course, and the Franklin and Marshall curriculum always included a wide variety of sciences. But providing equipment and faculty was expensive. These colleges may have begrudged the expense, but they were not hostile to science. Even Princeton looked for ten years before finding a wealthy patron to underwrite its science school.[13]

Laurence Veysey once posited that "in nineteenth-century America, educational and theological orthodoxy almost always went together."[14] If the science courses and parallel curricula at the three colleges modify that generalization, Swarthmore's experience utterly contradicts it. In harmony with their Hicksite Quaker founders, Swarthmore eschewed classical subjects in favor of scientific and vo-

---

tices in Four-Year Undergraduate Colleges of the U.S.: 1870–1915" (Ph.D. diss., Boston College, 1966), 54–55. For a work that incorrectly portrays McCosh as reluctant to promote science, see Robert V. Bruce, *The Launching of Modern American Science, 1846–1876* (New York: Knopf, 1987), 326.

12. Bucknell University, *Catalogue*, 1869–70 to 1889–90; Oliphant, 149–50; John Winter Rice, *A History of the Teaching of Biology at Bucknell University* (Lewisburg, Pa., 1952), 1–3. Bucknell awarded its first bachelor of science degree in 1863. Both programs permitted substitution of science courses for some of the classics required for the bachelor of arts. In the 1880s twenty-seven graduates received a Sc.B. or Ph.B., and seventy-seven received a B.A. Bucknell University, *Alumni Catalogue, 1851–1921* (Lewisburg, Pa., 1921), 16–25.

13. For evidence of the acceptance of science, see Franklin and Marshall College, *Catalogue*, 1869–70 to 1889–90; H. M. J. Klein, *History of Franklin and Marshall College, 1787–1948* (Lancaster, Pa., 1952), 52. See also Professor Stahr's comments in Franklin and Marshall College, Board of Trustees, Minutes (Franklin and Marshall Archives), 15 June 1886; Varnum L. Collins, *Princeton*, American College and University Series (New York: Oxford University Press, 1914), 307; Condit, 3–8.

14. Veysey, 25.

cational offerings. Both presidents in this period favored extensive electives and science programs: President Parrish had been a chemistry lecturer in Philadelphia; and President Magill, who had attended Brown University, was impressed by President Wayland's innovations there.[15] In a promotional pamphlet Parrish explained that the managers intended to feature science and to introduce "no unprofitable subjects of controversy" into the institution; it was "their firm belief that as solid and substantial learning is imparted upon subjects of practical interest, less importance will be attached to visionary ideas and less interest felt in useless speculations."[16] Yet Magill and Parrish both worried that excessive preoccupation with practicality would breed narrowness. In the *Friends Intelligencer* Parrish warned that "unless we wish to become mere machines of very perfect construction, adapted only to a single end, let this special training be preceded by a generous and liberal culture."[17]

Swarthmore's bachelor of arts program differed radically from those of the other three colleges. The first two years were heavily prescribed, but eliminating Greek and advanced Latin left time for additional work in history, English, German, mathematics, and physics. Two-thirds of the upper-class curriculum was elective; the only requirements were elocution, rhetoric and composition, political economy, French, and history. There was also a senior moral philosophy course that, as at the other colleges, provided an indoctrination in ethics with an emphasis upon the beliefs of the sponsoring denomination.[18] Thus, before Eliot instituted his supposedly revolutionary elective program at Harvard, theologically conservative Swarthmore had already decided that juniors and seniors could select two-thirds of their courses.

Even elementary Latin offended some Quakers; several students in the early years left because they refused to take it. Using the

15. Edward H. Magill, *Sixty-Five Years in the Life of a Teacher, 1841–1906* (Boston: Houghton Mifflin, 1907), 40–56, 204.

16. Edward Parrish, *An Essay on Education in the Society of Friends* (Philadelphia: J. B. Lippincott & Co., 1866), 68.

17. *Friends Intelligencer* 26 (10 July 1869): 293; Parrish, 88–89; Edward Magill to Edward Parrish, 3 May 1866, Parrish Presidential Papers (Friends Historical Library).

18. Swarthmore College, *Annual Catalogue*, 1870–71 to 1889–90; Ruth C. Enion, "The Intellectual Incubation of a Quaker College, 1869–1903" (Master's thesis, Swarthmore College, 1944), 45.

University of Minnesota and Cornell University for precedents, the managers then created a bachelor of letters degree that substituted modern foreign languages for Latin.[19]

From its inception Swarthmore offered a bachelor of science degree. In the 1870s the freshman and sophomore courses resembled those in the B.A., except that projection drawing and descriptive geometry replaced Latin. Science students did not have to take any of the classical languages, but the ability to read elementary Latin was an admission requirement. The upper-class program stressed physics and chemistry as well as additional work in mathematics and modern foreign languages. Future engineers took the scientific curriculum with additional work in drawing, applied mathematics, and physics; if they worked as engineers for three years after receiving the B.S., they received a civil engineering degree "in course." Teacher training provided another vocational alternative, which could be taken within a degree program or as a separate two-year certificate course.[20] Rhetoric and composition, elocution, political economy, and mental and moral philosophy were the only common upper-class courses for students across the three degree programs.

In the 1880s, President Magill grew increasingly worried about Swarthmore's academic reputation among other colleges. Its graduates were only admitted to the junior class at Harvard until 1881, when most students were held back a year to raise standards. The conflict over the normal and preparatory departments were two manifestations of the determination on the part of the president and the faculty to bring Swarthmore into line with outside criteria for college work. Eli Lamb, chairman of the managers' Committee on Instruction, sided with them against more conservative managers committed to preserving a distinctive guarded education. In the late 1880s, the managers agreed to eliminate the normal and secondary programs. Greek was added to the entrance requirements, and admission standards for Latin, mathematics, and natural science were raised. The science and engineering curricula became more distinctive with additional courses in engineering, science, and mathematics as well as

19. A number of letters from parents in the Magill Presidential Papers (Friends Historical Library) complain about the difficulty of the studies, especially languages. See, for instance, S. Bevins to Magill, 1882, box 2.

20. Swarthmore College, *Annual Catalogue*, esp. 1872–73; Swarthmore College, Stockholders, *Minutes of the Annual Meeting of the Stockholders*, 1873, p. 48.

a new science building and observatory.[21] Swarthmore was gradually adopting a more traditional curricula.

The rapid growth of knowledge potentially threatened the theological and moral bases of Protestant colleges. The label "natural philosophy" for early science courses indicates the antebellum coordination of biblical revelations with science. The moral philosophy course reiterated the compatibility of science and religion. However, Darwinian theory and demands for more specialized science courses threatened this peaceable kingdom after the Civil War.

Most faculty attempted to reestablish harmony by denying that Darwinism, properly understood, clashed with revelation. Professor John Stahr, a Reformed church minister who taught science at Franklin and Marshall from 1871 until his selection as president in 1890, declared that evolution only posed a danger to literal interpretation of scripture. He pointed out that evolutionary theory said little about ultimate origins and did not contradict the view that nature was a rational process. Stahr rejected the view that man was merely an improved gorilla, but he accepted Darwin's *Descent of Man* as a useful explanation of human development as long as it was not used to deny man's spiritual nature. Stahr was confident that thorough work in science posed no danger if approached properly. Skepticism results when "we persistently ignore, or at least forget the only Creator, begin below by induction, adhere only to tangible facts, stifle our deepest intuitions, and believe only what we can see." But if one had a strong faith and did not try to draw theological conclusions from science, faith would remain intact. Stahr believed it would be illogical for the study of nature to lead one away from its creator.[22]

Stahr's colleague, the Rev. Theodore Appel, also taught science and had a similar faith in its harmony with religion. Pointing out that understanding creation is a matter of faith rather than science, Appel limited science to the safe task of studying how divinely created matter

21. Homer D. Babbidge, Jr., "Swarthmore College in the Nineteenth Century: A Quaker Experience in Education" (Ph.D. diss., Yale University, 1953), 122–30, 158–83; Enion, 54; Swarthmore College, Committee on Instruction, Minutes (Friends Historical Library), 6 February–15 June 1885; *Phoenix* 6 (February 1887): 99.

22. John Stahr, "Evolutionary Theories and Theology," *Mercersburg Review* 19 (July 1872): 439–50 (quotation is on 449). The Rev. Justin Loomis, president of Bucknell from 1858 to 1879, expressed similar views to a Baptist audience. See National Baptist Educational Convention, *Proceedings*, 1870, pp. 51–56; Perry, 291–95.

assumed its present state. He shared Stahr's view that recent liturgical interpretations eliminated contradictions between religion and science.[23]

James McCosh maintained a similar position at Princeton. In his inaugural address, he challenged the repudiation of evolution by the leading Old School Presbyterian theologian, Charles Hodge. The president perceived that Darwinism neither dealt with original causation nor necessarily contradicted a general interpretation of Genesis. To McCosh, evolution was the method by which God works. He confidently maintained that "whatsoever is true is also good, and will in the end be favorable to religion."[24] Princeton's introductory geology course in the 1870s exemplified McCosh's belief that religion and science could coexist. Eminent geologist Arnold Guyot presented the subject straightforwardly, proceeding from the beginnings of the earth in a ball of gas through the appearance of man. He did not mention religion until the conclusion of the final lecture, when he put geology into a theological context. "Geological history is a grand history of life according to an inward law," he told students. "External laws will give varieties of animals but cannot create a species. The physical globe is merely a means to an end. Man is connected with the upper and invisible sphere, the connecting link between nature and the spirit-world."[25]

The heralded battle between science and religion was barely a skirmish on these campuses. These colleges would not have hired outspoken skeptics. Similar beliefs were shared by such leading scientists as Harvard's famous biologist, Asa Gray. Responding to

23. Theodore Appel, "Creation and Cosmogony," *Mercersburg Review* 24 (January 1877): 123–38.

24. Quoted from McCosh's *Religious Aspect of Evolution* in a book review in the *New Princeton Review* 6 (1888): 139; see also Veysey, 41–43; Joseph E. Illick, "The Reception of Darwinism at the Theological Seminary and the College at Princeton, New Jersey," *Journal of the Presbyterian Historical Society* 38 (September and October 1960): 152–65, 234–43; Gary S. Smith, "Calvinists and Evolution, 1870–1920," *Journal of Presbyterian History* 61 (Fall 1983): 335–52. The starting point for analyzing McCosh is the outstanding biography by J. David Hoeveler, *James McCosh and the Scottish Intellectual Tradition: From Glasgow to Princeton* (Princeton: Princeton University Press, 1981). On curriculum, see esp. chap. 7.

25. Arnold Guyot, Lecture Notes on Geology, recorded by William Barricklo, 1877–78 (Princeton University Manuscript Collection). Quote is from book 2, 18. Guyot's piety did not interfere with his ability to inspire young, less pious students into scientific careers. See William Berryman Scott to Leonard Jones, Neuchâtel, Switzerland, 12 January 1928, William Scott Papers (Princeton University Archives).

McCosh's request for names of candidates for a science position, Gray noted that "I should much like you to have a good Christian man."[26] Once hired, the scientist's freedom was shielded by confidence in the ultimate harmony of science and religion. The judicious scientist could camouflage potentially dangerous discoveries by avoiding the theological implications. Pious educators felt that ignoring modern science was a greater danger. As James McCosh wrote, "I have all along had a sensitive apprehension that the discriminating denunciation of evolution from so many pulpits, periodicals, and seminaries might drive some of our thoughtful young men to infidelity, as they clearly saw development everywhere in nature."[27]

Swarthmore College was free from such soul-searching about the relation of religion and science. Combining the Quaker faith in the goodness of nature and practical education, the founders had no qualms about scientific studies. President Parrish advertised that the institution "proposed to give greater prominence to the physical, natural, and chemical sciences than is common in ordinary colleges."[28] He lauded Herbert Spencer's conclusion that science was the knowledge most worth knowing and proudly emphasized that Quaker educators had long valued science over literature.[29]

Daily teaching of the social sciences and humanities was infused with religion and moral commitment. Since it was more difficult to make as clear a distinction between religion and subject matter, teaching in these areas was more intimately tied to one's worldview. Courses in the social sciences and nonclassical humanities splintered off from moral philosophy. President Hill's teaching at Bucknell illustrates the change. He inherited courses in moral philosophy, metaphysics, *Butler's Analogy*, constitutional law, and political economy. Hill soon dropped the first three, replacing them with psychology, ethics, and anthropology, and lengthened the political economy course. He also moved from recitations on a textbook to lectures supplemented by readings and discussion. A defender of the economic status quo, Hill taught laissez-faire economics and sought to cleanse students of na-

26. Gray to McCosh, 10 April 1874, McCosh Collection (Princeton University Manuscript Collection). McCosh's correspondent authored the renowned *Gray's Anatomy*. Veysey, 48; George M. Marsden, *The Evangelical Mind and the New School Presbyterian Experience* (New Haven: Yale University Press, 1970), 149.

27. Illick, 236, quoting McCosh's *Religious Aspect of Evolution*; Perry, 291–95.

28. Parrish, 63–64.

29. Ibid., 10–12.

scent socialist sympathies. Hill's offerings were a modernized version of the old senior courses, constituting half of the required senior work.[30]

Humanities and social science courses usually conveyed Victorian moralism. Joseph Dubbs, professor of history at Franklin and Marshall, saw "the true meaning of history as the development of the life of God in the world."[31] A colleague in literature claimed that his field was, next to religion, the most powerful and direct way to form character.[32] Another literature professor, the Rev. James Murray of Princeton, emphasized the morality of authors and their works in his lectures. Once he chronicled their sins, Murray could praise the literary value of authors like Byron and Burns and poems like *Don Juan*. History professor Charles Shields divided the past into four epochs: prehistoric, pre-Christian, Christian (or the "era of progress"), and millennial (or the "era of perfection"). Although he explained secular historical theories, he always returned to his quadripartite theological breakdown, concluding that the fourth era would usher in a Christian utopia. Professor Lyman Atwater blamed John Stuart Mill's regrettable radicalism on his "spiritualistic materialism."[33]

The board of managers regularly urged the Swarthmore faculty to increase their use of Quaker literature in courses. Typical of most faculty, the head of the philosophy department responded by selecting the textbooks that were "most in harmony with the views of Friends"—but little Friends literature found its way into courses.[34] At all four colleges, broadly accepted Protestant norms rather than denominationalism determined the values that were imparted.

Unfortunately, modern curricular debates are too often based on a simplified understanding of late nineteenth-century curricular change.

30. Parkman, 18–22, 50, 57–60; David Jayne Hill, As It Seemed to Me (ca. 1930, University of Rochester Library Special Collections, typescript), 156–57, 500–501; David Jayne Hill, *Lecture Notes on Economics and Politics* (Lewisburg, Pa., 1884). Hill published a pamphlet on "The Principles and Fallacies of Socialism." Bucknell University, *Catalogue*, 1885–86, pp. 15–18.

31. Joseph Henry Dubbs, *History of Franklin and Marshall College* (Lancaster, Pa.: Franklin and Marshall Alumni Association, 1903), 290. This well-written "house history" exhibits no overt assumptions about divine intervention. As with most of the faculty, such beliefs provided a vague glow rather than a rigid interpretation.

32. George Mull, "The Study of English Literature," *Reformed Quarterly Review* 36 (October 1889): 516–32.

33. Barricklo's notebooks from courses of professors Murray, Shield, and Atwater.

34. Babbidge, 188–97; Swarthmore, Committee on Instruction, 6 February 1885.

Most surveys of American history and of higher education depict conservative defenders of the classics and the prescribed curriculum engaged in mortal combat with forward-looking proponents of electives, science, and utilitarian education. An eager public presumably withheld their patronage of higher education until the reformers triumphed. The most influential advocate of this view is Frederick Rudolph, who clearly enunciated it in his influential *Curriculum.*

> The colleges were plagued by unpopularity and uncertainty of purpose into the 1870s and beyond. A developing rationale, even as the colleges headed unwittingly toward curricular chaos, made its appearance, however, not by some wand's stroke but because it could no longer be delayed. . . . They [the university builders] confronted the nervousness, the uncertainties, the disjunction between higher education and society in the way that great surgeons meet all but insurmountable medical challenges in movie and television drama. . . .
>
> Until the colleges succeeded in making curricular arrangements that supported *that* vision of America, they could not be popular or, although unpopular, very effective.[35]

Rudolph's book, published by the influential Carnegie Commission, is the resource most generalists draw upon to discuss the nineteenth-century curriculum.

These case studies do not support Rudolph's notion that colleges failed to respond to a palpable demand for university-style reforms. When alternative degrees were offered, most students remained in the bachelor of arts program. The four colleges established graduate programs but found few takers before 1890. Modest growth in the ministry, law, science, engineering, and medicine slowly increased enrollment, but if there was broad public demand for such reforms, it was circumspect.

Instead, as Colin Burke has suggested, these colleges faced greater demand for secondary and normal programs than for utilitarian and graduate programs.[36] All four colleges ran preparatory programs,

35. Frederick Rudolph, *Curriculum: A History of the American Undergraduate Course of Study Since 1638* (San Francisco: Jossey-Bass, 1977), 99–100. For a useful critique of Rudolph's book, see David Potts, "Curriculum and Enrollments," *History of Higher Education Annual* 1 (1981): 88–109.

36. Colin Burke, *American Collegiate Populations: A Test of the Traditional View* (New York: New York University Press, 1982), chap. 5.

and only Princeton could have survived solely on collegiate studies. Swarthmore established a normal program, and the other colleges considered adopting teacher training curricula. Swarthmore and Bucknell even sponsored elementary education for a period. These multifunctional institutions served many constituents who were not convinced that a college fit their own or their communities' needs. The denominations increasingly reserved their limited higher education funds for theological seminaries. Thus, college curricula should be judged in the context of a period when the most popular courses were essentially noncollegiate.

Rudolph's implication that colleges were restricted to a choice between a narrowly classical curriculum and that of the new universities caricatures late nineteenth-century higher education. As Stanley Guralnick has pointed out, science had long been a major part of college curricula, and the prescribed programs guaranteed that all students gained considerable exposure to science.[37] Even the rise of Darwinism did not deter the colleges from requiring extensive science courses. As Lewis Perry has observed, rigid opponents of evolutionary theory, such as McCosh's nemesis Charles Hodge, were atypical. The faculty at these colleges complacently absorbed Darwin's work with an optimistic belief that science would not contradict the mysteries of divine creation. These case studies strongly support Lewis Perry's assertion that "probably no subject in the history of American intellectual life has been more widely misunderstood than the reception of Darwin's theory of evolution."[38]

Religious conventions placed greater restrictions on those teaching the burgeoning humanities and social science courses. While scientists could dodge moral questions and had specialized journals, humanistic and social science issues were debated in the general theological and literary journals. Disciplinary organizations in the humanities and social sciences were still in their infancy in 1890, and their journals had not yet fully replaced the denominational quarterlies. Because faculty members at these colleges rarely challenged respectable Victorian political and moral thought openly, the exact boundaries of, and sanctions against, nonconformity are not clear.

These colleges do not fit Rudolph's account of institutions resisting change at every turn until forced to imitate universities. There was

37. Guralnick, 152–59.
38. Perry, 291–95 (quote is on 292).

resistance to change, and reducing the classics or dropping the prescribed curriculum was a bitter pill. But there was not the desperate resistance described by Rudolph. Indeed, Swarthmore, the college most dedicated to defending its denominational character, eagerly embraced the new curricular ideas. The four colleges added new areas of knowledge as they developed in science, the social sciences, and the humanities. Modern languages, a tradition at Franklin and Marshall, were soon added at the other three. Engineering programs were established at three of the four colleges. This was not revolutionary curricular change, but neither was it stasis. Louise Stevenson's vision of relatively constant reform, with each generation initially reforming and then defending the new status quo, is a more satisfactory model. Her study of the Yale faculty from 1830 to 1890 and David Hoeveler's biography of James McCosh show that the two leading "conservative" institutions of traditional historiography earnestly sought to integrate intellectual innovation and evangelical Protestantism.[39]

By 1890 the four colleges were converging on a new curricular consensus. Each offered modified B.A. programs with limited electives and parallel programs with reduced classics requirements. Rather than being caught in a dichotomy between obstinately resisting or slavishly following universities, these institutions reached workable reconciliations of their traditional missions and the dramatic expansion of knowledge.

39. Louise L. Stevenson, *Scholarly Means to Evangelical Ends: The New Haven Scholars and the Transformation of Higher Learning in America, 1830–1890* (Baltimore: Johns Hopkins University Press, 1986); and Hoeveler, 215–349.

5

Students as Gentlemen

Princeton, Franklin and Marshall, Bucknell, and Swarthmore today epitomize the American collegiate ideal. With handsome dormitories, dining halls, gymnasiums, athletic fields, and chapels, these tranquil campuses exude tradition and stability. They give the impression that a century ago or more students lived in a similar, if more rule-bound and homogeneous, environment. If such continuity is true anywhere, it should be for these prestigious residential liberal arts colleges.

Not surprisingly, the student bodies in the late 1800s were small by today's standards. The largest was Princeton, which grew from 264 when McCosh arrived in 1868 to 684 in 1890. The smallest was Bucknell, with seventy-one students as the 1880s closed. Franklin and Marshall ended the period with about 150 college students, as did Swarthmore. But enumerating college students overlooks the presence of subcollegiate classes on campus. At Bucknell and Swarthmore collegians were a minority during most of the period, and at Franklin and Marshall they barely outnumbered the academy and seminary students. Only Princeton was primarily collegiate, and even there preparatory classes were held in the 1870s.

By the 1880s a collegiate subculture was growing on these campuses, and its greatest promoter, the campus newspaper, decried the presence of these noncollegians. Having to share a campus with them affronted the emerging sense of collegiate dignity. In addition, a surprising number of collegiate students were not part of the community for the "normal" four years. Only about 40 percent of Swarthmore students completed their program in the 1870s and 1880s. At

Franklin and Marshall, 60 percent of students enrolled between 1853 and 1903 graduated. Catalogs regularly listed a considerable number of "special students," the euphemism for part-time students. The student bodies were neither as stable nor as purely collegian as they would later become.[1]

They were, however, racially, religiously, and ethnically homogeneous. Only one nonwhite student was recorded in the census at any of the colleges, West Indian–born William Granger of Bucknell. Each campus had difficulty enrolling as many students from the sponsoring denomination as most trustees desired, but the campuses were solidly Protestant. The rare surviving lists of religious affiliation show few Catholics and hardly any Jews. Student publications rarely mentioned ethnoreligious differences and showed little interest in doctrinal differences among Protestants. The *Princetonian* complained vigorously when denominationalism obstructed a faculty appointment: "That eminent and influential men should be prevented from coming to Princeton because in some of the less important points of Christian doctrine, or some of the external forms of Christian worship they differ with the majority of our faculty, is bigoted and absurd."[2] Although Germanic parents of Franklin and Marshall students and Scottish and Scotch-Irish parents of Princetonians may have selected those colleges because of ethnoreligious connections, the students seem to have created a broadly "American" culture that welcomed all "WASPs."

Official college rules mandated careful oversight of student life,

1. Homer D. Babbidge, Jr., "Swarthmore College in the Nineteenth Century: A Quaker Experience in Education" (Ph.D. diss., Yale University, 1953), 227; Franklin and Marshall College, *Catalogue of Officers and Students, 1787–1903* (Lancaster, Pa., 1903), viii. This collaborates the hypothesis of David F. Allmendinger, *Paupers and Scholars: The Transformation of Student Life in Nineteenth-Century New England* (New York: St. Martin's Press, 1975), 91–94.

2. *Daily Princetonian* 1 (22 September 1876): 7. Granger's race is recorded in the Decennial Census for Union County, Pennsylvania, 1880, reel 1175. Neither pictures, college records, nor censuses suggest the presence of other nonwhites. Strangely, only a few scattered records of students' denominational affiliation survived despite its importance to college authorities. Princeton yearbooks were the only regular source I found, published or unpublished. In these decades classes were 60–75 percent Presbyterian. The Episcopalians who vexed McCosh composed 12–15 percent of each class. Most of the rest were Protestant; about 1 percent were Catholics and none were Jewish in the years I sampled. However, 5–10 percent typically did not answer or called themselves pantheists, heathens, etc., possibly hiding skepticism or an unpopular faith.

but the limited facilities made these rules an ideal rather than a reality. Regulations for chapel services exemplify this dichotomy. Students at three colleges were required to attend chapel every weekday morning; these services also served as an assembly and a platform for visiting speakers. Quaker Swarthmore had a slightly different practice: scriptural readings followed by a period of silence just before bedtime. In the early 1870s, Princeton students had to attend Sunday afternoon Bible lectures (reinforced by a midweek review) funded by one of McCosh's Scottish-American supporters. Student misbehavior brought these to an unseemly end in 1876.

None of the colleges gave any thought to dropping compulsory chapel after Harvard did so in 1886. But the reality of the required Sunday observances was shaped by physical limitations. These were not campuses dominated by stately chapels; in 1865 only Princeton had a chapel, and it was modest. The other three colleges conducted their weekday services in assembly halls, some of them too small for the whole student body. The founders of Swarthmore consciously rejected having a meetinghouse on the grounds. (Traditionalists eventually won and constructed one.) Franklin and Marshall had only an austere room for services in the early 1870s. A drive to fund construction of a chapel fell afoul of the panic of 1873, and a small extension onto Old Main had to suffice. Bucknell students attended Sunday services in various Lewisburg churches until William Bucknell donated a chapel in 1885. In 1886 Princeton moved its services into an elegant new Romanesque chapel. College religion was coming to demand less austere piety and more ornate quarters.[3]

When it comes to those essential components of "traditional" college life, dormitories and dining halls, only Swarthmore provided room and board for virtually all of its students—and the paternalistic guidance that implied in Victorian society. With their deep commitment to guarded education, the backers of Swarthmore refused to open the institution until a mammoth stone building was completed in which all preparatory and collegiate students could eat and sleep.

3. H.M.J. Klein, *History of Franklin and Marshall College, 1787–1948* (Lancaster, Pa., 1952), 105–6; Thomas J. Wertenbaker, *Princeton, 1746–1896* (Princeton: Princeton University Press, 1946), 239–41, 335–36; H. C. Pitney, "Recollections," McCosh Papers (Princeton University Manuscript Collection); *Princetonian* 1 (19 October 1876): 6; Richard J. Walton, *Swarthmore College: An Informal History* (Swarthmore, Pa.: Swarthmore College, 1986), 10; J. Orin Oliphant, *The Rise of Bucknell University* (New York: Appleton-Century-Crofts, 1965), 148.

Fig. 10. God and man at Princeton: Marquand Chapel, built in 1882.

Other than a small number of "townies" who lived at home, all students lived under the same roof with the faculty. The 1870 census taker found President Parrish, six instructors, a matron, and a caterer living in the main building. In the summer of 1880 it housed eleven members of the faculty as well as numerous maids, laundresses, and cooks, according to the census.[4] In the dining room, the sexes dined together at tables presided over by a faculty member; this was followed by a chaperoned social hour. Steam heat, gas lights, and regular exercise were supposed to protect the health of staff and students, as dormitories were notoriously unhealthy. It was not fireproof, however, and it burned to the ground in 1881. Luckily, guarded education had wealthy supporters; Swarthmore was financially strapped, but funds immediately appeared to supplement insurance and to rebuild Old Main.

4. Bureau of the Census, Decennial Census, 1870 and 1880, for Springfield Township; Walton, 5–13.

Fig. 11. A mixed-sex table group at Swarthmore, 1884.

Such carefully structured in loco parentis could not exist at the other campuses. Bucknell required all students to live on campus, except for the 15 percent or so who lived at home. However, unless one wished to dine with the preparatory students, students had to leave campus for their meals. At one-half to two-thirds of the cost of campus dining, students could join a club and eat at a boardinghouse.

Franklin and Marshall, perhaps influenced by German tradition, had no dormitory facilities at first. The 1869–70 catalog listed thirteen students living at home; the other fifty-nine lived in boardinghouses, each generally run by a married woman and accommodating five to ten students. Only two students lived apart from other students, and they may have been living with relatives who had a different last name. These were not "bachelor pads," but neither was this guarded education. In the early 1870s the college purchased a large boardinghouse, but a majority of the students continued to live either at home or in private rooms.

Most surprisingly, Princeton did not fulfill this collegiate ideal. It had long required students to live on campus if there was space, but as early as the 1840s there were too few rooms. The doubling of enrollment during McCosh's presidency forced increasing numbers of students to live off-campus. The 1870 and 1880 censuses show student boardinghouses dotting the town, many of them apparently run by students. Ever since the commons had been disbanded in 1855, groups of about fifteen students had formed eating clubs that made private arrangements with local landlords. Woodrow Wilson, for instance, was one of fourteen students who constituted "The Alligators" and rented a house across the street from the campus. These informal organizations were usually temporary, but after an attempt to restore the campus dining halls failed and fraternities were banned in the mid-1870s, permanent eating clubs with their own buildings began to be incorporated.

McCosh squeezed the housing situation further when he moved students out of Nassau Hall. Only three of the buildings constructed during his twenty-year presidency were dormitories. One was an elegant Victorian Gothic structure that appealed to wealthy students. Appalled by the growing opulence of the campus, McCosh had a more modest and cheaper alternative constructed to attract poorer students, especially those preparing for the ministry.[5] Since McCosh was educated in Scottish universities where students lived in private "digs," it was not second nature to him to make dormitories a high priority. But neither was he deviating as far from American practice as one might assume.

Such departures from the conventional image of the denominational college partially stem from economic limitations. Except for some liberal Quakers, authorities at all four colleges wanted chapels. But assembly halls and local churches provided acceptable alternatives while money was limited, whereas science buildings were expensive facilities for which no alternatives existed. Each college constructed and equipped at least one in the 1870s and 1880s, and several built observatories. These required a considerable outlay and commitment to science, and meant forgoing other facilities. Except at

5. Wertenbaker, 324–35; Henry Wilkinson Bragdon, *Woodrow Wilson: The Academic Years* (Cambridge: Belknap Press of Harvard University Press, 1967), 29–36; James W. Alexander, "Undergraduate Life at Princeton—Old and New," *Scribner's Magazine* 21 (June 1897): 667–69.

Swarthmore dormitories and dining halls were sacrificed. Young alumni were more eager to contribute gymnasiums and athletic fields.

Boardinghouses were still a respectable middle-class institution, usually cheaper than college-run equivalents.[6] Running what was, in effect, a huge hotel was an administrative burden. In addition, even if dormitories were considered good for the soul, they were a mixed blessing for the body. Alarming numbers of their residents had died from various maladies over the years. Later would come "the boardinghouse evil" and wealthy donors eager to contribute neo-Gothic dormitories, but between the Civil War and 1890 only an institution with a unique commitment to social isolation, like Swarthmore, acted fully in loco parentis.

The growing desire of students for a genteel life-style met with the strongest resistance from Swarthmore authorities. In its first years Swarthmore emphasized the gentler, more optimistic side of Quakerism. President Parrish believed "the innate innocence of children furnishes the key to that method of development which is beginning to be recognized by enlightened educators."[7] Complaints about his permissiveness contributed to Parrish's removal. His successor was Edward Magill, a former New England schoolmaster who was ready to impose the rules desired by more conservative managers. His "Laws of Swarthmore College Relating to Students" were required reading for all students, who chafed for years under rules that even forbade male and female students from walking together on the grounds. In addition to the usual restrictions on drinking, smoking, and profanity, Swarthmore banned dancing, music in any form, and most art, and required "plain speech" and "plain dress." In 1882 the faculty prevented formation of a glee club on the grounds that it might perform bawdy songs. That same year a student request to play baseball with other colleges met a similar fate, although occasional intercollegiate matches were permitted.[8] When the managers rejected the gift of a

6. John Modell and Tamara Hareven, "Urbanization and the Malleable Household," *Journal of Marriage and the Family* 35 (August 1973): 467–79.

7. Quoted in Babbidge, 88–89.

8. See Edward Parrish to Martha Tyson, 19 November 1869, Parrish Presidential Papers (Friends Historical Library), for an example of Parrish defending his ideas. Babbidge, 96, 139–43; Emily Cooper Johnson, *Dean Bond of Swarthmore* (Philadelphia: J. B. Lippincott Co., ca. 1930), 133–35; *Phoenix* 1 (April–May 1882), 2 (December 1882). The minutes of the faculty and the trustees are very helpful. See esp. Swarthmore College, Faculty, Minutes (Friends Historical Library), 3 December 1877, 25

piano for the lobby of the main building in 1886, the student newspaper reminded them that the type of student at Swarthmore had "undergone a radical change in the last two decades. Young Friends perform on all kinds of musical instruments, just the same as people belonging to other denominations."[9]

When enrollment dropped severely, the managers finally considered complaints from students and recent graduates. The investigation brought some relief. President Magill began holding informal weekly conferences with students. The *Phoenix* liked the idea, though it doubted that give-and-take was possible with Magill. Two other reforms pleased students more. The first was the hiring of Dean Elizabeth Bond, who expunged many of the most stringent rules and retrieved the banished piano for the lobby.[10] Second, the presence of preparatory students in the same building encouraged the continuance of a rigorous form of in loco parentis that affronted the collegians' dignity. The *Phoenix* editorialized that "ultimately one of the two things must happen, *either the Prep must go, or the college man will go*."[11] The board of managers phased out the former in 1890. The *Phoenix* approvingly commented that "there has begun an era of reformation at Swarthmore, and we sincerely hope that the good will go on."[12]

Similar though less intense conflicts occurred on other campuses where the responsibility for discipline rested more fully with the faculties. In the 1870s disciplinary actions were taken at most of their weekly meetings. Students often appeared before the faculty either to confess or to defend themselves.[13] In one case, Anthony Comstock appeared before the Franklin and Marshall faculty to display obscene literature that had been intercepted on the way to a student. Another

---

February 1878, 25 March 1878, 6 May 1878, and 26 October 1882. For another example of Quaker "guarded education," see Opal Thornburg, *Earlham: The Story of the College* (Richmond, Ind.: Earlham College Press, 1963).

9. *Phoenix* 6 (June 1886): 19.

10. Babbidge, 144–53; Johnson, 61–238; *Phoenix* 6 (October 1886).

11. *Phoenix* 6 (December 1886): 66–67.

12. *Phoenix* 9 (January 1890): 102.

13. Veysey's depiction of the faculty penchant for extracting confessions is borne out in these colleges' records, but his attribution of an authoritarian mentality seems severe. The tradition of religious confession and the need for an excuse to lighten unenforceably severe formal penalties may better explain it. Laurence R. Veysey, *The Emergence of the American University* (Chicago: University of Chicago Press, 1965), 35.

student was expelled for having been "guilty of a crime the punishment of which he avoided only by marriage."[14]

Most problems were more mundane, such as intoxication, smoking, leaving campus without permission, and creating general disturbances. The faculty sought to control the movement of students and reviewed student requests for school holidays and parental requests for home visits. Students sometimes succeeded in getting classes canceled in order to see a circus or take part in a political parade, but just as often they failed. Behavior apparently affected grading; at Franklin and Marshall the faculty invoked a system of demerits, and the *Princetonian* complained that "all marking should be strictly on scholarship."[15] Most Princeton students broke the rules. Half admitted drinking alcohol, and a majority had smoked, danced, played cards, and attended the theater at a time when college authorities opposed all of these activities.[16]

Princeton students ran afoul of the combined forces of the Presbyterian press and the faculty during a short-lived attempt to revive the commons. The *Princetonian* complained: "It is quite generally known that the *Observer* [a New York City Presbyterian newspaper] lifted its voice, and our billiard tables were removed. . . . [Now there is] the appearance of a letter in the *Evangelist*, protesting, on temperance grounds, against the use of wine-sauce on puddings." The next issue reported: "The [faculty] Committee on Morals, Discipline, and Diet (apparently) has banished the sparkling but seductive 'wine-sauce' from the festive boards of the College Commons. . . . The spectacle of three eminent scholars and theologians seriously devoting themselves to the petty business for which the Committee on Morals and Discipline seems to have been constituted, is sufficient to excite laughter in gods and men."[17]

Such assiduous faculty paternalism declined in the 1880s. The Franklin and Marshall, Princeton, and Bucknell faculty minutes show markedly fewer disciplinary cases. Most such cases in the 1880s in-

14. Franklin and Marshall College, Faculty, Minutes (Franklin and Marshall Archives), 10 March 1881, September 1878, and 10 March 1881.

15. *Princetonian* 10 (26 October 1885).

16. Princeton University, *Nassau Herald* (1888), 77–78. Polls in other years revealed similar behavior.

17. *Princetonian* 1 (30 November and 14 December 1876). This controversy may have contributed to the students turning away from the commons and to its collapse the following year.

volved absence from or inattention in class and chapel, or intoxication; there are few signs of student rebellion or of faculty enforcement of minor rules. With looser oversight, the smoldering discontent at Bucknell and the near-strike by Princeton students in the 1870s were not repeated in the next decade.[18] Tolerance of the multiplying student organizations helped reduce student-faculty tensions.

The changing approach to fraternities illustrates an important shift in faculty attitudes toward student conduct. The growth of these secret societies disrupted campuses across the country in the 1860s and 1870s as authorities tried to suppress them. At Bucknell, President Loomis destroyed Phi Kappa Psi and Theta Delta Chi in 1871, but Sigma Chi fought back and its supporters helped oust the president. His successor, President Hill, rescinded the ban on fraternity membership, and two immediately resurfaced. At Princeton, President McCosh also warred with secret societies and succeeded in dismissing five members of the Society of Love and Pleasure. As at Bucknell, Princeton fraternities had powerful alumni backers, including wealthy alumni from New York. But despite an alumni protest meeting at Delmonico's, the ban stood. McCosh's idea of forming a third literary society and his brief experiment with a college dining hall were unpopular alternatives. The formation of "eating clubs" served a similar if somewhat less pernicious purpose, which McCosh eventually accepted. Franklin and Marshall required students to sign a pledge to abstain from fraternities; but two of the boarding arrangements in Lancaster secretly turned into fraternities, and their existence was eventually tolerated. Even Swarthmore accepted fraternities in 1888.[19]

Thus, in the 1880s college authorities reduced their often futile attempts to control student life. Usually championed by younger faculty and alumni, fraternities and other student organizations gained more tolerance, if not full acceptance. The activities later threatened

18. The threatened strike was reported in William B. Scott, Some Memoirs of a Paleontologist (ca. 1930, Princeton University Manuscript Collection, typescript), 47.

19. Lewis Edwin Theiss, *Centennial History of Bucknell University, 1846–1946* (Williamsport, Pa.: Grit Publishing Co., 1948), 167–69; Oliphant, 180–81; Wertenbaker, 322–23; Princeton University, Faculty, Minutes (Princeton University Archives), 20 November 1875; Princeton University, Trustees, Minutes (Princeton University Archives), 22 December 1875; J. David Hoeveler, *James McCosh and the Scottish Intellectual Tradition: From Glasgow to Princeton* (Princeton: Princeton University Press, 1981), 262–64 and 347; Franklin and Marshall College, *Catalogue*, 1873–74; Klein, 126.

to become the center of collegiate life. But in the late 1880s, most college authorities were grateful for their beneficial effect on student behavior.

Students created a new style of social life. The antebellum extracurriculum consisted of literary societies and extemporaneous student activities, which included occasional rebellions. As younger students disappeared from the campuses and collegians developed a more genteel self-image, pranks and rebellions gave way to formally organized activities. Fraternities, musical groups, and athletic clubs appeared sporadically in the 1860s and became fixtures by the 1880s.

College authorities were upset by the threat the new groups posed to the popularity of literary societies, which remained the dominant student organizations through the 1870s. Campus authorities viewed them as essential complements to the classical curriculum. Declamations and debates offered opportunities to deal with contemporary political and social issues that got little classroom attention. The societies' libraries contained recent or popular works neither used in courses nor held in the college library. These collections often outnumbered those of college libraries and were more accessible.[20]

The literary societies held an honored place in the college community, strongly supported by faculty and older alumni. Before 1880 most students joined, and the faculty reserved one evening a week for their meetings, a practice that was maintained long after their popularity declined. The academic prizes at the colleges were awarded by the societies. Their alumni dinners and debates were a feature of commencement. Their prestige was indicated by possession of impressive buildings at Princeton and at Franklin and Marshall and of private rooms at Swarthmore and Bucknell.[21]

The literary societies lost their preeminence in the 1880s. The broadened curriculum and improved college libraries impinged on their role, and other activities competed for attention. Bucknell's reinstated fraternities and Princeton's new eating clubs provided al-

20. See Bucknell University's Theta Alpha Literary Society, Minutes (Bucknell University Archives). The proceedings of the Princeton and Swarthmore literary societies are also available in their archives.

21. Catalogs give detailed information about the literary societies. The minutes mentioned above are helpful, as is the history of a Franklin and Marshall society: Henry J. Young, *Historical Account of the Goethean Literary Society, 1835–1940*, Franklin and Marshall College Studies, no. 3 (Lancaster, Pa., 1941).

Fig. 12. The Franklin and Marshall Glee Club on the road, 1890.

ternative sources of fellowship. Franklin and Marshall's firmer stand against social alternatives, however, preserved much of the strength of the Goethean and Diagnothian societies until the turn of the century. Literary societies, which had competed fiercely in their heyday, were forced to sponsor joint publications and debates to remain viable. The number of meetings declined in the 1880s as the societies became a specialized interest of a minority. The secretary of Theta Alpha at Bucknell unwittingly made an important point when he recorded, "no society [meeting tonight] owning to big blazing bonfire and lively time on the campus in honor of the great football victory over Dickinson College."[22]

Students' energies went increasingly into other activities, particularly athletics. Although students had always played games informally, in the 1860s and 1870s organized intercollegiate sports caught their imaginations. In 1869 Princeton played Rutgers in what is usually considered the first intercollegiate football game. Swarthmore students fielded football teams in the 1870s; Bucknell followed suit in 1883, and Franklin and Marshall in 1887. Baseball and track teams

22. Theta Alpha, Minutes, 2 November 1888; Oliphant, 156–59, 170–72. Bucknell's *College Herald* (1870–80) and Franklin and Marshall's *College Student* (1880–1915) were both published jointly by the literary societies. Young, 35–55.

competed sporadically before becoming permanent fixtures in the late 1880s.

Most older faculty and trustees were ambivalent about these developments. Puritan strictures against exercise gave way to a belief that exercise promoted morality and health. The opportunity to reverse the perception that college was harmful to one's health attracted college authorities, but most favored European-style gymnastics. The first structure Swarthmore erected after completing the main building was a gymnasium. At Princeton, the first addition to the campus under McCosh was a gymnasium that he welcomed for its potential in "promoting morality and preventing mischief by fully occupying the physical energy of our youth."[23]

The presidents and faculties of the 1860s and 1870s were less enamored of the student-initiated intercollegiate spectator sports, fearing that they encouraged gambling and discouraged scholarship. President Loomis banned baseball at Bucknell, and McCosh tried to limit the travels of Princeton's baseball team. By the 1880s, most faculty members accepted athletics and shifted their attention to gaining control over the student-run teams. Princeton's Committee on Athletics and the Musical Clubs was, according to Ronald Smith, the first faculty committee in the country devoted to regulating the new organizations. McCosh initiated several unsuccessful attempts to forge intercollegiate agreements regulating athletics.[24]

Public support for organized athletics had been growing since the 1840s and the English muscular Christianity movement provided a religious rationale for athletics. Many younger faculty and most students supported the new ethos. At Bucknell, Loomis's successor lifted the ban on baseball. McCosh tempered his criticisms after realizing the promotional possibilities. Soon he was encouraging an alumnus to stir up support in Kentucky, as one of their native sons, "Mr. Ballard[,] has won us great reputation as Captain of the foot ball

23. James McCosh to R. Bonner, 29 December 1870, McCosh Papers (Princeton University Manuscript Collection). See also McCosh's address in Princeton College, *Opening Exercises of the Gymnasium* (Princeton, 1870) for his approach to exercise.

24. For a valuable analysis of the struggle between students and authorities to control intercollegiate athletics, see Ronald A. Smith, *Sports and Freedom: The Rise of Big-Time College Athletics* (New York: Oxford University Press, 1988), chaps. 9 and 10. On these four colleges, see W. Bruce Leslie, "The Response of Four Colleges to the Rise of Intercollegiate Athletics, 1865–1915," *Journal of Sport History* 3 (Winter 1976): 213–22.

Fig. 13. Princeton plays Yale before a fashionable crowd in New York City, 1889.

team which beat both Harvard and Yale."[25] Muscular Christianity was winning converts.

Football—not yet very popular with the general public—emerged as the collegiate game. Enthusiasm reached a fever pitch at Princeton in the mid-1870s, with the Yale game becoming a major social event in New York for which the Rev. Henry Ward Beecher shortened his Thanksgiving sermons. Teams at the Pennsylvania colleges led more precarious existences. In 1885 President Magill, an opponent of intercollegiate athletics, received a self-congratulatory letter from a like-minded fellow president proclaiming that "we can now rejoice together over the symptoms discernible in Princeton, Harvard, Yale

25. McCosh to Logan Murray, 2 December 1878, McCosh Papers (Princeton University Archives). The faculty minutes at all four colleges show numerous requests by athletic and other organizations for permission to practice, perform, or travel. On the changing attitudes toward exercise and athletic organizations, see Melvin L. Adelman, *A Sporting Time: New York City and the Rise of Modern Athletics, 1820–1870* (Urbana: University of Illinois Press, 1986), 269–86.

and of *their* growing disgust with *such* muscular culture."[26] The president's joy was premature; by 1890 football was an obsession at all four colleges.

Student interest in athletics was erratic at first. Bucknell's *College Herald* editorialized that walking provided sufficient exercise for young scholars. But soon all of the student newspapers were avidly supporting their teams. The lament in the *Phoenix* that laziness reigned supreme at Swarthmore reflected the paper's support of muscularity. The student press enthusiastically embraced the new athleticism, often draping athletics in moralistic Victorian language.[27] Woodrow Wilson's editorials in the *Princetonian* typified the boosterism that dominated student newspapers. Of seventy-two editorials attributed to his pen, twenty-two concerned athletics. Wilson glorified victory, lambasted those who failed to support athletics, criticized teams' failures, and carped about victorious rivals.[28] Similar editorials appeared regularly in all the campus newspapers in the 1880s. Whether or not the Napoleonic wars were decided on the cricket fields of Eton and Harrow, fin de siècle American worship of the active life was surely fostered on college playing fields.

Students created a variety of organizations. Dramatic productions ran afoul of some administrators, but student thespians persisted and won some important adherents. President Hill's wife helped Bucknell's drama club, and even James McCosh, after prolonged hostility, eventually conceded that there was some redeeming virtue to drama.[29] Banjo clubs, glee clubs, and orchestras also overcame religious prejudice. As with athletics, student newspaper editors felt justified in freely criticizing performances and students who did not attend.

Students even institutionalized religious activities. College religious societies predated the Civil War, but in the 1870s they exhibited a new style and vigor. For example, Princeton's Philadelphian Society, founded in 1825, gained new energy in the mid-1870s when it dropped

26. J.H.A. Bomberger (Ursinus College) to Edward Magill, 8 April 1885, Magill Papers (Friends Historical Library); *College Herald* 6 (November 1875).

27. For instance, fourteen years after Bucknell's paper lauded walking, its successor was wildly supporting football; *University Mirror* 8 (October 1889); Adelman, 252–55.

28. Arthur S. Link, ed., *The Papers of Woodrow Wilson* (Princeton: Princeton University Press, 1966), 1:260–479.

29. Donald Marsden, *The Long Kickline: A History of the Princeton Triangle Club* (Princeton, 1968), 3–9; Theiss, 199–202.

its sectarian Presbyterian ties and opened membership to all Protestants. The society participated in revivals that periodically swept the campus, sent student groups to visit potential converts, and held fervent evening meetings. In his early years McCosh imported evangelists like Dwight Moody to spark revivals; later, student organizations initiated them.[30]

Student religious organizations developed intercollegiate connections. Princeton student Luther Wishard pioneered the collegiate branch of the YMCA by organizing delegates from twenty-one colleges at the YMCA's 1877 national convention. The death of a pious Princeton graduate two years later inspired a bequest that gave Princeton the first campus YMCA building in the country. Branches were soon established at Bucknell and at Franklin and Marshall. The Swarthmore board of managers, still uncomfortable with evangelical Protestantism, rejected a student application to create a YMCA in 1888.[31]

Princetonians also played a prominent part at Dwight Moody's Northfield conferences and in its stepchild, the Student Volunteer Movement. Wishard convinced Moody to establish a summer collegiate conference at Northfield, Massachusetts, in 1885, where several Princetonians promoted student missionary work. The result was the Student Volunteer Movement, through which students of various evangelical faiths shouldered "the white man's burden." Bucknell also sent a delegate to Moody's conference and established a campus branch of the Student Volunteer Movement.[32]

Student publications reflected the changing nature of student life.

30. Philadelphian Society, *Constitution and By-Laws* (Princeton, 1874). Later versions have less sectarian membership requirements. See the *Princetonian* 10 (29 January 1886) for notice of one intercollegiate meeting. William M. Sloane, ed., *The Life of James McCosh* (New York: Charles Scribner's Sons, 1896), 229–30. Revivals were also reported at Franklin and Marshall and at Bucknell, but details survive only of those at Princeton. *Princeton College Bulletin* 12 (May 1901): 84–85; Charles H. Hopkins, *History of the YMCA in North America* (New York: Association Press, 1951), 285; John T. Duffield, *Historical Discourse on the Second Presbyterian Church of Princeton* (Princeton, 1897). McCosh reported fully on one to the trustees on 26 June 1876, noting particularly the Episcopalians' tepid response. The Princeton records are also the only ones that give much indication of actual religiosity. Scattered reports suggest that about one-half of the students were actively religious in the 1870s, with the figure rising to about two-thirds during a revival.

31. Hopkins, 276–85; Philadelphian Society, *One Hundred Years, 1825–1925* (Princeton, 1925); Theiss, 202–3; Babbidge, 111–18.

32. Hopkins, 287–304; Fred L. Norton, *A College of Colleges* (New York: Fleming B. Revell, 1889), 287–99; James F. Findlay, Jr., *Dwight L. Moody: American Evangelist,*

In the 1870s most were published by the literary societies and generally echoed the faculty viewpoint, opposing fraternities, encouraging scholarship, and attacking breaches of piety and discipline. When the *Princetonian* began in 1876, it had a different style, aggressively promoting a gentlemanly student image, supporting student organizations, and reporting about other campuses. By the mid-1880s, the student papers on all four campuses were also enthusiastically promoting the new student life-style. Heightened self-consciousness of a discrete student subculture and intercampus rivalries bred uniformity in student life. Students were seeking acceptance from peers, not challenging the prevailing faculty and trustee values; there was no debate on economic or political beliefs between students and the authorities.[33] As in most periods, the generation gap opened up over style rather than substance.

Sole reliance on newspapers to understand student life can exaggerate the hegemony of the active college life because they were written by those most enthralled with the new style. Clearly, a minority of students were involved in more intellectual pursuits. The literary publications that sprung up in the 1880s give the impression of a more studious undergraduate life. The different styles coexisted, sometimes in the same student. A football fanatic like Woodrow Wilson also founded a debating club, wrote on political theory, and read voraciously. The literary magazines provide the only written evidence of a studious alternative to the life-style chronicled in the newspapers.[34]

Newspapers also shed little light on the role of women at coeducational Bucknell and Swarthmore; their content differs little from publications at Princeton and at Franklin and Marshall, both all-male. Life on these campuses confirms Helen Horowitz's conclusion that

1837–1899 (Chicago: University of Chicago Press, 1969), 341–54; Oliphant, 178–79.

33. These conclusions are based on a reading of student newspapers. Unfortunately, no diaries were available for this period even though a number have survived from the 1840s and 1850s for Franklin and Marshall, Princeton, and Bucknell. Apparently student diaries became less common or less durable after the Civil War.

34. Franklin and Marshall's *College Student* and Princeton's *Nassau Literary Magazine* were particularly vigorous. Debating remained a popular activity. Helen L. Horowitz, *Campus Life: Undergraduate Cultures from the End of the Eighteenth Century to the Present* (New York: Knopf, 1987), chap. 3, is an intriguing account of campus "outsiders." Horowitz's unsystematic but wide-ranging research delineates strains that cannot be detected on a single campus, or even on four. For an insightful account of the new student life-style, leading to withdrawal from public life and political issues, see Louise

"the female equivalent of the college man began to emerge only in the 1890s."[35]

A wide gulf opened between the self-concepts of the colleges' supporters and authorities and those of the students. A generation gap is a constant in higher education, but the twenty-five years after the Civil War witnessed a particularly deep cultural divide. Each college's supporters had a distinctive combination of denominational, ethnic, and life-style identities. Between 1865 and 1890 much of the money given to these institutions was intended to promote Scottish and Scotch-Irish Presbyterianism, German Calvinism, traditional Baptism, or Hicksite Quakerism, respectively. These traditions connoted life-style variations within the general canon of Protestant piety. Though money and students were sent to these colleges to promote one of these visions, the students soon fostered quite different and less distinctive ones. The theme of student life may be unintended results—at least, unintended by parents, supporters, and older faculty.

Ethnicity and denominational distinctiveness were subverted by students' self-image as archetypal Americans. Students seldom differentiated among their WASP colleagues. The frequent protestations of college democracy were reasonably accurate among the overwhelming majority of students who were white Protestants. In place of piety and denominational distinctiveness, most students embraced "muscular Christianity" (in reality, Protestantism). Avoidance of display was replaced by stylishness. Especially at Bucknell and Princeton, an upbeat, exuberant gentility replaced subdued mid-Victorian mannerisms. Religiosity was expected, but it was now expressed in less self-deprecating ways, coexisting comfortably with athletics and affluence in the emerging student subculture.

The generational conflict on campuses mirrored broader cultural changes in eastern Protestant society. Many younger faculty and alumni shared the students' views on life-style and athletics. As time passed

---

L. Stevenson, "Preparing for Public Life: The Collegiate Students at New York University, 1832–1881," in Thomas Bender, *The University and the City* (New York: Oxford University Press, 1988).

35. Horowitz, 201; Rosalind Rosenberg, "The Limits of Access: The History of Coeducation in America," in John Faragher and Florence Howe, eds., *Women and Higher Education in American History* (New York: W. W. Norton, 1988), 111–12, reaches a similar conclusion.

they became more influential in college life, and by the late 1880s, resistance to the new style was crumbling. Most younger faculty, alumni, and students applauded, while the older generation grudgingly admitted that student behavior had improved and settled for regulating student-run activities. George Peterson found a similar pattern at New England colleges, where student life on different campuses converged on a distinct collegiate subculture.[36]

The emergence of the student culture has been vividly described by historians, usually as a liberation from the repressive tradition of in loco parentis. This, however, somewhat confuses official college rules with the reality of most campuses.[37] As David Allmendinger found in antebellum New England colleges, financial limitations made fully residential campuses rare. At these four postbellum Middle Atlantic campuses, the requisite facilities for acting in loco parentis were also only partially in place. While faculties sought to enforce moral codes, the lack of on-campus dining halls and residences meant that, except at Swarthmore, students had considerable de facto autonomy. These case studies bolster Allmendinger's hypothesis that romantic college campuses are less a venerable collegiate tradition than a twentieth-century creation.[38]

Focus by historians on the partly mythological liberation from in loco parentis has obscured the fact that the new student life-style, rather than being primarily a democratic liberation from authority, was more fundamentally a product of rising student wealth. Investing considerable time and money in activities was only feasible for affluent students. All four colleges issued ritual denunciations of luxury and paeans to hardworking, impecunious scholars, especially those training for the ministry. But the grain of student life ran in the opposite direction. This was most visible at Princeton, where President McCosh publicly agonized over the increasing proportion of Episcopalians, a barometer of student opulence. The appearance of servants and elegant eating clubs in the 1880s confirmed McCosh's

36. George E. Peterson, *The New England College in the Age of the University* (Amherst, Mass.: Amherst College Press, 1964), 82–86.

37. Frederick Rudolph, *The American College and University* (New York: Vintage Books, 1962), 87. Most writings on post–Civil War colleges have echoed Rudolph's imagery. For instance, Veysey, 67.

38. David Allmendinger pointed out that historians had drawn excessively on the experiences of Harvard and Yale, whose wealth made their antebellum campus life atypical.

fears. As David Hoeveler said, "Evangelical and democratic Princeton was dying even before he left, and he had had something to do with that fact."[39] Signs of wealth, slightly less extreme, appeared on the other three campuses as well. The cultures promoted by the founders and traditional supporters of the colleges were being challenged by a new generation that had grown up in the homes of the incipient white-collar professional class. Its growing demand for college education would foment even more dramatic changes after 1890.

39. Hoeveler, 347. Marilyn Tobias depicts a similar change of class origin and student culture at Dartmouth in *Old Dartmouth on Trial: The Transformation of the Academic Community in Nineteenth-Century America* (New York: New York University Press, 1982), chap. 3.

Part Two

CONVERGENCE AND COSMOPOLITANISM, 1890–1917

6

Piety versus Prosperity in the Protestant College

Between 1890 and World War I the ambitions of presidents, faculty, wealthy alumni, and students converged to change higher education dramatically. The expansion of professional and managerial positions in the burgeoning American economy created wealthy new potential constituents for colleges and universities. As the baccalaureate degree became part of what defined the new national upper and upper-middle classes, they financed a restructuring of the institutional forms and social meaning of higher education that is still evident.

Before 1890, the four colleges in this study depended on donors motivated by ethnoreligious loyalty who expected the colleges to promote a distinctive identity. After 1890, that changed. Many students of the 1870s and 1880s had rejected the values of such sponsors and developed a college life consonant with the less denominationally centered Protestantism and less pious life-style of the emerging urban upper-middle class. After graduation many prospered in professional and managerial jobs; colleges that cultivated their loyalty reaped rewards.

These four colleges emerged among the winners from this period of change. By the standards of 1890, they were thriving and secure in 1917. Their success is most simply measured by enrollment increases, ranging from two and one-third times at Franklin and Marshall to Bucknell's tenfold growth (Table 7).

Endowments grew apace. At the outbreak of the war they ranged from $5,000,000 at Princeton to $500,000 at Franklin and Marshall. Each college had cultivated an affluent constituency; the resulting funds were never as plentiful as the faculty and loyalists wished, but

Table 7. Total Baccalaureate and Graduate Enrollments, 1890–1917

	Bucknell	F&M	Princeton	Swarthmore
1889–90	71	136	653	193
1899–1900	315	164	1194	208
1909–10	527	241	1,400	359
1916–17	715	319	1,555	444

SOURCE: These figures were compiled from college catalogs and other publications.

they were far beyond their resources in 1890 or those of most other colleges in 1917. Their place among the leading colleges was confirmed and enhanced by grants from the foundations dispensing Rockefeller and Carnegie dollars.

Part Two examines the social origins and educational effects of the new collegiate affluence. Chapter 6 analyzes the changing sources of control and support. Doing so requires teasing out complex interactions beneath such seemingly discrete labels as denomination, ethnicity, alumni, community, and philanthropist. To elucidate these interactions, Chapter 6 examines the four colleges seriatum. Chapters 7, 8, and 9 integrate the case studies to analyze the impact of the changing constituencies on college governance, the curriculum, and the students.

Between 1890 and World War I, Princeton became one of the colleges most valued by the Protestant elite. This connection with affluence, which had worried President James McCosh in the 1880s, solidified after the turn of the century. The College of New Jersey had been tied to Scottish and Scotch-Irish Presbyterianism since its founding. In the 1870s and 1880s President McCosh capitalized on the connection to court wealthy fellow Scots in New York, Philadelphia, and Pittsburgh. By distancing the college from Princeton Theological Seminary and Old School Presbyterianism, he associated Princeton with a version of Presbyterianism that was more familiar to mainstream Protestants.

The college's denominational bonds weakened after 1890. This was simplified by the absence of legal, and only the barest financial, connection between denomination and college. The traditional association was protected by the charter provision that one-half of the trustees be clergymen; no denominational affiliation was specified, but the self-perpetuating board normally appointed Presbyterians.[1] Until the turn of the century, the general assembly received reports on the state of religion and morals at the college and routinely recommended that Presbyterians send money and students to Princeton.[2] The New Brunswick Presbytery annually awarded two minor prizes to Princeton students and supported about four preministerial students in the 1890s and 1900s. Even this provision atrophied; the presbytery reduced its scholarships from $100 to $80 in 1892 and to $70 in 1898. The *Observer*, the leading New York Presbyterian newspaper, decreasingly treated Princeton as one of its own.[3]

The college continued its commitment to undergraduate training for future ministers and ministers' sons. They once were a significant segment of the student body, but now their numbers were dwarfed by those entering secular careers. The college granted free tuition to all ministerial candidates based on old scholarships that, by the mid-1890s, no longer covered the cost. In 1896 a faculty-trustee committee voted to make up the difference because scholarship students, two-thirds of whom were ministerial candidates or sons of ministers, outperformed their peers and provided an indispensable moral influence if Princeton was "to maintain her character as an institution under evangelical religious influence." Their presence comforted those uneasy with Princeton's growing Episcopalian enrollment and reputation as a "rich man's school."[4] Such sentiments were embodied in a letter from an alumnus praising a speech by

1. The charter allowed up to twenty-seven trustees, with at least twelve clerical and twelve nonclerical members. Princeton University, *Charters and By-Laws of the Trustees* (Princeton: Princeton University Press, 1883). In practice the seats were divided evenly, with 56 of the 112 trustees elected from 1800 to 1896 being clerics. Princeton University, *General Catalogue, 1746–1896* (Princeton: Princeton University Press, 1896), 6–12.

2. *Princeton College Bulletin* 1 (June 1889): 90; Frederick Loetscher, "A Century of New Jersey Presbyterianism" (typescript of address, 16 October 1922). A copy is in the Presbyterian Historical Society. The general assembly officially controlled Princeton Theological Seminary, which had separated from the college in the early 1800s.

3. Presbytery of New Brunswick, Minutes, 1876–1907 (Presbyterian Historical Society, Philadelphia). See esp. 4 October 1892, 19 October 1898, 23 October 1902. *New York Observer*, 72–73 (1894–95). In the 1920s the Presbyterian Board of Education ceased listing Princeton.

4. Princeton University, Trustees, Minutes (Princeton University Archives), 13 February 1896; Thomas J. Wertenbaker, *Princeton, 1746–1896* (Princeton: Princeton University Press, 1946), 331.

President Francis Patton (1888–1902), which "ought to send a great many boys to Princeton. It touched just the right key for the conservative laity of the West."[5]

But addresses that pleased conservative laity mattered less and less. Presbyterianism was liberalizing, and the proportion of Presbyterians among Princeton students was declining. About three-fourths of the students in the 1870s were Presbyterians, and about 60 percent in the 1880s and 1890s. The class entering in September 1901 was 56 percent Presbyterian. By 1911 it was down to 41 percent, while 24 percent were Episcopalians. Only 30 percent of students entering in 1915 were Presbyterians. In the 1920s Episcopalians and Presbyterians were about even, together constituting about two-thirds of each class.

Like Presbyterianism, Scottishness and Scotch-Irishness became less distinctive after the turn of the century. John Ingham found that the heavily Scotch-Irish Pittsburgh iron and steel elite became major supporters of Princeton. These elite families originally were attracted by Princeton's ethnoreligious distinctiveness, but increasingly they valued its ability to blend Scotch-Irish Presbyterians into the Anglo-Episcopalian elite.[6]

Presbyterians of Celtic descent continued to play a major role, but increasingly their tie to Princeton came from being alumni, a status shared by other Protestants. Ministers, especially faculty at the college or the theological seminary, dominated the Princeton alumni association for fifty years after its creation in 1826. Alumni from outside the local community, mostly laymen, started taking an active role in the 1870s and came into conflict with McCosh when the New York Association of Princeton College Alumni opposed his fraternity ban. They failed, but even McCosh recognized their potential and soon was promoting the establishment of local alumni associations and championing their representation on the board of trustees.[7]

5. Ethelbert Warfield to M. Taylor Pyne, 17 December 1889, AM 245 (Princeton University Archives). Warfield became president of Lafayette College, and Pyne became the most powerful Princeton trustee.

6. Princeton University, *Nassau Herald*, 1885–1915; John N. Ingham, *The Iron Barons: A Social Analysis of an American Elite, 1874–1965* (Westport, Conn.: Greenwood Press, 1978), 94–95.

7. Princeton, Trustees, 22 December 1875. For his promotion of alumni, see James McCosh to James W. Alexander, 27 November and 9 December 1885, McCosh Papers (Princeton University Archives); Howard B. Maxwell, "The Formative Years of the University Alumni Movement as Illustrated by Studies of the University of Michigan and Columbia, Princeton, and Yale Universities" (Ph.D. diss., University of Michigan, 1965), 167–75.

Unlike the McCosh era, when donors were primarily nonalumni inspired by ethnoreligious affiliation, in the 1890s alumni identity inspired most contributions. Publication of the first alumni directory in 1888 symbolized the growing group consciousness. When enrollment doubled between 1886 and 1892 without a corresponding increase in the endowment, New York alumni established a permanent alumni fund. In the sesquicentennial celebration of 1896, alumni donations were the primary benefactions; outside gifts failed to materialize. Alumni even paid several professors, including Woodrow Wilson, "under the table" to keep them at Princeton.[8]

As president, Wilson's attempt to utilize ethnic loyalty backfired spectacularly. He courted Andrew Carnegie with the sentiment that Princeton "has been largely made by Scotsmen,—being myself of pure Scots blood, it heartens me to emphasize the fact,—and she is thoroughly Scottish in all her history and traditions in matters educational."[9] Wilson dreamed of a library or law school. Unfortunately, Carnegie spotted a small valley at the foot of the campus and donated a lake instead. Wilson bitterly retorted, "We needed bread and you gave us cake," and banned student rowing.[10]

The board of trustees had squelched McCosh's earlier request for alumni representation, but the alumni became insistent in the late 1890s and threatened to withhold donations. In March 1900, the trustees approved a plan for indirect representation. But in April the first issue of the *Princeton Alumni Weekly* demanded direct representation, as did the Western Association of Princeton Clubs. In October, the trustees agreed to add five members elected by the alumni, effectively eliminating the requirement that one-half of the board be clergymen. Trustee Elijah Craven had his opposition inscribed in the board's minutes. Craven exemplified the older trustees. After graduating from the college and the seminary in the 1840s, he served several New Jersey pastorates and was secretary of the Presbyterian Board of Publications for seventeen years. Elected to the

8. Maxwell, 178–82; Princeton College, *Alumni Directory* (1888); Henry Wilkinson Bragdon, *Woodrow Wilson: The Academic Years* (Cambridge: Belknap Press of Harvard University Press, 1967), 227. See also Cleveland H. Dodge to Professor William Berryman Scott, 22 January 1901, Scott Papers (Princeton University Archives).

9. Woodrow Wilson to Andrew Carnegie, 17 April 1903, in Arthur S. Link, ed., *The Papers of Woodrow Wilson* (Princeton: Princeton University Press, 1972) 14:412.

10. John M. Mulder, *Woodrow Wilson: The Years of Preparation* (Princeton: Princeton University Press, 1978), 163.

Fig. 14. Woodrow Wilson and the donor of the lake, Andrew Carnegie, 1906.

board of trustees in 1859, Craven served until his death in 1908. He saw no reason for changing Princeton's practices or augmenting the power of younger alumni. Although an alumnus, Craven was more committed to preserving the traditional social and moral tone of the campus than to competing socially and academically with other institutions.[11]

Trustees like Craven were a shrinking minority, in fundamental conflict with the wealthier young graduates of recent classes. President Patton's failure to fulfill the hopes expressed in taking the name "university" in 1896 exacerbated the conflict, and in 1902 younger alumni on the board of trustees and faculty ousted him. They replaced him with Woodrow Wilson, the first nonclerical president (though the son of a Presbyterian minister), whose less traditional Presbyterianism merged more easily with vigorous promotion of the university. In 1906 another charter revision further reduced the pro-

11. Maxwell, 190–95; Ingham, 149–51; Bragdon, 22; *Princeton Alumni Weekly* (April 1900); Princeton, Trustees, 19 October 1900. The addition increased the size of the board from twenty-five to thirty and effectively reduced the ministers' traditional 50 percent share.

portion of ministers and, in effect, the role of traditional Presbyterianism on the board of trustees.[12]

During his first year in office Wilson triumphantly toured the alumni clubs, where he unfolded ambitious plans for new dormitories, laboratories, a gymnasium, a graduate school, and curricular innovation that depended upon their beneficence. The national system of alumni clubs and the *Alumni Weekly* beat the drums. Administering the elections for alumni representatives to the board of trustees forced Princeton to hire a secretary of the university, who maintained alumni records and provided direct communication with the administration. Creation of the Association of Class Officers in 1904 streamlined the process. Wilson began distributing the heretofore secret annual reports of the president and treasurer to the alumni.[13]

The president successfully used the machinery of alumni support to finance his dreams, including an ambitious curricular innovation.[14] On 18 March 1905 he announced his "preceptorial" system (small-group instruction requiring fifty additional faculty members) to the Princeton Club of Western Pennsylvania. An alumni Committee of Fifty opened a Wall Street office and soon secured the requisite $12.5 million.[15]

Wilson discovered that alumni power could be a two-edged sword, however, when his ideas diverged from the dominant alumni mentality. He had become increasingly concerned over the exclusionary membership policies and anti-intellectualism of the eating clubs. In December 1905 he presented a special report on the "Social Coordination of the University," proposing to abolish the highly selective clubs and replace them with an Oxbridge "college system" of quadrangles whose membership would be chosen randomly and in which

12. See Chapter 7 for a detailed account of Patton's demise. Princeton, *Charters*, 1906. The number of ministers mandated on the thirty-member board was reduced from twelve to eight.

13. Princeton, Trustees, 13 December 1900 and 10 June 1901; E. C. Richardson to Edwin G. Conklin, 5 December 1911, Conklin Papers (Princeton University Archives); Varnum L. Collins, *Princeton*, American College and University Series (New York: Oxford University Press, 1914), 356, 374.

14. Bragdon, 357; Maxwell, 196–212. During Wilson's eight-year administration the university's annual disbursements rose from $200,000 to $700,000, an increase largely financed by the alumni.

15. Maxwell, 216–22; Bragdon, 288, 304. Wilson did, however, have a pledge from wealthy classmates to cover the deficits.

faculty would mix socially. Whereas Wilson had carefully consulted the alumni about his earlier plans, he kept this secret until the trustees approved it in June 1906.[16]

Initially most alumni accepted Wilson's plan as a fait accompli. But when several influential faculty joined the *Alumni Weekly* editors in opposition, resistance snowballed among the younger alumni and converted several influential trustees. Fund-raising ground to a halt. With the expense of the preceptorial program draining funds and the panic of 1907 undercutting philanthropy, even trustees who shared Wilson's dislike of the clubs could not support constructing expensive quadrangles. Four months after approving the plan with only one dissent, the board asked Wilson to withdraw it. Wilson tried to go over the trustees' heads by appealing to the alumni, especially those in the Midwest who saw the clubs as bastions of the East Coast elite. He also received some support from the older classes, which had not rallied to his preceptorial plan but predated the eating clubs. However, his old allies on the *Alumni Weekly* staff and among the younger alumni steadfastly defended the clubs' social role. At the June 1908 meeting, a trustee committee report exonerated the clubs, criticizing only their most flagrant abuses. Wilson accurately ascribed his defeat to the same people who made his earlier successes possible.[17]

Wilson depended upon relatively young alumni. When fund-raising was arranged by classes in 1906, organizations were created for all classes dating back to 1870. The oldest graduates represented were only in their late fifties. But the recent graduates had impressive resources; in 1904 an Alumni Dormitory Committee successfully raised funds for a dormitory from the twelve youngest classes.

Princeton systemized alumni solicitation in the decade before World War I. The trustees created a Graduate Council to bring alumni to the campus and to control the *Alumni Weekly*. Fund-raising shifted

16. Bragdon, 319–35. The wider ramifications of the plan are discussed in Laurence R. Veysey, *The Emergence of the American University* (Chicago: University of Chicago Press, 1965), 241–48. For an excellent account drawing fully on the Wilson Papers, see Mulder, 187–203.

17. Princeton, Trustees, 10 June and 17 October 1907; Maxwell, 231–49; *Princeton Alumni Weekly* 8 (25 September–23 October 1907); scattered correspondence, 8 July–19 November 1907. Woodrow Wilson Papers (Library of Congress Manuscript Division), box 35. One alumnus offered to finance an experimental quadrangle but Wilson declined, fearing that only club rejects would join. In the 1950s Princeton built an alternative to the clubs and appropriately named it Wilson Quadrangle.

from concentration upon a few hundred men during Wilson's presidency to a broader canvas that netted 2,635 contributions in 1916. The university could rely on an increasingly broad base of alumni support; but as Wilson found out, this meant that alumni opinion mattered. Wilson's successor, John Grier Hibben, reconciled most of the alumni and faculty factions that had been split by Wilson's attempt to abolish the clubs. Alumni, especially a moderate-sized group of wealthy, regular contributors, had to be reckoned with before launching new ventures.[18]

Thus Princeton, after 1890, successfully turned its prestige as a colonial college and its Scotch-Irish Presbyterian connections into a prodigious financial base headed by New York businessmen. As Scottishness and Scotch-Irishness blended with other northern European ethnic identities, Princeton's ethnic distinctiveness faded. While many students had Scottish blood and were brought up in the Presbyterian church, it was the alumni connection that now galvanized financial support. The demanding ties of Old School Presbyterianism were exchanged for a broad Protestantism centered on a modernized Presbyterianism and Episcopalianism. Its prestige in the upper class provided a financial base few colleges could match.

Like Princeton, Franklin and Marshall College served an ethnically and religiously distinct clientele, though one with considerably more limited means. Founded to serve German-Americans in the Lancaster area and legally tied to the German Reformed church, the college continued to serve and be defined by those groups after 1890. Acceptance of formal denominational control had rescued Franklin and Marshall from financial crisis in 1866; but after 1890 the affiliation stifled growth by limiting outside solicitation.

Denominational control was exercised through the thirty trustees, all elected by the Eastern Synod from 1866 until 1891. Then the Eastern Synod agreed to reduce its share to twelve, giving nine seats to its offshoots, the Potomac and Pittsburgh synods. This left nine not tied to the denomination that could be given to potential donors from other denominations, usually Lancasterians. Since nominees from the board of trustees were always accepted by the synods, it was virtually a self-perpetuating body. The only regular synodical actions on the college were annual approval of the catalog and a statement

18. Maxwell, 223–30, 257–77.

urging support by church members. There was no criticism in the minutes.

Unfortunately, legal affiliation and official praise did not result in formal financial support. The only direct assistance was an annual recommendation that congregations hold a special service with a collection for the college. The results were modest, and as educational costs rose denominational contributions became increasingly inadequate. The centennial of Franklin College in 1887 provided an opportunity to solicit denominational funds; but the college encountered strong competition for funds from foreign and domestic missions, the theological seminary, and local church construction. Two donors gave the college an observatory and ten thousand dollars, but the drive to endow the presidency dragged on for two years. In contrast, alumni and citizens of Lancaster quickly raised the money for a gymnasium after a successful football season.[19]

A $500,000 drive begun in 1896 again failed to rally rank-and-file denominational support. General Watts de Peyster, whose only connection with the college seems to have been friendships with a trustee and the librarian, offered to fund a library if McKinley defeated Bryan. Otherwise, the campaign lagged, delaying construction of a badly needed science building. A special synodical Committee on the Endowment of Franklin and Marshall had little success. In 1898, after raising only four thousand dollars in two years, the committee charged that the church had "not responded to the demands of the College, as the necessities call for."[20] After two more unsuccessful years the committee asked to be disbanded. Meanwhile, personal donations from the trustees underwrote the new science building, which was finally completed in 1902. But the cost of laboratory equipment and the failure of the Potomac Synod to meet its pledge left the college twenty-one thousand dollars in debt.[21]

19. Reformed Church in the United States, *Acts and Proceedings of the Eastern Synod, 1889–1916*. The Eastern Synod approved the trustees' nominations except in 1888, when it rejected two of three nominees. I have been unable to attach any significance to this rejection. Franklin and Marshall College, Board of Trustees, Minutes (Franklin and Marshall Archives), 19 June 1883, 18 March 1884, 12 June 1888; Reformed Church in the United States, *Reformed Church Messenger* 56 (1888); H.M.J. Klein, *History of Franklin and Marshall College* (Lancaster, Pa., 1952), 115–23.

20. Reformed Church, *Acts*, 1898, 58; Klein, 127.

21. Reformed Church, *Acts*, 1896–1901; Klein, 129; *Reformed Church Messenger* 71 (9 October 1902).

The college was somewhat more successful at the fiftieth anniversary of the unification of Franklin and Marshall colleges in 1903. The goal was to erase the debt on the science building and raise $150,000 for the endowment. Two young Reformed ministers canvassed congregations for four years before successfully completing the drive. The difficulty encountered by these agents, even with enthusiastic support from the *Reformed Church Messenger* and *Reformed Church Review*, indicated the limits of denominational fund-raising. This became painfully obvious when the General Education Board pledged $50,000 of Rockefeller money if the college raised $308,000 in matching funds. With credit for $106,000 already collected, $202,000 more was needed. The three synods pledged $50,000, but collecting the pledges was so difficult that William Hensel, president of the college's board of trustees, threatened to resign. He attacked the church membership in the *Reformed Church Messenger*, pointing out that a Presbyterian congregation in Lancaster (whose membership included four trustees) had contributed more than the three synods combined. President Apple was also blunt in his 1916 report to the synods: "It is to be regretted that more than $25,000 out of the $50,000 proposed to be raised within the bounds of the synods was not secured; and that the task of the College was made harder in gathering this amount from other sources to meet the obligation of the General Education Board."[22]

To deal with this denomination-wide problem, the eleven Reformed educational institutions created a joint promotional organization in 1915. Franklin and Marshall's share of the first campaign was to be $200,000, which the General Education Board offered to match with $100,000. Despite using Reformed ministers as agents, the congregational canvass failed. Only four fortuitous bequests from affluent individuals secured the matching funds.[23]

The failure to support the college cannot be attributed to denominational opposition; the synodical meetings and journals consistently

22. H. H. Apple, *Report of the Board of Trustees of Franklin and Marshall College to the Eastern, Potomac, and Pittsburgh Synods* (Lancaster, Pa., 1916).

23. The other ten institutions in the Association of Schools, Colleges, and Seminaries of the Reformed Church were Franklin and Marshall Academy, the theological seminary, Ursinus College, Allentown College for Women (all in Pennsylvania), Heidelberg University and Central Theological Seminary of Ohio, Masanutten Academy in Virginia, Hood College in Maryland, Catawba College in North Carolina, and Mission House in Wisconsin.

praised it. The *Messenger*, the denominational weekly, warmly supported the institution. In the course of an attack upon one of Harvard's innovations, the editors boasted that Franklin and Marshall produced "a better all around scholar than if he had taken the same course at Harvard."[24] In the 1890s and 1900s, articles regularly urged members to send their sons and donations to the college. Reciprocally, Franklin and Marshall professors frequently wrote for the *Reformed Church Review*, the denomination's scholarly quarterly, and the college continued to advertise in the *Messenger* into the 1920s.

A 1902 editorial in the *Reformed Church Messenger* revealed the problem. By urging a few rich families to step forward to contribute to the college so that the rest of the denomination could concentrate upon its "regular benevolent work," the editors implicitly admitted that the rank-and-file Reformed membership did not feel an obligation to the college. The denomination was a relatively small and rural one. In 1894 the eight synods had 221,000 communicants and 123,000 unconfirmed members in 1,646 congregations and raised a total of $258,000 for benevolent purposes. Even though Franklin and Marshall was the best-known Reformed institution, the money had to be divided many ways, and much of the Franklin and Marshall share went to the academy and the theological seminary.

As with Presbyterianism, the German Reformed church was inextricably twined with ethnicity. Explicit "Germanness" declined rapidly during the nineteenth century in both the denomination and the college. It was a German-American culture, with emphasis on the latter, by 1890. There was little ethnic flavor at the college, and most students and faculty strongly supported American participation in World War I. The record enrollment in 1920 suggests that the college was not tainted by its ethnic tradition.

As at Princeton, descendants of the founding ethnoreligious group were blending into a broader Protestant culture. Despite behavioral convergence, they continued to play an important role in the institution. Virtually all of the trustees elected by the synods had Germanic names, as did some of the trustees elected by the board.

Lancaster Presbyterians, sharing civic and Calvinist traditions, probably occupied the other seats. From the beginning, localism had mixed with ethnoreligious motives to support the college. Local donors came to the rescue several times when the denomination fal-

24. *Reformed Church Messenger* 64 (19 March 1896): 9.

tered. The board usually selected Lancasterians with Anglo names to fill the non-Reformed seats. The Eastern Synod's choices were also usually from the Lancaster area. Few were from Philadelphia or Pittsburgh.

Thus, Franklin and Marshall's fate depended heavily on the Lancaster economy, which slipped badly in the 1890s as its iron, cotton, and cigar industries declined. It recovered by the turn of the century due to the rapid growth of new small industries and nearby Hershey chocolate. In 1901 Lancaster was the fourth largest manufacturing center in Pennsylvania behind Philadelphia, Pittsburgh, and Reading.[25] This financial base helped Franklin and Marshall outdistance many colleges, but left it behind the three in this study that tapped Philadelphia and New York.

Despite its good reputation in the Reformed church, the college had to depend upon a few affluent individuals for financial support. Before 1910, most benevolence was inspired by denominational and local ties; none of the four major donors in the previous twenty-five years were alumni.[26] In this respect George Baer, the infamous railroad and mining magnate and Franklin and Marshall's best-known former student, was a transitional figure. Born to a German-American family in western Pennsylvania, he was a completely Anglicized lawyer who became a close associate of J. P. Morgan, whose interests Baer was defending in his famous dispute with Theodore Roosevelt. Having briefly attended Franklin and Marshall, Baer foreshadowed the blending of ethnoreligious loyalty and the alumni relationship. After 1910, most donations were inspired by the alumni connection.

The alumni association, founded in the 1830s, was dominated by local clergy and college faculty until the 1890s. Establishment of branches in several Pennsylvania and Maryland towns broadened its geographic and generational range. The average age of its activist Advisory Council was only forty-eight. The association became very active as the jubilee of 1903 approached, publishing annual reports and an obituary record, procuring a Phi Beta Kappa chapter, and

25. Reformed Church Messenger 71 (30 October 1902); see also 24 July 1902, 27 May 1909, and 16 June 1910. Joseph Dubbs, *A History of the Reformed Church German*, The American Church History Series (New York: Christian Literature Co., 1895), 416–23. Trustees' names and addresses are listed in the catalogs. John W. Loose, *Heritage of Lancaster* (Woodland Hills, Calif.: Windsor Publications, 1978), 114–44.

26. In the 1880s and 1890s the major donors were Charles Santee, George W. Fahnestock, Watts De Peyster, and James H. Hood; none were alumni.

talking optimistically of doubling the enrollment. But after the jubilee the president and trustees let the alumni spirit languish, and their publishing efforts ceased.[27]

The new president, Henry Apple, shared the young alumni's dream of growth. He tried to revive their interest and create a new balance of power on the board of trustees.[28] In 1911 he recommended reducing the synods' share of the thirty seats from twenty-one to nine, allocating six to the alumni association. Apple hoped to gain more support from non-Reformed alumni and qualify Franklin and Marshall for faculty pensions from the Carnegie Foundation for the Advancement of Teaching without relinquishing the denominational relationship. The trustees rejected Apple's proposal, and the composition of the board remained unchanged until 1921. No further alumni publications appeared until 1925, reflecting their estrangement.

Thus, Franklin and Marshall retained a structure that provided modest support, but far less than its most ambitious supporters wanted. Its ethnoreligious connection provided a steady flow of students; large numbers of non-Reformed did not attend until the 1910s.[29] Franklin and Marshall received support from some wealthy Lancasterians and could call on the loyalty of a primarily rural church. But that tie restricted appeals to the wealthy in Philadelphia or Pittsburgh. The greatest potential for financial assistance existed in cultivating

27. The chairman of the first advisory council graduated only ten years earlier, and the average age was about forty-eight. Three of the nine were ministers. Franklin and Marshall, Trustees, June 1901; Franklin and Marshall College, Alumni Association, *Printed Report* (1902–5); Franklin and Marshall College, *Catalogue of Officers and Students, 1787–1903* (Lancaster, Pa., 1903), 133–53. On Baer, see John N. Ingham, "Masters of the Mill: Innovation and Social Class in the Nineteenth-Century Iron and Steel Industry" (unpublished manuscript, 1985), 383–84, 403.

28. In Apple's first year he collected a remarkable amount of money, and the *Reformed Church Messenger* (16 June 1910) proudly exclaimed that "the beauty of it all is that these generous donors are sons of the Reformed Church." Since the "sons" numbered only three or four, this munificence did not indicate broad-based church support.

29. There were apparently no official records kept on the students' religious affiliations. The only record I located was President Thomas Apple's report to the board of trustees of 11 June 1889 in which he noted that 96 of 107 students were members of the Reformed church. Changes in Franklin and Marshall Academy and in its relation to the college strongly suggest a decline in the proportion of Reformed students at the college after 1910. Charles Stahr Hartman, "Franklin and Marshall Academy 1872–1943" (Unpublished Master's essay, Johns Hopkins University, 1948), 45–72.

the younger alumni. Many had grown up in the German Reformed tradition, but increasingly they related to the college as alumni who wanted it to emulate other colleges. The church, through the board of trustees, chose to keep the college close to its original clientele rather than promoting the new alumni spirit that sponsored more rapid growth at the other three colleges.

In contrast to Franklin and Marshall, Bucknell grew dramatically and departed from its educational traditions. In 1890 it had only seventy-one undergraduates and a classical curriculum. By World War I Bucknell had over seven hundred students and a panoply of curricular options. Contrary to conventional expectations, the transformation was directed by a traditional Baptist minister.

The period began inauspiciously with the departure of a dynamic young president, David Jayne Hill, and the death of its principal benefactor and namesake, William Bucknell. For eight years after the "coup" of 1882, William Bucknell single-handedly underwrote the university. His contribution of a chapel, an observatory, a dormitory, a laboratory building, scholarships, and an endowment worth about $250,000 was a substantial windfall for a college of less than one hundred students. He expected that, given the physical plant, the college would pay its current expenses from tuition. This conservative fiscal approach corresponded with President Hill's disinterest in enlarging either the enrollment or the expensive science programs.[30]

Hill's successor, the Rev. John Harris, had a different vision. Harris recruited a freshman class for September 1890 that outnumbered the sophomore, junior, and senior classes combined. After William Bucknell's death, Harris turned to the trustees for donations, but he found that because they were primarily clergy and educators, they could not underwrite his plans. Harris resolved that future members of the board would be wealthy businessmen and professionals. Apparently the trustees acquiesced, as only one of the twenty-four trustees selected in the next seventeen years was a clergyman. In 1908

30. J. Orin Oliphant, *The Rise of Bucknell University* (New York: Appleton-Century-Crofts, 1965), 149; Lewis Edwin Theiss, *Centennial History of Bucknell University, 1846–1946* (Williamsport, Pa.: Grit Publishing Co., 1946), 207–8; John H. Harris, *Thirty Years as President of Bucknell with Baccalaureate and Other Addresses* (Washington, D.C.: privately printed, 1926), 8–10.

Harris could boast that "the Board is composed for the most part of business men."[31]

The Lewisburg area, a minor railroad and manufacturing center and county seat for an agricultural area, supplied a few prosperous trustees like Harold McClure, a district judge and local bank director. The college had not been dependent on the Lewisburg area since 1882, when William Bucknell's coup had shifted power to Philadelphians. However, many of the Philadelphians Bucknell brought in were the very ministers Harris hoped to phase out. In the search for businessmen, Harris was unable to entice many Philadelphians. More of the new trustees Harris recruited in his early years were Baptist businessmen or professionals from small Pennsylvania towns like Lewisburg. A few of the affluent new trustees came from further afield, such as John Stetson of haberdashery fame. But the best-known Baptist, John D. Rockefeller, declined to join the board.[32]

Rockefeller did, however, help fund Harris's ambitions through the American Baptist Education Society, which was created in 1888 to funnel his money to the University of Chicago and administer matching grants to other Baptist institutions of higher education.[33] In 1891, the society granted Bucknell $10,000 if it could raise $90,000. William Bucknell's survivors contributed $22,500, the Pennsylvania Baptist Education Society added $10,000, and a drive in Lewisburg netted $13,000. The remainder came so slowly that Harris needed an extension. Harris and seventeen voluntary alumni assistants gathered the requisite pledges by July 1892, but it took six more years to collect the money and obtain the matching funds.[34]

31. Bucknell University, *Bucknell University Bulletin*, ser. 7, no. 4 (1908–9). See also Bucknell University, *Alumni Catalogue* (Lewisburg, Pa., 1926), 6; Harris, 7–8. In 1890 eleven of the twenty-three trustees were clerics.

32. Charles M. Snyder, *Union County, Pennsylvania: A Bicentennial History* (Lewisburg, Pa.: Colonial Printing House, 1976), 94–99; Bucknell University, *Bucknell University Bulletin*, Announcements, ser. 7, no. 9 (1908–9); Bucknell University, *Memorials of Bucknell University, 1919–1931* (Lewisburg, Pa., 1931), 161–79; Bucknell University, Board of Trustees, Minutes (Bucknell University Archives), 17 June 1902 and 23 June 1903.

33. Albert H. Newman, *A History of the Baptist Churches in the United States*, American Church History Series, vol. 2 (New York: Christian Literature Co., 1894), 476–78; Paul M. Limbert, *Denominational Policies in Higher Education*, Teachers College Contributions to Education, no. 378 (New York: Teachers College Press, 1929), 37–39; National Baptist Educational Convention, *Proceedings* (1870 and 1872). An attempt to create a national Baptist educational organization in the 1870s collapsed for lack of funds.

34. Bucknell, Trustees, 23 June 1891; Oliphant, 198; Harris, 32–33; American

By the end of the decade a wealthier board of trustees and a more active alumni organization responded more quickly to Harris's ambitions. In May 1899 Rockefeller approved a $15,000 grant to Bucknell; the $60,000 in matching funds were raised by January 1901. Harris immediately proposed another fund drive, and in November the society pledged $25,000 of Rockefeller's money to be matched by $75,000. Eight trustees contributed $40,000 and seventeen other donors added $30,000, leaving only $5,000 to be gathered from minor contributors.[35]

The Rockefeller grants enabled Harris to combine entrepreneurial goals and denominational commitment. Whereas denominational ties restricted growth at the other colleges in the 1890s, John D. Rockefeller single-handedly reversed that for Baptist colleges. Harris promoted expansion while maintaining a traditional vision of a denominational college. One of Harris's first presidential acts was to address the Northumberland Baptist Association to repair local denominational ties neglected by his predecessor. Harris preached to Baptists across the state and often in temporarily vacant local pulpits. Along with several professors and trustees, he participated in the Northumberland Baptist Association. The association maintained a standing committee on Bucknell that annually inspected the college and recommended it to the membership's favor.[36] In his first campaign to increase enrollment, Harris distributed ten thousand leaflets through Baptist associations in New Jersey and Pennsylvania. The trustees' Committee on Publication annually inserted advertisements in the published proceedings of both Baptist associations, a practice continued at least until World War I.[37] Harris felt no tension between

Baptist Education Society, Correspondence (American Baptist Historical Society, Rochester, N.Y.), 20 June 1898.

35. H. L. Morehouse to John H. Harris, 10 May 1899, Harris Papers (Bucknell University Archives); Bucknell, Trustees, 20 June 1899, 9 January 1902, and 8 January 1903; American Baptist Education Society, Correspondence, 4 November 1901; Oliphant, 200.

36. Bucknell University, *Charter and By-Laws* (Lewisburg, Pa., 1956), 36–38; Northumberland Baptist Association, *Minutes* (1881–1916). In 1915 the president, five professors, and one trustee participated in the association's functions.

37. Bucknell, Trustees, 10 January 1889, 8 January 1891, 20 July 1891, 11 January 1894, 10 June 1910, 15 January 1915, and 13 June 1916; Theiss, 212–20; Oliphant, 196. Between 1891 and 1902 the budget for publicity increased from $87 to $1,638. I could not locate statistics on the students' religions, which makes it impossible to know what effect the public relations campaign had on the proportion of Baptists at Bucknell.

mammon and denominationalism. He fully accepted the charter stipulation, which remained in effect until 1926, that four-fifths of the trustees be Baptists; he just insisted on wealthy Baptists.

The convenient convergence of denominationalism and expansionism ended in 1902 when Rockefeller created the General Education Board to administer his educational philanthropy without preference for Baptists. The American Baptist Education Society collapsed, leaving denominational fund-raising in disarray. Fortunately for Harris, he had already capitalized on the Rockefeller money to transform Bucknell.

The loss of Rockefeller support caused Bucknell to begin loosening its denominational ties. The Pennsylvania Baptist Education Society continued to sponsor a number of ministerial students in Bucknell's preparatory and collegiate classes. However, these students made up a smaller proportion of the rising enrollment. The founding of Temple University in 1886 ended Bucknell's exclusive claim upon Pennsylvania Baptists.

Bucknell began to recruit actively outside the denomination. It purchased advertising in eighty-five weekly and daily newspapers and sent public relations dispatches to newspapers in New York, Philadelphia, and Pittsburgh. In 1906 the university increased its publication budget in order to send literature to all secondary school principals and normal school graduates in eight neighboring states. In 1911, for example, in addition to 30,000 leaflets to Baptist associations and 2,700 letters to ministers and alumni, the Committee on Publication distributed the *Bucknell Bulletin* to 17,000 high school graduates.[38]

The incentive to reach beyond Baptist circles was further encouraged by the continuing inability of northern Baptist educators to replace the American Baptist Education Society. Northern Baptists were the last major denomination to create a single coordinating body (the Northern Baptist Convention, founded in 1907), and their educational efforts suffered. In reaction to the faculty pension plan offered by the Carnegie Foundation, the northern Baptist colleges unsuccessfully tried to create their own retirement benefits. Four years later the Northern Baptist Convention created a Board of Education, but it did not raise money until after World War I—and

38. Oliphant, 196–97; Bucknell, Trustees, 17 June 1902, 11 January 1906, 21 June 1910, 20 June 1911, 15 January 1915, and 13 January 1916.

then with only limited success. Northern Baptist priorities had shifted from controlling colleges to sending Baptists to colleges and supporting theological seminaries.[39]

After 1902, explicitly Baptist appeals for funds supplied less of the university's needs. In 1904 Andrew Carnegie donated $30,000 to construct a library. Three years later President Harris, frustrated by the lack of dormitory space, began another $100,000 drive. Progress was slow, and the president waited until he had the lure of matching funds before his next pursuit of mammon in 1911. The General Education Board offered $35,000 to be matched by $135,000, the first infusion of Rockefeller money since 1902. Bucknell raised the sum in two years, with the trustees contributing over half.[40]

Alumni began to replace denominational grants and nonalumni Baptist trustees as dependable sources of largesse. When an early fund drive for a gymnasium stalled, Harris decided that "the main difficulty was that it was an alumni undertaking and nearly all the alumni were ministers who were unable to do much."[41] The president set out to change this situation by shaping the curriculum to appeal to the sons of businessmen and lawyers. He was also an early champion of alumni representation on the board of trustees. In 1892 the trustees designated the seven alumni already serving on the board as alumni representatives, whose successors would be elected by the alumni association. Since five of the seven trustees so designated were Baptist pastors, this was neither an immediate threat to the older leadership nor an immediate solution to Harris's problem. The first elected alumni representative took his seat in 1896, but none of the eight trustees appointed over the next dozen years were alumni. Then between 1909 and 1919 ten of the fourteen new trustees were alumni.[42] Most had to be Baptists, but, as at Princeton and at Franklin and Marshall, denominationalism was being submerged under alumni status. Unlike those two colleges, however, the emergence of alumni

39. Limbert, 39–42; Oliphant, 247–55; Bucknell, Trustees, 16 June 1908. In the 1920s the proportion of Baptists on the board of trustees was reduced from 80 percent to a mere majority after further unsuccessful fund-raising in the denomination.

40. Oliphant, 202–7; Bucknell, Trustees, 14 January 1904, 21 June 1904, 22 June 1909, 12 January 1911, 20 June 1911, and 9 January 1913.

41. Harris, 17.

42. Bucknell, *Alumni Catalogue*, 5–6; Harris, 7–8, 43–45; Bucknell, Trustees, 8 January 1891, 23 June 1891, 14 January 1892, 11 January 1893, and 10 January 1895.

power was not a vehicle for ethnic blending; Bucknell had been dominated by those with English names since its founding.

The alumni became noticeably more active and self-conscious after 1890. Between 1885 and 1895, seven new alumni clubs were founded, and the proportion of offices held by ministers declined considerably. The trustees' Committee on Publication began distributing newsletters to keep the alumni informed of university affairs. Athletics became a rallying point, especially after Christy Mathewson '02 became a major league baseball star. In 1908, one hundred alumni formed "The Bucknellians" in order to "make every Alumnus directly responsible for the success or failure of her athletics" by paying for professional coaches and providing athletic scholarships.[43] The *Alumni Monthly* began in 1914 with an initial circulation of 2,800; the following year Bucknell published its first alumni catalog.

President Harris's policy of creating an affluent board of trustees and alumni body resulted in dramatic growth. During his thirty-year presidency from 1889 to 1919, there were remarkable physical changes: college enrollment increased from seventy-one to over seven hundred, the endowment grew from $200,000 to $800,000, and the campus was transformed. His tenure demonstrates that a traditional denominational college and ministerial president could pursue the entrepreneurial fiscal policies usually associated with Veblen's "captains of erudition" on university campuses.

The years between 1890 and 1917 were a watershed for all four of the colleges in this study, but most dramatically for Swarthmore. It began the period as the one most alien from other colleges; its authorities had just decided to close the preparatory and normal schools but remained ambivalent about emphasizing collegiate work. In 1890 Swarthmore was tied to a small sect that was Anglo-American, but whose beliefs dictated a more distinct life-style than ethnicity did at Princeton and at Franklin and Marshall. Within fifteen years Swarthmore was at the center of national controversies about football, and by 1917 it was on the verge of becoming a national model for liberal arts colleges.

Founded by Hicksite Quakers to provide a "guarded education" that protected their traditional life-style and beliefs, Swarthmore re-

43. Open letter from "The Bucknellians," 15 July 1908 (Bucknell University Archives).

mained under control of a wholly Hicksite board of managers until the 1910s. Like Princeton and Bucknell, the denominational relationship was informal (the only attempt to place Swarthmore under the control of a Quaker Meeting was rejected by the managers in 1895), but the leaders of the college expected Swarthmore to serve the denomination.[44] The first question students filled out on the admission form asked whether the applicant or either parent was a Friend. Until 1898 an affirmative answer brought a 25 percent tuition reduction. Even with that, only about half of the students before 1898 were Friends; the proportion dropped to about one-third by 1907.[45]

Since Friends had no professional clergy, ministerial training was never a function of Swarthmore. Thus, the task of cultural transmission fell to teachers in Friends schools, making teacher training a high priority at Swarthmore in the 1890s even though the normal department had been abolished in 1886. The managers permitted the faculty to eliminate Swarthmore's preparatory school in 1890, a decision facilitated by a bequest that enabled the Hicksites to open George School.[46] The *Friends Intelligencer* lavished attention on Swarthmore with a weekly column as well as news stories and letters to the editor about the institution. The college reciprocated with weekly advertisements reaffirming that Swarthmore was "under the care of Friends."

Swarthmore entered the 1890s torn between those wishing to compete with other colleges and those wanting to protect a threatened

44. Swarthmore College, Board of Managers, Minutes (Friends Historical Library), 17 September and 12 December 1895.

45. Scattered copies of the 1884 application appear in the Edward Magill Presidential Papers (Friends Historical Library), box 6. George Booth to Charles De Garmo, 1896, De Garmo Presidential Papers (Friends Historical Library). The *Friends Intelligencer* 42 (26 September 1885): 522–23, estimated that Friends made up 50 percent of the student body. In 1906 and 1907 89 of 258 entering students were Friends. "President's Report to the Stockholders," in Swarthmore College, Stockholders, *Minutes of the Annual Meeting of the Stockholders* (1906, 1907). Even in the late eighteenth and early nineteenth centuries, the Friends had trouble filling their secondary schools and admitted a number of outsiders—a practice which suggests that some non-Friends came to Swarthmore via the Friends schools. Sydney V. James, *A People Among Peoples* (Cambridge: Harvard University Press, 1963), 274–78.

46. John M. Moore, ed., *Friends in the Delaware Valley: Philadelphia Yearly Meeting, 1681–1981* (Haverford, Pa.: Friends Historical Association, 1981), 107; Richard J. Walton, *Swarthmore College: An Informal History* (Swarthmore, Pa.: Swarthmore College, 1986), 10.

life-style. The financial system discouraged growth. Once the initial capital was raised through the original stock issue in the 1860s, the college was expected to support itself. Gifts from a few rich managers covered the annual deficits, and when the main building burned in 1881 they made up the difference between the insurance and the rebuilding costs.

The only major fund drive between 1869 and 1902 was an 1887 campaign to endow a professorship. It took President Magill almost a year to raise the money through small donations; when he did, three wealthy managers endowed three more chairs. There were no further additions to the endowment for fifteen years. In a college featuring science and engineering programs that required expensive equipment, this was a severe handicap.[47]

The dominant managers rejected expansion; in 1899 the college's total expenses were only six thousand dollars more than they had been a quarter-century earlier. This represented both the limits and the potential of Swarthmore. Joseph Wharton, Isaac Clothier, and some other managers presided over fortunes. Wharton was a nickel and pig-iron tycoon who helped found the forerunner of Bethlehem Steel and the Wharton School at the University of Pennsylvania. Clothier founded the famous Philadelphia department store with an Orthodox Friend, Justus Strawbridge. Other managers carried such famous Philadelphia names as Shoemaker, Roberts, and Biddle. They were loyal Hicksite Friends who served Swarthmore for years; this generation remained in power until 1902 and held the college to a modesty that conformed to their beliefs.[48] Swarthmore was tied to a small minority group and to the Philadelphia region. But the attendance of these Hicksite offspring guaranteed Swarthmore's continuing connection with some very wealthy families in one of the nation's leading cities.

These few wealthy Hicksites were crucial because the rank and file

47. Homer D. Babbidge, Jr., "Swarthmore College in the Nineteenth Century: A Quaker Experience in Education" (Ph.D. diss.: Yale University, 1953), 184–88, 230. See also the board of managers' annual report to the stockholders, available at the Friends Historical Library. Edward Magill, *Sixty-Five Years in the Life of a Teacher* (Boston: Houghton Mifflin, 1907), 210–17.

48. Swarthmore College, Executive Committee, Minutes (Friends Historical Library), 5 February 1888; Babbidge, 183–88; Magill, 217–20; Ingham, 388–403; Philip S. Benjamin, *The Philadelphia Quakers in the Industrial Age, 1865–1920* (Philadelphia: Temple University Press, 1976), 55–56.

offered little financial support. As with Franklin and Marshall College, the affiliation with a rurally based denomination provided a distinct mission that imposed financial and cultural limits. Unlike most Protestant denominations, the Quakers were shrinking. From the Hicksite separation of 1827 to 1900, the Hicksite Philadelphia Yearly Meeting shrank by almost 40 percent while Philadelphia's population grew fivefold. While the Orthodox Friends were fewer in number and suffered similar losses, that sect had a larger share of wealthy urban Friends. Wharton and Clothier were exceptions. Rank-and-file Hicksite philanthropy was unlikely to go toward the higher education of an urban few. Preparatory and normal schools were more in line with most Hicksites' interests.[49]

The conflicting purposes and financial limitations eventually led to crisis. After abolishing the preparatory and normal schools, the managers hedged their bets by hiring Charles De Garmo, a nationally recognized expert in pedagogy, as president in 1891. His conception of teacher training proved to be more academic than the managers liked, and his interest in emulating prestigious colleges fit neither their ideology nor their pocketbook. After seven uncomfortable years, De Garmo resigned and the managers replaced him with William Birdsall, principal of Friends' Central School in Philadelphia. He represented "the position of Friends, with whom *education is a religious concern*, and who would make the development of character always a primary consideration."[50] Most younger Friends who planned to attend college defined character differently.

In 1902 declining enrollment and rising deficits led to Birdsall's return to secondary education and a dramatic alteration of the managers' educational, social, and financial policies. The leading Hicksite educator in the nation was Joseph Swain, president of Indiana University; in desperation, the managers offered him the presidency. Swain agreed, on the conditions that he would control faculty appointments and that the managers would increase the endowment from $400,000 to $1,000,000 within three years.[51]

This acceptance of the academic revolution mirrored a changing

49. Benjamin, 3–25.

50. *Friends Intelligencer* 57 (1900): 613.

51. Babbidge, 210–16. Joseph Swain to Howard C. Johnson, 31 March, 12 May, 17 May, and 9 June 1902, Swain Presidential Papers (Friends Historical Library). Swain admitted that while he and his wife "have both remained Friends we have been away from a Friends Meeting for a number of years."

philosophy and life-style among the new generation of Hicksite leaders. In the 1890s and early 1900s the Hicksites revised their rules, gained new members, and moved away from Quietism and plainness. Cultural defensiveness was replaced by a more dynamic Quakerism that surrendered much that was distinctive. Swarthmore faculty and graduates articulated their new vision in the *Friends Intelligencer* and other forums, agreeing with Swain that "modern Quakerism must adopt any improved method of modern civilization that does not violate its principles and reject any tradition that does not bear the test of modern scholarship."[52]

Swain's election did not end the denominational relationship; rather, its meaning shifted. The attitudes of Hicksites elected to the board of managers changed significantly in the years after Swain's inaugural, while a close relationship between college and denomination continued. Swain continued to court the Friends and their secondary schools, calling the latter educationally equal but morally superior to other preparatory institutions and reminding the denomination that the failure to provide high-quality higher education was causing many young Friends to leave the faith. Still wanting Swarthmore to produce teachers for its schools, the Friends General Conference began to endow a department of pedagogy in 1906. But by 1910 the conference had collected only a fraction of the required funds, and the campaign had to be rescued by a few individuals.[53] The *Friends Intelligencer* continued diligent reporting of campus events, as well as its "Swarthmore College Notes" column.

The denominational relationship no longer demanded a distinct life-style. As with the rejection of ethnicity at Princeton and at Franklin and Marshall, students and alumni increasingly valued Swarthmore for its conformity to national collegiate values rather than for providing an alternative. As denominational membership decreasingly conveyed a distinctive life-style, alumni status became a more important identity, one that encompassed Swarthmoreans of all denominations. All managers were Friends until the 1930s, but increasingly they identified with Swarthmore as alumni.

52. *Friends Intelligencer* 55 (20 June 1903): 393. A supporting editorial is on 390. Several editors had Swarthmore connections. Moore, 104–11.

53. Babbidge, 195–97; Swarthmore College, *The Register of Swarthmore College, 1862–1914* (Swarthmore, Pa., 1914), 28. For an early demand for alumni representation on the board of managers, see *Friends Intelligencer* 39 (7 October 1882): 534–35; see also 65 (9 September, 24 October, and 21 November 1908).

Fig. 15. The new academic order at Swarthmore: Joseph Swain with (left to right) Nicholas Murray Butler, Joseph Wharton, and Isaac Clothier.

The absence of older alumni (the first class graduated in 1873) delayed the victory of the new college culture that repelled the older managers. The early graduates created an alumni association in 1882, the same year as the first of their number was elected to the board of managers. A few alumni participated in the life of the college in the 1890s as faculty or managers, but there was not a strong alumni organization until after 1900. Even then their numbers were low. In 1900 there were still only 421 alumni, and less than 100 alumni over the age of forty. At least 40 percent of the graduates were female—in an era when most families contributed to the husband's alma mater. When a young member of the Clothier family endowed a chair of physics in 1905, it was the first major alumni donation. William Sproul, class of 1891 and a future governor of Pennsylvania, followed with thirty thousand dollars for an observatory two years later. Between 1902 and 1914, four regional Swarthmore alumni clubs were created to represent those outside the Philadelphia area for the first time. The number of alumni managers slowly increased, becoming a majority after World War I.[54]

Foundation money offered temptations to loosen the denominational tie. Rejection by the Carnegie Foundation forced the managers to try to establish their own pension fund to remain competitive in faculty recruitment. Two years later they acknowledged failure and dropped the requirement that managers be Friends in order to qualify the faculty for the Carnegie pension. The managers pledged that Swarthmore would remain under de facto Friends' control, and no non-Friend was elected for several decades; but the legal tie to Quakerism was gone. In 1909 the General Education Board offered a matching grant to Swarthmore, on the condition that the stockholder system be abolished. The shares were duly turned in and the stockholders disbanded in 1910.[55]

One gift created a dilemma for those favoring increased acceptance of the world. In 1907 a wealthy Friend, Anna Jeanes, best known for her contributions to African-American schools, left Swarthmore a sizable bequest on condition that the college ban intercollegiate athletics forever. A committee of managers weighed the offer and sampled the opinion of college presidents across the country. A debate raged over the issue in the *Friends Intelligencer* as well as in national journals. Some Friends vigorously opposed intercollegiate athletics and especially the relatively violent game of football. But others, primarily alumni, came to the defense of athletics. A young alumnus from the influential Clothier family retorted that "after all, what does a broken bone here and there amount to compared to the great amount of good which football accomplishes."[56] Although the man-

54. Society of Friends, *Proceedings of the Friends General Conference* (1906), 99–101; Swarthmore College, *Annual Catalogue*, 1910–11, p. 3.

55. Edward Magill to Andrew Carnegie, 15 July 1905, Magill Papers (Friends Historical Library); Swarthmore, Executive Committee, 13 April 1906; *Friends Intelligencer* 65 (5 and 12 December 1908); Swarthmore College, Stockholders, *Minutes*, December 1909, December 1910; William I. Hull, "History of Swarthmore College" (ca. 1940, Friends Historical Library, typescript), 2:23–25. In practice the majority of stockholders surrendered their privileges to the managers in the 1890s. General Education Board, *Report of the Secretary*, 1916–17, pp. 9, 23.

56. *Friends Intelligencer* 65 (28 March 1908), 203; see also 4 January, 1 February, 14 March, and 21 March; Swarthmore College, *Papers on the Bequest of the Late Anna T. Jeanes* (Philadelphia: Franklin Printing Co., 1907); Burton R. Clark, *The Distinctive College: Antioch, Reed, and Swarthmore* (Chicago: Adams Publishing Co., 1970), 178–83.

agers finally rejected the bequest, they compromised with denominational opposition by canceling football and basketball for a year while they tried to eliminate the worst abuses. By 1915 the *Friends Intelligencer* included sports news in its "Swarthmore College Notes," suggesting a growing acceptance of athletics in the denomination.[57]

Swarthmore had embraced modern college life and the financial benefits that could accompany it if a college had access to the wealthy. In 1916 Swarthmore became one of the first non-Baptist colleges to receive a second allotment of Rockefeller money. The General Education Board offered $125,000 toward the fiftieth anniversary Jubilee Fund if Swarthmore raised $625,000. The alumni organized by class and gender for the first time and raised $160,000. The managers more than doubled that figure. It is not clear how much of the managers' share was contributed by alumni, but Swarthmore clearly was cashing in on long-standing upper-class connections whose financial potential was no longer limited by Hicksite traditions. In this fund drive Swarthmore compared itself to the most prestigious small liberal arts colleges. During Swain's presidency, the campus was transformed and the endowment increased from $400,000 to $3,000,000, the third highest per student in Pennsylvania. Swarthmore was becoming very attractive to the Philadelphia elite.[58]

Swarthmore's acquiescence to a student request for military training in World War I showed how fully Swarthmore had accepted modernity and left its Hicksite roots behind. The managers initially rejected a student petition demanding the formation of a Student Army Training Corps on campus but relented when Swain warned of sharp enrollment declines. No other Quaker college accepted a SATC unit, and the *Friends Intelligencer* lambasted Swarthmore for surrendering its principles. Nearby Haverford, also a Quaker school, "stuck to its guns" (to reverse a metaphor), and its enrollment fell to sixty-five students in the fall of 1918.[59]

57. *Friends Intelligencer* 65 (13 June and 3 October 1908) and 72 (1915). For two accounts of the controversy with different emphases, see Benjamin, 40–48, and Ronald A. Smith, *Sports and Freedom: The Rise of Big-Time College Athletics* (New York: Oxford University Press, 1988), chap. 15, "The Swarthmore Case: An Addendum on Freedom." Benjamin looks at the bequest in terms of Swarthmore straying from Quaker tradition, while Smith stresses the implicit assumption that students are no longer to control athletics.

58. E. Digby Baltzell, *An American Business Aristocracy* (New York: Collier Books, 1962), 356.

59. Swarthmore College, Board of Managers, "To the Undergraduate Men of Swarthmore College," Swain Presidential Papers; Walton, 26–28; Gregory Kanner-

Swarthmore preserved enrollments but set off a bitter debate. The arguments provoked a new activist spirit in Quakerism, one that provided Swarthmore with a modernized denominational mission. Swarthmore faculty were leaders in movements that reunited the Orthodox and Hicksite Friends and created the American Friends Service Committee in 1917. The Quaker service orientation coexisted with football and other trappings of mainstream campus life and enabled Swarthmore to combine a semblance of its earlier distinctiveness with the academic revolution.[60]

On the surface, these case studies repeat the conventional account of the decline of denominations and the rise of alumni, businessmen, and foundations. But that description is superficial. Beneath these broad labels are more subtle interactions among the groups shaping the relationship between colleges and their communities.

The new possibilities for institutional aggrandizement were unsettling. Those wanting expensive, fashionable facilities had to find new sources of revenue. Between 1890 and 1917, the aspirations of most presidents, faculty members, and younger alumni intersected to change the colleges dramatically. The explosion of knowledge, the example of the leading universities, and the emergence of an academic culture gave faculty and presidents new models to emulate. New professional requirements, growing wealth, and changing life-styles created alumni willing and able to support an institution that fit their educational and social needs. But these forces had a wrenching impact on the relationship of the colleges to their traditional constituents.

Increasingly, the wealth that could finance such ambitions was in the hands of urbanites. The combination of congregational canvasses, individuals motivated by ethnoreligious loyalty, and local boosterism that financed more modest visions of higher education before 1890 no longer sufficed. Princeton developed the greatest access to urban wealth, drawing particularly on New York, Philadelphia, and Pittsburgh. Wealthy Philadelphians underwrote Swarthmore's new eminence. Bucknell combined support from some Philadelphians with that from wealthy rural and small-city Pennsylvania Baptists to underwrite substantial growth. Franklin and Marshall, limited by legal

---

stein, ed., *The Spirit and the Intellect: Haverford College, 1833–1983* (Haverford, Pa.: Haverford College, 1983), 25.

60. Herbert Hadley, "Diminishing Separation," in Moore, 138–53.

denominational ties, received little support outside the Lancaster area and remained the smallest and poorest of the four. Formal contributions from denominational organizations and churches had rarely been significant. In the 1880s and 1890s, the denominations increasingly turned their limited educational funds to theological seminaries. Formal denominational relationships became fiscal liabilities, except while Bucknell received Rockefeller money through the American Baptist Education Society.

Each college had been founded to promote denominational identity. At Princeton and at Franklin and Marshall, denominationalism was tied to ethnicity; at Swarthmore, to a distinct life-style. In the 1870s and 1880s, students increasingly shunned cultural uniqueness for a student life that ignored distinctions among Protestants of northern European ancestry. After 1890, as these students became prosperous alumni, they valued the colleges for assisting their acceptance into this culture rather than for promoting ethnic or denominational distinctiveness. Colleges founded to protect cultural pluralism had become agents promoting Anglo-Protestant upper- and upper-middle-class culture.

Increasingly it was the alumni identity, rather than an explicitly ethnoreligious one, that inspired loyalty and financial contributions. Graduates' growing self-consciousness and ability to give were demonstrated by their broad-based and predictable benefaction in the 1890s and 1900s. Only Franklin and Marshall, inhibited by the Reformed church, failed to cultivate alumni. Although the colleges continued to invite wealthy outsiders to contribute and serve on their governing boards, they relied more and more upon their own graduates. The new foundations and their matching grants provided a powerful incentive that ambitious college leaders could use to mobilize wealthy alumni and trustees.

Using the labels "ethnicity," "denomination," and "alumni" obscures the nature of the change. The majority of alumni grew up in the ethnoreligious group that sponsored the college. But at these colleges, that background had less and less behavioral significance; a similar student life-style dominated all four colleges. "Alumni" became virtually a surrogate for "generation." As graduates, most entered an upper-middle class in which it was essential to be a Protestant of northern European ancestry; but denominational and ethnic differences within that group were losing their importance. As Stuart

Blumin has shown, distinctions within the middle class were becoming more finely tuned in the late nineteenth century, and a visible upper-middle class was emerging, one increasingly defined by college degrees.[61]

Hidden beneath the behavioral homogeneity was considerable structural continuity, as suggested by the continuity of the charters. Swarthmore's dramatic revolution occurred while all its managers were Friends. Bucknell mushroomed without changing its stipulation that 80 percent of its trustees be Baptist. Princeton's and Franklin and Marshall's trustees continued to be dominated by the founding groups. Instead, the key was occupational and generational change, replacing clergy and traditional laymen on the boards with a new generation of wealthy businessmen, bankers, and lawyers and attracting their children to the college. Not until the immediate prewar years did the proportions from the founding groups drop significantly.

The entrepreneurial success of these four colleges might be explained in terms of their having responded to the needs of society. But they responded to some groups while disregarding or discarding others. The Anna Jeanes bequest is only the most dramatic expression of a deep cultural conflict. These case studies demonstrate that groups with competing visions fought to control colleges that particularly responded to wealthy urbanites who could finance more expansive visions of higher education. The colleges responded to society selectively, consciously cultivating those who could help them shape a new educational order.

61. Stuart M. Blumin, *The Emergence of the Middle Class* (New York: Cambridge University Press, 1989), chap. 8.

7

Presidential Power and Academic Autonomy

Rising expectations of donors and institutional size complicated colleges' governance. As their missions shifted away from protecting a distinct version of Protestantism and toward regional, and even national, competition for prestige among affluent Protestants, the relationships of governing boards, presidents, and faculty changed. The result was conflict. By World War I, as these colleges adapted to their modified missions, all four became more bureaucratized with roles more clearly differentiated and face-to-face community no longer a feasible ideal.

The declining role of denominations and clergy in college governance was the most visible change, though its effect on the behavior of governing boards defies expectations. Franklin and Marshall, the most determinedly denominational college, had the least intrusive trustees after 1890. Whereas the board of trustees ran many daily operations in the 1860s and 1870s, it was relatively unobtrusive after John Stahr became president in 1889. Thereafter the board usually met only during commencement week. Its Committee on Instruction was authorized to visit classrooms and oversee academic affairs, but in practice it made only cursory annual visits. The committee's reports invariably praised the faculty's work and seconded their request for additional equipment and instructors. There is little evidence of conflict between the faculty and the board of trustees; only one faculty request was rejected in this period.[1]

1. They rejected a faculty recommendation favoring coeducation. Franklin and Marshall College, Board of Trustees, Minutes (Franklin and Marshall Archives), 1890–1922.

After 1890, the trustees influenced Franklin and Marshall primarily through the power of the purse. The denomination's financial limitations and the board's refusal to permit presidents to court alumni in effect vetoed curricular innovation. The trustees, for instance, approved faculty proposals to bolster science offerings and to create a bachelor of science degree. But lack of funding stunted the science program for decades, leaving Franklin and Marshall as one of the last colleges in Pennsylvania to institute a B.S. degree.[2] The fact that Franklin and Marshall had the fewest students and most limited curriculum of the four colleges on the eve of World War I was due, not to denominational hostility, but to the financial limitations of the relationship with the German Reformed church and dependence on the Lancaster area.

At Bucknell, trustees allowed more autonomy after the 1882 coup. Most of the trustees William Bucknell appointed lived hours away, mainly in Philadelphia, making meetings infrequent and campus oversight difficult. Although many were clergy, any inclination toward pastoral oversight was discouraged by distance. When wealthy businessmen joined the board in the 1890s and 1900s, the pattern of noninterventionist trustees was already established. The decline of clergy from 48 percent to 25 percent of the trustees in the 1890s improved fund-raising without changing the board's campus role. By 1890 responsibility for most affairs had already passed to the president.

The most intrusive oversight was on the campus without clergy. Only Swarthmore's governing board intervened in campus life persistently after 1890. Its determination to maintain guarded education was facilitated by the fact that many managers lived only a short railroad ride from campus. Their intrusion into campus affairs during the 1890s resulted in regular clashes with the president and the faculty. When President Magill retired in 1889, he was replaced by a noted Herbartian psychologist, Charles De Garmo. The managers were originally attracted by his reputation in teacher training and hoped he would revive the normal department. However, De Garmo wanted to move education courses—and Swarthmore—into the collegiate mainstream. While De Garmo and the faculty sought to raise Swarthmore's standing in the academic world, the managers contin-

2. Franklin and Marshall, Trustees, 1890–1922; Richard Schiedt, "The Natural Sciences Then and Now," *Reformed Church Review* 7 (April 1903): 196–213.

ued to emphasize guarded education within Hicksite traditions. They pressed him to enforce strict social regulations, increase Bible instruction, and maintain a high proportion of Quaker students and faculty. The managers were so sensitive to deviations from Quaker traditions that they called a special meeting before accepting a donation of two pianos. The conflict intensified in 1897 when the board rejected faculty proposals to permit students to attend off-campus church services and to create honor scholarships. De Garmo's annual report expressed regret over the failure of Swarthmore to meet competition from other schools, and he resigned a few months later to accept a chair at Cornell University.[3]

The managers chose a more compatible successor, William Birdsall, the principal of a Friends secondary school and an ardently traditional Quaker. Birdsall launched an extensive recruiting drive with special emphasis on convincing midwestern Friends to send their children to Swarthmore rather than to state universities. Despite Birdsall's vigorous recruiting and his popularity among older Friends, he could not attract enough younger ones. Enrollment declined, and the percentage of male students dropped to 40 percent of the class of 1902. For students, faculty, and some alumni, the increasing disparity between Swarthmore and prestigious colleges became painfully obvious. Birdsall resigned in 1902 and returned to secondary education.[4]

Joseph Swain's arrival marked the end of the attempt by the managers to mold the school to traditional Quaker ideals. He accepted the presidency on the condition that the board would raise more money and fewer objections. The board's executive committee continued to meet monthly, and a visiting committee inspected the campus weekly. But the managers delegated much more power to the

3. Homer D. Babbidge, Jr., "Swarthmore College in the Nineteenth Century: A Quaker Experience in Education" (Ph.D. diss., Yale University, 1953), 200–206; Richard J. Walton, *Swarthmore College: An Informal History* (Swarthmore, Pa.: Swarthmore College, 1986), 15; Swarthmore College, Board of Managers, Minutes (Friends Historical Library), 14 October 1895, 12 September 1896, 8 March 1897, 21 September 1897, and 6 December 1897; Swarthmore College, Executive Committee, Minutes (Friends Historical Library), 21 September 1897.

4. Joseph Swain to Howard Johnson, 12 May, 17 May, and 9 June 1902, Swain Presidential Papers (Friends Historical Library); Babbidge, 206–9; Swarthmore College, *The Register of Swarthmore College, 1862–1914* (Swarthmore, Pa., 1914). I found no records that indicate whether Birdsall was able to raise the proportion of Quaker students.

president and the faculty. The managers' powerful instruction committee followed suit. In the 1890s it had even reviewed requests for minor pieces of equipment and actively participated in faculty appointments. A decade later, the committee no longer considered minor administrative details, and it shared the major decisions with President Swain. By 1915 the committee rubber-stamped the president's appointments and exercised discretion only in matters with major financial ramifications.[5]

The other serious case of trustee intervention occurred, surprisingly, on the most university-oriented campus. At the very time Princeton was becoming a research university, disputes brought it national attention and trustee intrusion. The first incident resulted from dissatisfaction with the leadership of McCosh's successor, the Rev. Francis Patton, a conservative theologian who had been the prosecutor in the famous Briggs heresy trial. Although Patton did not impose his orthodox religiosity on the campus, his lackadaisical administration delayed movement toward university status, so valued by some powerful faculty and alumni. The drift particularly frustrated younger faculty who had trained in graduate schools and expected Princeton to embrace university values. By 1900 some of them created, over Patton's objections, a committee to reform the curriculum. By blocking its proposals, Patton forced a showdown. Dissident faculty joined with some former classmates of the McCosh era, by then rich and influential trustees, to force Patton out of office. He accepted a generous "golden parachute" in June 1902, and the trustees immediately elected one of the conspirators, Professor Woodrow Wilson, as his successor.[6]

After four years of spectacular success, Wilson became embroiled in two disputes that nudged him out of Princeton and into politics. The quadrangle system proposal (see Chapter 6) and a dispute over

5. Swarthmore, Executive Committee, 1890–1914. See Chapter 6 for details of the Swain appointment. Swarthmore College, Committee on Instruction, Minutes (Friends Historical Library), 1895–1916; Walton, 16–24.

6. John M. Mulder, *Woodrow Wilson: The Years of Preparation* (Princeton: Princeton University Press, 1978), 156–57; Henry Wilkinson Bragdon, *Woodrow Wilson: The Academic Years* (Cambridge: Belknap Press of Harvard University Press, 1967), 203, 274–79; William Berryman Scott, Some Memoirs of a Paleontologist (ca. 1930, Princeton University Manuscript Collection, typescript), 710–12; Howard Segal, "The Patton-Wilson Succession," *Princeton Alumni Weekly* (6 November 1978): 20–24.

locating the graduate school both created alliances between factions in the faculty and on the board. Wilson consulted only three faculty members before submitting his quadrangle plan to the trustees in June 1907. After a summer of alumni attacks, Wilson finally sought faculty support and won a preliminary vote, 80–32. The minority included older alumni faculty who opposed Wilson's desire to replace the eating clubs with residential colleges. Unfortunately for Wilson, these alumni faculty, although less prestigious in the academic world than the younger nonalumni faculty, had close ties with some of the trustees. His plan was rejected.[7]

Eventually a similar split occurred in the battle over planning the proposed graduate college. Professor Andrew West gained exceptional power under Patton and, after administering a spectacular sesquicentennial celebration in 1896, was named dean of the graduate college. The trustees gave him almost complete autonomy over the incipient program and, to keep him from accepting an offer from MIT, promised generous financial support. West loyally supported Wilson's expensive undergraduate curricular reforms, assuming that the next priority was his graduate school. When Wilson turned instead to the quadrangle plan, West felt betrayed and began to use his considerable influence with the trustees against Wilson. Grover Cleveland, chairman of the trustee's Committee on the Graduate School and West's intimate friend, was particularly influential in the dean's behalf.[8]

Two bequests that offered to finance conflicting versions of the graduate college set off the second stage of the battle. Wilson envisioned graduate students living in the center of the campus and adding sophistication to undergraduate life. West, enamored with the ambiance of Oxford and Cambridge, wanted a self-contained graduate college with sumptuous social amenities. Both wanted to

7. Mulder, 187–203; Bragdon, 321–29; Scott, 1009; Edward G. Conklin, "Departmental Colleague," in William S. Myers, ed., *Woodrow Wilson: Some Princeton Memories* (Princeton: Princeton University Press, 1946), 28–29; Woodrow Wilson to George C. Fraser, 16 April 1907; Arthur S. Link, ed., *The Papers of Woodrow Wilson* (Princeton: Princeton University Press, 1966–), 17:110–11; Laurence R. Veysey, *The Emergence of the American University* (Chicago: University of Chicago Press, 1965), 241–48.

8. Bragdon, 270–72, 312–16; Willard Thorp, "The Cleveland-West Correspondence," *Princeton University Library Chronicle* 31 (Winter 1970): 69–102. Cleveland named his Princeton residence Westland in the dean's honor.

thrust the collegiate tradition upward into graduate education, but their differences set off a celebrated conflict.[9]

Again Wilson sought faculty support when he began to lose ground with the trustees. A number of faculty, especially three senior professors recently recruited from rival universities, disliked West's emphasis upon amenities. In 1908 they helped Wilson force West to accept oversight by a faculty committee. After Cleveland's death the trustees' Committee on the Graduate School also rallied to Wilson's cause, but the whole board sided with West by a 14–9 vote in 1909. Wilson threatened to resign, splitting the trustees and delaying final action. He then toured alumni clubs and found that, although the New York and Philadelphia alumni opposed him, he had support elsewhere. With Wilson on the verge of at least partial victory, a third bequest left several million dollars to fulfill West's plan. A few months later Wilson resigned to run for the New Jersey governorship, leaving behind a bitterly divided college.[10] His campus battles gave him a handy if exaggerated political image as an opponent of privilege.

Princeton's trustees overruled a majority of the faculty in both instances. Fund-raising efforts and the controversies brought alumni and trustees intrusively into university affairs. For fifteen tense months after Wilson's resignation in 1910, a trustee served as acting president. During the interregnum the faculty argued with the trustees over chapel attendance and fellowships. The faculty finally requested that the board appoint representatives to meet with a faculty committee to promote "mutual understanding upon policies combining administrative and educational features."[11] After considerable agonizing, the trustees elected (on a 17–9 vote) John Hibben, a former Wilson intimate who had sided with West. Hibben's election caused two of Wilson's allies to resign from the board and withdraw their financial support. Several faculty members also left and others con-

9. For a detailed account, see Willard Thorp et al., *The Princeton Graduate School* (Princeton: Princeton University Press, 1978), 103–51; see also Mulder, 203–18. The commonality of the protagonists' views is convincingly argued in Veysey, 241–48. For West's romantic vision, see Andrew F. West, *The Graduate College of Princeton* (Princeton: Princeton University Press, 1913).

10. Bragdon, 354–56, 361–79; Scott, 1007; Edward G. Conklin, "As a Scientist Saw Him," in Myers, 59–60.

11. Princeton University, Faculty, Minutes (Princeton University Archives), 16 May 1912; also 13 May 1912. On chapel attendance, see 21 September, 5 and 20 November, 4 and 12 December 1911; also 15 January 1912.

sidered doing so, fearing that Hibben's election meant continued domination by the trustees and by faculty who supported West and were unsympathetic to true university values.[12]

Their fears proved to be unfounded. Hibben conciliated the warring factions, and most Wilson supporters remained at Princeton. West's critics gained places on the faculty and trustee committees overseeing the graduate college. Hibben voluntarily surrendered the president's prerogative over faculty appointments and increased the power of faculty committees.[13]

The decade of trustee activism at Princeton did not create a tradition of intervention. Faculty stars, now valued for their national reputations, lost the battles but won the war. By 1917 the board rubber-stamped most faculty decisions on academic and social affairs. By bringing peace to the campus President Hibben encouraged the trustees to limit their role to major financial and policy matters.[14]

On all four campuses, pastoral oversight by the governing boards was replaced by financial control by 1917. The proportion of clergy on the boards declined—but at these four colleges there was surprisingly little correlation between clerical trustees and board intervention.[15] The two denominational colleges with heavily clerical boards had the least intrusion, while the one without clergy and the one moving toward university status experienced considerable trustee intervention. Clerical and nonclerical trustees both pulled back from intrusive campus oversight in the 1880s and 1890s. Thus, the rising proportion of businessmen and nonclerical professionals did not create the sharp break from pastoral habits. Generational change was much more significant. Younger trustees, regardless of profession, did not expect the colleges to protect a distinctive life-style, were more comfortable with the new student culture, and granted more autonomy to the president and faculty. Presumably, they were also

12. Bragdon, 405; Scott, 103–4, also 454–56 for his impression of the trustees' power.

13. Bragdon, 405–8; Scott, 455–56; Varnum L. Collins, *Princeton*, American College and University Series (New York: Oxford University Press, 1914), 289.

14. Princeton University, Trustees, Minutes (Princeton University Archives), 1890–1916.

15. The percentage with clerical training at Bucknell declined from 48 percent to 25 percent in the 1890s and then remained at that figure until World War I. Princeton's clerical proportion dropped from 48 percent to 24 percent between 1900 and 1915. Franklin and Marshall, although under legal control of a denomination, had about one-quarter clerical trustees throughout the period.

more used to bureaucratic administration with clearly separated functions. On the other hand, rapid growth and the concomitant fund-raising created conflicts that extended the power of wealthy lay trustees (especially if they were alumni) into campus life. The lesson for presidents and faculty was that autonomy and financial support were enhanced by avoiding controversy.

Presidents controlled their campuses if they kept their institutions within the bounds of propriety. Increasingly they were promoters, campaigning for new buildings and programs and inspiring donors to match their rivals. Even Franklin and Marshall's quiescent President Stahr continually pressed the trustees for new facilities and appointments.[16] Presidents Harris, Swain, and Wilson tried to shape governing boards that would support growth and their policies. At Bucknell, Franklin and Marshall, and Princeton, the president was an ex officio member of most trustee committees before 1900. At Swarthmore the board of managers initiated policy until Joseph Swain's arrival in 1902. Although not formally appointed to trustee committees until 1910, Swain immediately took the initiative and made managers spend their time reacting to his recommendations. Strong presidents like Swain, Harris, Wilson, and Apple cultivated an image of efficiency that fit business expectations.

The policies of the new entrepreneurial presidents suited the desire of many faculty members for institutional growth, but presidents came to share less and less else with faculty. The role of the president evolved from head of the faculty to chief administrator of the institution. The presidents' withdrawal from teaching most concretely demonstrated the estrangement. Swarthmore's President Swain was the first to abandon teaching. His two immediate predecessors taught several courses, though neither carried the heavy load that President Magill bore in the 1870s and 1880s. Similarly, Francis Patton and Woodrow Wilson taught one or two courses at Princeton each semester, a significant reduction from James McCosh's backbreaking load. Wilson participated actively in departmental meetings and activities. President Hibben initially taught an ethics course but eventually dropped that last remnant of McCosh's keystone senior course. At Franklin and Marshall, Henry Apple stopped teaching in 1914,

16. See Franklin and Marshall, Trustees, June 1894.

but a colleague's death forced him back into the classroom the next year.[17] The tradition of a heavy presidential teaching load lasted longest at Bucknell, where John Harris taught all philosophy courses and averaged ten to fifteen hours a week in the classroom. His ethics lectures gave Harris weekly contact with every senior. Through these courses and a Sunday morning Bible class, Harris maintained an old tradition long after it was discarded at the other campuses. When Harris retired in 1919, it passed from the Bucknell scene too.[18]

Institutional growth and trustee and faculty withdrawal from former duties made the executive function more onerous. After 1900, presidents repeatedly requested administrative assistance. The Princeton trustees refused to give President Patton a secretary, so he wrote all of his own letters. Woodrow Wilson had to be satisfied with undergraduate assistants until he suffered a partial physical collapse in 1906 and the trustees finally approved a full-time secretary. By 1916 Princeton employed sixteen full-time administrators.[19] In 1900 Swarthmore hired a combination registrar and presidential secretary who also corrected sophomore essays and ran the Friends Historical Library. President Swain personally administered all scholarships, admissions, and purchases during his first four years in office. In 1906 he convinced the managers to raise the administrative budget, and he created several full-time administrative positions over the next decade. Swain's correspondence reveals a major shift; his attention was increasingly taken up by architects, planners, and investors, and his relation to campus affairs was mediated through student and faculty committees.[20] In 1902 President Stahr secured a part-time registrar to relieve Franklin and Marshall faculty from maintaining

17. Swarthmore College, *Annual Catalogue*, 1890–91 to 1915–16; Princeton University, *Catalogue*, 1890–91 to 1915–16; Franklin and Marshall College, *Catalogue*, 1890–91 to 1920–21; Myers, 21–45.

18. Lewis Edwin Theiss, *Centennial History of Bucknell University, 1846–1946* (Williamsport, Pa.: Grit Publishing Co., 1946), 258; John H. Harris, *Thirty Years as President of Bucknell with Baccalaureate and Other Addresses* (Washington, D.C., 1926), 52–55, 77–79; Bucknell University, *Catalogue*, 1890–91 to 1921–22; Bucknell University, Board of Trustees, Minutes (Bucknell University Archives), 8 January 1914.

19. Scott, 710; Bragdon, 313; Princeton, Trustees, 10 June 1891 and 19 October 1900; Princeton, *Catalogue*, 1915–16.

20. Birdsall to Albert Myers, 22 May 1900, Birdsall Presidential Papers (Friends Historical Library); Swarthmore, Executive Committee, 6 October 1905; Swarthmore, Committee on Instruction, 2 May 1916; letter copybook, 17 August 1903–12 January 1904, and selected correspondence, 1917–18, Swain Presidential Papers.

student records. The next year, Stahr's request for a full-time assistant was granted only after an investigation by a trustee committee. But President Apple's requests for additional personnel and a centralized accounting system in the 1910s were readily approved.[21]

These requests were more than responses to growth. Franklin and Marshall and Swarthmore in the 1910s were the size of Princeton in the 1870s. The new administrative positions reflected changing approaches to organization. They also resulted from trustee determination that student life continue to be regulated after faculty backed away from that duty. The result, as Laurence Veysey has argued, was an extensive bureaucracy unknown in European universities.[22]

The model of the entrepreneurial administrator-president spread rapidly, even to small colleges. While Patton seemed to confirm the notion that dynamic presidents had to be laymen, the careers of the Revs. John Harris, John Hibben, and Henry Apple demonstrate that clerical presidents could also be aggressive institution builders. Harris was a particularly fascinating combination of old and new conceptions of the presidency. His heavy teaching load and deep involvement in Baptist affairs continued traditional presidential functions. But his penchant for growth at any cost based on vocationally oriented curricula and vigorous public relations resembled the approach of Veblen's "captains of erudition." His administrative style was also transitional. Harris modeled himself upon older presidents who discharged a variety of functions single-handedly, yet even he eventually built a small bureaucracy.[23]

Harris ruled the faculty autocratically for thirty years, from 1889 to 1919. Under earlier presidents the faculty met weekly to record grades, deal with disciplinary cases, and discuss general matters. Harris only called the faculty together five or six times a year, bragging that such "meetings were strictly for business, whereby much time

21. Franklin and Marshall, Trustees, 1902, pp. 85–86, June 1903, January 1904, 1913, pp. 238–47; H.M.J. Klein, *History of Franklin and Marshall College, 1787–1948* (Lancaster, Pa., 1952), 142; Franklin and Marshall, *Catalogue*, 1919–20; Henry H. Apple, *Report of the President of Franklin and Marshall College* (1910).

22. Veysey, 314–15.

23. J. Orin Oliphant, *The Rise of Bucknell University* (New York: Appleton-Century-Crofts, 1965), 193–96, 227; Harris, 91–92; Bucknell, *Catalogue*, 1889–90 to 1919–20. Under Harris's leadership Bucknell grew from an enrollment of less than one hundred to nearly six hundred, making it the sixth largest college in Pennsylvania.

was saved and harmony promoted."[24] "Harmony" meant eliminating opportunities for faculty dissent. Decisions pertaining to individual faculty members were conveyed from Harris through department chairmen he appointed. Harris regulated faculty activity closely, even ordering a biologist to remove questions on reproduction from his exams. Another time he directed professors Lindemann and Davis to exchange sporty caps for respectable derbys. One professor recollected that "if one adjective were chosen to describe the Harris regime at Bucknell, it most probably would be *austere*."[25]

Harris made himself the only line of communication between the faculty and the trustees. He served on the board of trustees for several years before his election as president and, in 1894, was appointed an ex officio member of all trustee committees. The faculty did not send a single remonstrance to the board during Harris's thirty years in office. The remarkable display of apparent harmony demonstrated Harris's determination to delegate as little authority to faculty committees as possible. Dissatisfaction brewed beneath the surface; when Harris retired, the trustees immediately approved a reorganization establishing eight faculty standing committees and authorizing monthly faculty meetings.[26]

By 1917 similar administrative structures and presidential roles were developing at all four campuses. Princeton's size required greater complexity, but bureaucratization also proceeded on the three smaller campuses. The presidents built power bases and clearly differentiated themselves from the faculty. The managing boards increasingly restricted themselves to major policy decisions, especially financial ones. Routine matters that trustees and faculty dealt with in the 1870s and 1880s were delegated to the presidents, who, assisted by growing

24. Harris, 51; Bucknell University, Faculty, Minutes (Bucknell University Archives), 1889–1917.

25. John Rice, "Reminiscences," 1963, in Harris Papers (Bucknell University Archives). The faculty minutes confirm Rice's observations. Quote is on 24; emphasis is his.

26. The only admonition from the board to the faculty I found from 1890 to 1917 was a trustee resolution "that the members of the College Faculty be required to attend the Daily Services." This may have also originated from Harris, as he was a member of the Committee on Instruction and Discipline that made the motion. Bucknell, Trustees, 19 June 1894. Bucknell was the only one of the four colleges that did not have faculty committees by 1915.

administrative staffs, increasingly controlled institutional policy after 1890.[27]

Increasing presidential power was a mixed blessing for faculty. The creation of an administrative staff released them from onerous chores. Faculty and presidents shared a commitment to institutional growth and actively sought support for it. But the growing professional self-consciousness of academics often clashed with presidential prerogatives.

In the 1870s and 1880s governing boards played active roles in faculty appointments at these four colleges. After 1890 they increasingly ceded the prerogative to presidents and even the faculty. At Bucknell, the trustees delegated the power to President Harris and their Committee on Instruction and Discipline; in practice the committee's role was minor. Harris apparently made appointments with little faculty consultation.[28] The board of trustees at Franklin and Marshall delegated the responsibility to a standing committee, but its role is unclear.[29] The board of managers, acting through the instruction committee, controlled appointments at Swarthmore until Swain became president in 1902. His recommendations were routinely approved by the committee.[30] President Patton, apparently from disdain for administrative drudgery, delegated the decisions to Princeton's department chairmen. For instance, Professor Woodrow Wilson selected his only colleague in the new department of jurisprudence and political economy. As president, Wilson occasionally preempted the departments, but under his successor the faculty gained nearly complete control.[31]

27. For formal recognition of these expanded powers and duties of the presidency, see Princeton University, *Charters and By-Laws of the Trustees* (Princeton: Princeton University Press, 1906), which revised the 1883 statement on presidential duties. Franklin and Marshall College, Faculty, Minutes (Franklin and Marshall Archives), 19 June 1913 (recording board of trustees action); Babbidge, 210–16; Joseph Swain to Howard Johnson, 12 May, 17 May, and 9 June 1902, Swain Presidential Papers.

28. Bucknell, Trustees, 1889–1917; Bucknell, Faculty, 1889–1917.

29. Franklin and Marshall, Trustees, 1890–1917.

30. Swarthmore, Committee on Instruction, 1890–1916. See especially a letter from Birdsall to Abby Miller read into the minutes of 1 March 1900. Isabelle Bronk to Birdsall, 20 March, 29 March, and 4 April 1901, Birdsall Presidential Papers.

31. Woodrow Wilson to Winthrop Daniels, 16 May and 30 May 1892, in Link, ed., *Papers of Wilson*, 7:634–38; Princeton, Trustees, 1890–1902, confirms that this was typical procedure. Bragdon, 294–305; Myers, 14, 57.

Not surprisingly, the criteria for faculty appointments increasingly stressed training in graduate schools rather than theological seminaries. But, at least for the 1870s and 1880s, the significance of this transition has been exaggerated. Until the late 1800s theological seminaries offered the most advanced scholarship in the areas that became the humanities and social sciences. Until the disciplines matured and the graduate schools grew, hiring seminary graduates was appropriate and unavoidable. It was not until the 1890s that the universities began to offer an adequate alternative professional model and supply of Ph.D.'s. Between 1870 and 1890 the number of American faculty tripled from about five thousand to over fifteen thousand. Only one doctorate was awarded in the United States in 1870, and 1888 was the first year in which the number passed one hundred.[32]

After 1890, graduate schools rapidly surpassed the theological seminaries in the subject areas relevant to undergraduate education, and theological training became much less common for faculty. Even Harris and Patton, the most traditionally pious of the presidents, hired few faculty from seminaries. Franklin and Marshall moved away from clerical faculty more slowly. In 1909 nine of its fourteen faculty members were ordained ministers, and virtually all had studied in the Reformed theological seminary adjacent to the college in Lancaster. This high percentage resulted from the long tenures of several professors and the small science program; few faculty hired after 1910 had degrees in divinity.[33] The ministerial tradition remained stronger in the trustees' choice of presidents. Woodrow Wilson, the son of a Presbyterian minister, was the only one of the six presidents who served at Franklin and Marshall, Princeton, and Bucknell between 1890 and 1917 who had no theological training. (Since the Society of Friends did not have a ministry, Swarthmore's presidents were laymen.)

Instead of hiring theological seminary graduates, the colleges found another way to recruit faculty with denominational and institutional loyalty: they appointed nonclerical alumni. The alumni connection

32. Burton J. Bledstein, *The Culture of Professionalism* (New York: W. W. Norton, 1976), 269–77; Colin Burke, *American Collegiate Populations: A Test of the Traditional View* (New York: New York University Press, 1982), 247–48.

33. Princeton University, *General Catalogue, 1746–1896* (Princeton: Princeton University Press, 1896), 18–21; Franklin and Marshall, *Catalogue*, 1909–10; *Student Weekly* 1 (16 September 1915): 15.

was nearly synonymous with religious affiliation to the sponsoring denomination. In addition, an alumnus had spent four years under the "proper" influences and could be expected to observe the basic Protestant amenities. President Harris was the most addicted to home-grown products: over 80 percent of his appointments were alumni. He maintained that "the best men for us [were] our own men," whereas outsiders took "years before they became an integral part of the life of the Institution."[34]

Harris selected promising undergraduates as potential faculty and encouraged them to attend graduate school. When he had the funds to begin a civil engineering program, he sent a promising student, Charles Lindemann, to Harvard and upon Lindemann's return entrusted him with establishing the program. Several years later Walter Rhodes went to the University of Michigan for graduate study in electrical engineering with a similar promise, and in 1907 he returned to open the department. Harris assisted some students by convincing trustees to donate fellowships to support graduate work. Others were less fortunate; in 1915 he informed a young alumnus in the biology department that budgetary problems made this a good time to begin graduate study. The instructor borrowed money and enrolled at Columbia. The extreme inbreeding delayed Bucknell's accreditation by the American Association of Colleges until 1927 and by the American Association of University Women until 1931.[35]

Franklin and Marshall College was less insistent on employing its own graduates, but most of its faculty had studied at the Reformed theological seminary in Lancaster. Although dependence upon the seminary continued into the twentieth century in the humanities, most science and social science professors appointed after 1890 arrived with some professional training or took leaves for additional university study.[36]

With neither clergy nor many alumni to call upon, Swarthmore recruited university-trained scientists from its inception. Faculty in

34. Harris, 49–51; quote is on 50. This was a public policy. "The policy of the Institution has been to employ its own graduates; requiring these however to pursue advanced work in Universities." Bucknell University, *Bucknell University Bulletin*, Announcement 1908, ser. 7, no. 4.

35. Theiss, 227–30; Harris, 43–51; Rice, "Reminiscences," Harris Papers; Bucknell University, *Alumni Catalogue* (Lewisburg, Pa., 1921); Oliphant, 257–58.

36. Klein, 120–206; Franklin and Marshall, Trustees, 1887–1915.

other subjects were hired from Friends secondary schools through the 1890s, although there was a growing emphasis on advanced degrees and alumni status. President Swain also went further afield and recruited some respected scholars such as John Miller, an astronomer from Indiana University.[37]

At Princeton, President Patton followed McCosh's example of recruiting young alumni who had spent several years in graduate school. But Woodrow Wilson and his dean, Henry Fine, wanted to compete academically with universities and gave no preference to alumni. During Wilson's eight-year presidency, the percentage of alumni in the total faculty dropped from 68 percent to 41 percent; the proportion in the junior faculty plummeted from 78 percent to 29 percent. There were only twelve alumni in the first group of forty-nine young preceptors, thirty-seven of whom had Ph.D.'s. Wilson also hired Princeton's first Catholic and Jewish faculty. Concern with university status resulted in recruiting two Cambridge University mathematicians and in luring professors away from Missouri, Chicago, Pennsylvania, and Yale. But even for Wilson, concern with character was not totally excluded in favor of scholarly standards; he wanted scholars who were "clubbable" gentlemen.[38]

As doctorates became valuable commodities for institutional reputations, colleges began awarding honorary degrees to their own faculty. All four colleges used this device to bolster their faculties' credentials. Although this had gone on before, it was especially widespread between 1890 and 1910 at these colleges and nationwide. By World War I the requirements for awarding honorary degrees were more standardized, and incestuous honorary degrees fell into disrepute as faculties began to fill with earned doctorates.[39]

College teaching became a more distinct vocation at all four campuses after 1890. In the 1870s and 1880s the existence of preparatory and normal programs blurred the distinction between secondary and higher education and the identity of college faculty; the threat dis-

37. Swarthmore, *Register*; *Phoenix* 6 (May 1886): 15; *Friends Intelligencer* 43 (16 May 1885), 50 (7 October 1893), 57 (31 March and 23 June 1900); selected correspondence, 1898–1902, Birdsall Presidential Papers.

38. Bragdon, 305; Mulder, 171–77.

39. See the alumni registers for lists of honorary degrees. For national practices, see Frederick Rudolph, *The American College and University* (New York: Vintage Books, 1962), 396–97.

appeared in the following decades. Princeton eliminated its short-lived preparatory school in the early 1880s. Swarthmore dropped its normal program in the 1880s and its preparatory classes in the early 1890s. Bucknell and Franklin and Marshall retained their secondary schools, but college faculty were rarely asked to teach in them after 1890.

Growing use of administrative staff and faculty committees eliminated duties that had once consumed faculty time. In the 1870s and 1880s the faculties, meeting as a whole, passed judgment upon changes in courses, disciplinary cases, admissions policies, and other details of campus life. Beginning in the 1890s, such responsibilities were delegated to ad hoc or standing faculty committees or to newly established registrars and deans.[40] Faculty regulation of student behavior shifted from disciplining individuals to regulating organizations. After 1890 the number of discipline cases brought to the faculty dropped markedly. But the obsession of students with extracurricular life, especially athletics, became a thorn in the side of all faculties. They set up rules requiring good academic standing of participants, limiting the number of athletic contests and road trips, approving organizational constitutions, and overseeing the finances of the frequently insolvent student groups.[41] Faculties tentatively began to share some responsibility for regulation with students through honor systems, joint committees, and student governments.[42]

The academic structure also became more compartmentalized. Departments had existed in name for decades, but most had only one or two members and few functions before 1900. Institutional growth and disciplinary specialization made departments functional at Princeton during Wilson's presidency. Departments started playing a role at Bucknell and Swarthmore by 1910. Smaller Franklin

40. For the inner workings of one such committee, see Woodrow Wilson's notes from the Committee on Discipline, for which he was secretary from 1891 to 1899. Link, *Papers of Wilson*, vols. 7 and 8, includes his notes for the first four years. Catalogs list faculty committees shortly after 1900 at Franklin and Marshall, Princeton, and Swarthmore. None are listed at Bucknell until John Harris left in 1919.

41. See for instance, Princeton, Faculty, 18 November 1892, 25 October and 1 November 1893, 17 April 1905; Swarthmore, Faculty, 16 February 1903; Bucknell, Faculty, 21 January 1902, 9 May 1903, 15 June 1903, 18 June 1910, and 26 May 1917; Franklin and Marshall, Faculty, 19 September 1906.

42. Princeton, Faculty, 18 January 1893; Link, *Papers of Wilson*, 8:415–16; Swarthmore, Faculty, 17 November 1902, 2 March 1914, 15 June 1914; Bucknell, Faculty, 13 June 1903; Franklin and Marshall, *Catalogue*, 1916–17.

and Marshall did not divide academic duties along departmental lines until the 1920s.[43] These colleges experienced a limited form of the internal differentiation that characterized the emerging universities.[44]

While faculty duties and departmental structure became well established in this period, academic freedom and tenure were barely extant in these institutions. Despite a lack of de jure protections, faculty enjoyed surprising de facto security. Woodrow Wilson's voluminous papers give a comprehensive picture unavailable for other presidencies. They disclose that, under special powers granted to him by the trustees to reorganize the faculty, he dismissed a French professor for lackadaisical teaching. The resulting outcry forced Wilson to grant him an extra year. Thereafter Wilson was loath to use that power and, except for one forced retirement, removed no other professors. Both terminations resulted from inadequate teaching rather than issues of academic freedom.[45] If other presidents removed faculty, the limited records hide the action. The long careers suggest that arbitrary termination was rare. Princeton was the first to offer formal security by creating a tenure system in 1915.

Only one clear violation of academic freedom surfaces in the records of the four colleges. German-born Franklin and Marshall professor Richard Schiedt publicly supported his homeland in World War I from the outbreak of hostilities. After American intervention the board of trustees declared that it "neither could nor would tolerate divided allegiance in the teaching force of the College" and appointed a committee to deal with the errant professor. Schiedt resigned shortly thereafter, in spite of one trustee's vigorous objections.[46] This action, brought on by the passions of war and the vulnerability of an institution with a German heritage, stands out as an

43. Princeton, Faculty, 2 December 1903; Collins, 289–90; Myers, 63; Bucknell, *Catalogue*, 1901–2 to 1910–11; Swarthmore, *Catalogue*, 1902–3 to 1908–9; Franklin and Marshall, *Catalogue*, 1905–6 to 1922–23.

44. See Veysey, 320–24, for an excellent discussion of departmentalization in the universities.

45. Mulder, 162–63; Bragdon, 295–96. See, for instance, Woodrow Wilson to Professor Arnold Cameron, 11 November 1903, Wilson Papers (Library of Congress Manuscript Division); Arthur S. Link, "That Cobb Interview," *Journal of American History* 72 (June 1985): 13.

46. Franklin and Marshall, Trustees, 23 November 1917; Richard Schiedt, "Germany and the Formative Forces of the War," *Reformed Church Review* 19 (1915): 19–48.

Fig. 16. Franklin and Marshall faculty, 1913. Professor Schiedt is second from the left in the middle row, and President Stahr is on the far right in the middle row.

exception. Although records do not show how many nonconformists were not hired or were stifled after being hired, overt violations of academic freedom were uncommon. The creation of the American Association of University Professors (AAUP) in 1915 provided procedural recourse for some; faculty from Swarthmore and Princeton joined immediately, and a Bucknell professor joined in 1920.[47]

The creation of vested pensions provided more tangible security for faculty. The absence of dependable retirement benefits no doubt caused great anxiety to any faculty member who was not independently wealthy. Trustees sometimes awarded limited ad hoc pensions. At the turn of the century they became more common, though small. President Magill and Professor Beardsley, each of whom served Swarthmore for over thirty years, received $500 annually. Freeman Loomis, a professor at Bucknell for thirty-five years, received $600 and a room in his first year of retirement; the sum was reduced to $400 the second year and to $200 the third.[48]

47. Association of American University Professors, *Bulletin* 1 (1915), 6 (1920). In 1920 there were seventy-four members from Princeton and eleven from Swarthmore.

48. Swarthmore, Executive Committee, 13 April 1906; Bucknell, Trustees, 20 June 1899, 19 June 1900, 18 June 1901.

Establishment of the Carnegie Foundation for the Advancement of Teaching in 1906 radically improved the situation. The foundation offered faculty pensions to all nonsectarian institutions. Princeton qualified immediately. Swarthmore, after failing to establish its own pensions, dropped the formal requirement that managers be Quakers in order to qualify. Bucknell did not apply to the foundation, opting for an ultimately unsuccessful scheme to establish pensions among Baptist colleges. Franklin and Marshall's board rejected President Apple's plan to reduce the number of trustees elected by the Reformed synods in order to qualify. But when ex-President Stahr retired from the faculty in 1915, he received a twelve-hundred-dollar pension—higher than any previously awarded. All four colleges either joined the pension fund or were forced to consider alternatives.[49]

The Carnegie pension, tenure systems, and the AAUP increased formal faculty security. Departmental structures and the elimination of nonteaching duties protected faculty from unprofessional pressures. Clearly the professionalized faculty who were starting to dominate by 1917 had gained considerably more autonomy than their predecessors. The results of professionalization for salary, standard of living, and social status, however, were less positive.

Professionalization brought higher pay and greater privileges for well-known faculty, as colleges came to value their academic reputations. This increased bargaining power was demonstrated most dramatically at Swarthmore. The board of managers cut faculty salaries by 10 percent for several years around the time of the depression of 1893. But a decade later they capitulated to the demands of Professor John Lowes, who threatened to accept an offer from Indiana University unless the managers pledged one thousand dollars annually for the English section of the library and gave him an assistant.[50] Astronomer John Miller conditioned his acceptance of a Swarthmore

49. Henry Pritchett, "The Policy of the Carnegie Foundation," *Educational Review* 32 (June 1906): 83–93; Carnegie Foundation for the Advancement of Teaching, *Reports* 1 (1906): 21; 4 (1909): 19–21; Swarthmore, Executive Committee, 13 April 1906; Bucknell, Trustees, 16 June 1908; Bucknell, Faculty, 18 June 1910; H. H. Apple, *Report of the President of Franklin and Marshall College*, 1911.

50. Swarthmore, Committee on Instruction, 9 March 1896, 14 April 1896, 18 September 1906. Lowes accepted an offer from Harvard several years later. See *Friends Intelligencer* 60 (20 June 1903): 393 for an expression of the need to pay more to meet competition from universities.

Fig. 17. Swarthmore professor John Miller and his telescope.

appointment upon the purchase of a 24-inch telescope. Having arranged this, President Swain conveyed the good news and added, "But remember this is a Friends' College and thee should give up thy smoking. Please wire thy acceptance." When Miller balked at giving up the noxious weed, Swain backed down.[51]

In 1892 the University of Illinois offered Woodrow Wilson its presidency at $6,000, twice his Princeton salary. President Patton resisted making a counteroffer to avoid "invidious distinctions" among the faculty. He finally raised Wilson's salary to $3,500 and gave him an assistant. Five years later, to counter an offer to head the University of Virginia for $4,000 and a house, several trustees created a secret annual $2,500 subsidy. A decade later such enticements were com-

51. "Quaker Astronomer: John A. Miller," clipping from *The Sky* (March 1941), Faculty Papers (Friends Historical Library).

mon: a trustee openly built a rent-free house that lured an eminent University of Pennsylvania biologist to Princeton rather than Yale.[52] In 1914 a noted botanist successfully demanded "facilities for carrying forward my chosen lines of investigation, and freedom to control the number and character of students accepted to work in my classes."[53] Bucknell and Franklin and Marshall continued to rely heavily upon their own graduates and were less involved in bidding for faculty.

Star professors clearly benefited from the new academic marketplace. Those lacking a national reputation or working in institutions not seeking one fared less well. Salaries remained fairly static. At Bucknell and at Franklin and Marshall, professional salaries rose slightly but remained in the $1,500 range. Swarthmore paid its established professors about $2,000 in the 1890s and 1900s; their pay rose to about $3,000 after 1910. Wilson's $3,500 made him the highest paid Princeton faculty member in the early 1890s. A quarter-century later, that would still have been higher than the salaries of all but a few full professors recruited from other universities at about $4,000.

The academic star system meant that salary disparities among faculty grew considerably. In 1890 the highest paid professors typically received about 25 percent more than the lowest paid, and there were relatively few faculty in the lower ranks. Except for the stars, that relative equality among senior faculty continued. But the number of junior faculty grew rapidly at Swarthmore and Princeton. In 1915 Swarthmore had fourteen professors, each making about $3,000; eight assistant professors in the $1,500–2,000 range; and fourteen instructors receiving $800 to $1,200. Princeton hired large numbers in the lower two ranks at similar salaries. Wilson hired his preceptors at salaries ranging from $1,400 to $2,000 in 1905. When Princeton created a tenure system for assistant professors in 1915, they received a salary of $2,000. Princeton also hired a number of "assistants," presumably graduate students, at $425.

The differential between presidential and faculty salaries also grew. Before 1890, presidents made only marginally more than professors.

52. Link, *Papers of Wilson*, 7:609–35, 10:481–531; Bragdon, 227; Myers, 57–58; Mulder, 135–56.

53. George Shull to Edwin G. Conklin, 16 June 1914, Conklin to John Hibben, 15 January 1915, and Hibben to Conklin, 27 January 1915, Conklin Papers (Princeton University Archives).

Franklin and Marshall's John Nevin made $1,500 in the 1860s, while his colleagues received $1,200. James McCosh made $4,000 when Princeton professors were paid $3,400. But his successor was making $8,000, twice the salary of any professor except Wilson, when he left office in 1902. John Harris and Joseph Swain also made about twice the salary of their faculty colleagues. Only President Apple of Franklin and Marshall remained in the same salary range as his faculty.[54]

Faculty were relatively well paid in comparison with the average American. In 1890 the mean income of American clerical workers was $848, and for industrial workers it was $486. The highest salary at these four colleges in the 1890s was Woodrow Wilson's $3,500. Typical salaries for professors ranged from $1,400 to $2,000. Presidential salaries were about equal to Wilson's professorial pay. By 1910 the national average for clerical workers was up to $1,156; for industrial workers, $630. The highest paid professors were receiving $4,000, with most between $1,500 and $2,200. When the rank of assistant professor emerged, the pay was typically about $1,500. Thus, the average faculty member remained well ahead of clerical workers and far ahead of industrial workers, but the differential was declining.[55]

How can these figures be reconciled with frequent complaints about impoverished faculty? The exaggerated laments served the purposes of university reformers seeking financial support for the new academic order. But there was some basis for the deeply felt sense of deprivation. Faculty salaries were in relative decline. Salaries in many other occupations rose sharply between 1890 and World War I, a rise matched in academia only by stars. This was part of a long-term relative decline; Colin Burke estimates that faculty made 7.5 times as much as the average unskilled laborer in 1850, a ratio that declined to 5.2 in 1890, 3.3 in 1920, and about 2 in recent decades.[56] In

54. Salaries derived from trustees minutes and scattered institutional histories.

55. In an excellent article, Frank Stricker found strikingly similar figures for faculty in the better-paying colleges nationally. He estimates inflation for faculty at only 1 percent between 1890 and 1914; salary increases were real gains. Frank Stricker, "American Professors in the Progressive Era: Incomes, Aspirations, and Professionalism," *Journal of Interdisciplinary History* 19 (Autumn 1988): 231–57; Bureau of the Census, *Historical Statistics of the United States* (Washington, D.C.: U.S. Government Printing Office, 1975), 168. For another measure, see National Bureau of Economic Research, *Income in the United States: Its Amount and Distribution, 1909–1919* (New York: Harcourt, Brace, & Co., 1921; reprint, New York: Arno Press, 1975), 102–3.

56. Burke, 232–33.

addition, faculty families usually conformed to the middle-class ideal of a single breadwinner; multiple-earner working-class families could, in favorable conditions, approach the income of professional families. Young faculty in the new junior positions could find themselves temporarily behind working-class families when few faculty would have doubted their right to incomes several times greater than those of the working class.

Worse for the faculty psyche, the average American was not their frame of reference. Many of their neighbors were doctors, lawyers, and businessmen, whose incomes were rising rapidly. The trustees and many students came from upper-class families that were making the greatest gains in a booming economy. Even the highly paid Princeton faculty suffered by comparison in a community that attracted a growing number of plutocrats after Grover Cleveland retired to it from the White House in 1897.[57] Faculty compared themselves with other professionals and corporate executives—in other words, with their neighbors and students' parents—and most were not keeping up. Like many professionals in the Progressive Era, professors felt squeezed from above and below by the working class and the wealthy.

The two institutions that openly bid in the new academic marketplace paid higher salaries. But correlation is not causation. While the two colleges most committed to the academic revolution, Princeton and Swarthmore, paid higher wages, that differential largely preceded the reforms. In the late 1860s an educationally traditional Princeton paid about twice the salaries offered to faculty in Lewisburg or Lancaster. Once Swarthmore decided to be solely a college in about 1890, it began to pay about one and one-half times that of the two other Pennsylvania colleges, while Princeton continued at about twice their salaries. When Princeton and Swarthmore both plunged into academic reform at the turn of the century, the differentials remained. The main difference was that a few academic stars negotiated higher salaries, but large numbers of young faculty were slotted into new junior categories—thus keeping the average differential about the same. Rather than the academic revolution lifting salaries, the causation may be reversed; already affluent colleges were the ones that could take part.

57. Frank Stricker reached similar conclusions about the disparity between faculty laments and their relative comfort. Stricker, 251–56; Mulder, 188.

Although professionalization did not bring high salaries for most faculty, many apparently lived well. Unfortunately, it is difficult to measure their economic status. Many faculty probably brought family money with them and lived beyond their salary. Because the census dropped direct measures of wealth after 1870, faculty wealth in later decades is a matter of conjecture. The most useful indicator that can be teased from the census is the number of servants living with the family, which was recorded in all five extant censuses from 1860 through 1910.[58] Over the whole period, faculty were twice as likely to have servants (58 percent) as their neighbors (29 percent), and over six times as likely as the community (9 percent). Faculty were three times more likely than their neighbors to employ more than one servant, and thirteen times more likely than the community (Table 8).

If the figures are broken down by period, there is evidence that the relative standing of faculty members declined after 1890. From 1860 to 1880, 77 percent of faculty homes included servants; this declined to 46 percent for 1900 and 1910. The proportion of the

Table 8. Servants Living in Households, 1860–1910

No. of Servants	Faculty	Neighbors	Community
None	41.9%	71.5%	90.7%
1	32.1	19.8	7.1
2	16.2	6.4	1.4
3+	9.8	2.4	0.6
	N=315	N=517	N=927

SOURCE: United States Census, 1860, 1870, 1880, 1900, and 1910; see note 58 and Chapter 3, notes 3–7.

58. For the methodology used to analyze the 1860, 1870, and 1880 census data in Tables 8 and 9, see Chapter 3, notes 3–7. The latter censuses used were 1900 (reels 982, 1406, 1423–25, and 1488) and 1910 (reels 896–97, 1338–40, 1352–55, and 1423). I located about two-thirds of the faculty in 1900 and 1910. "Neighbors" are the five households listed above and below the faculty member; "community" is the college's political unit. In 1900 and 1910, that was Lancaster City, Princeton Township and Borough, Lewisburg Borough, and Swarthmore Borough. In selecting "neighbors" and "community," I used sampling ratios that would yield about fifty cases for each category at each college.

Home ownership was not a meaningful category because some of the most affluent faculty rented, perhaps from the college. I counted "domestics," "companions," "nurses," and "housekeepers" as "servants," which biased the data against my conclusion.

neighbors with servants remained between one-quarter and one-third. In the community the percentage dropped from 11 percent to 7 percent.[59] If servants continued to be an accurate indicator of wealth after 1870, faculty continued to be affluent in the following decades, but their relative advantage declined—slightly in comparison with the general community, sharply in comparison to their neighbors. Fewer twentieth-century faculty enjoyed the luxury of servants, though they were still dramatically more likely to have servants than the average American.

Comparing the professions of faculty neighbors to those of the community provides another indicator of status (Table 9). Throughout the period, faculty neighborhoods were about three times more likely to contain professionals or proprietors of large enterprises (23.5 percent) than the community in general (8.8 percent). Fewer of their neighbors were manual workers and small businessmen (47.7 percent) than was typical in the general population (65.9 percent). The elusive category "none" (in which I included the retired) probably masks a greater disparity between faculty neighbors and the general community. It seems that many reporting "none" who lived near faculty were independently wealthy, a condition sometimes indicated by phrases like "living on own income." "None" in other parts of town was often linked with indicators of poverty.

Thus, most faculty in these colleges lived in affluent neighborhoods among doctors, lawyers, ministers, and businessmen, and many were able to hire servants. Their income, wealth, and household structure clearly distinguished them from most of the community. However, after 1890 the differential, as measured by salaries and servants, was decreasing, suggesting that although faculty continued to live in elite neighborhoods, their position within those neighborhoods declined.

Thus, professionalization was not synonymous with prestige and wealth; rather, it signified change in reference groups and adjust-

59. In the 1900 and 1910 censuses street addresses were recorded, enabling me to choose those living within five houses on the same street. This makes the 1900 and 1910 neighbor cohort a better sample but skews comparisons with the data from the 1860, 1870, and 1880 censuses, biasing the data in favor of my thesis. For that reason I have not compared the figures in tabular form. The resulting data indicated that the percentage of neighbors with servants declined minutely from 28.6 percent to 28.0 percent. If I had continued the sampling method as used for 1860–1880, the resulting data would probably show that the proportion of neighboring households containing servants declined modestly.

Table 9. Occupations of Faculty Neighbors and the Community, 1860–1910

Category	Neighbor 1860–1910	Community 1860–1910	Neighbor 1860–1880	Community 1860–1880	Neighbor 1900–1910	Community 1900–1910
Professional	14.7%	5.3%	7.3%	3.8%	19.5%	6.8%
Large Proprietor	8.8	3.5	7.3	3.0	8.8	3.9
Small Business/Craftsmen	29.6	37.7	33.6	42.0	25.8	33.2
Semi- and Skilled Manual	6.0	6.9	4.6	3.2	6.9	10.7
Unskilled Manual	12.1	21.3	14.9	21.1	13.1	21.4
Keeping House	9.3	10.6	15.6	15.3	4.5	5.7
None	16.5	10.8	11.1	6.8	19.5	14.9
Other	3.2	4.1	5.7	4.9	1.9	3.3
	N=571	N=927	N=262	N=470	N=309	N=457

SOURCE: United States Census, 1860, 1870, 1880, 1900, and 1910; see notes 58 and 59 and Chapter 3, notes 3–7.

ment to a nationalizing society. With the academic revolution, faculty, like other professionalizing groups, moved along the spectrum from "localism" toward "cosmopolitanism." Their predecessors had participated in a local and regional intellectual life that was largely composed of nonacademics. A professionalized academic culture became a viable alternative in this century as a truly national society and economy emerged. University-trained faculty were part of a national and even international academic life but were probably more isolated intellectually from nonacademic professionals.

The advantages of academic professionalization have often been exaggerated by denigrating the intellectual role of religion in nineteenth-century colleges. As seen above, however, theology provided an umbrella for concerns later labeled the humanities and social sciences. Denominational organizations and publications provided sources of social and intellectual community that were not carried on by younger professors. Franklin and Marshall faculty members published prolifically on various subjects in the *Reformed Church Review*. Richard Schiedt, for instance, regularly published articles on science and politics. Faculty often served on the editorial board. But by 1915 only the older faculty participated. The *Presbyterian (and Reformed) Review* and the *Princeton College Bulletin* provided similar outlets for Princeton's professors. After Wilson became president, faculty published almost solely in the new disciplinary journals. The Northumberland Baptist Association remained a focal point for some senior members of Bucknell's faculty.[60] Some Swarthmore faculty played important roles in liberalizing Quakerism and healing the Orthodox-Hicksite split through summer schools, articles in the *Friends Intelligencer*, and activism within the Meeting. They were leaders in the creation of the American Friends Service Committee in 1917, and two Swarthmore history professors, William Hull and Jesse Holmes, were part of the five-man delegation to the All Friends Conference held in London in 1920.[61] Involvement in denominational activities

60. *Reformed Church Review* 1–20 (1897–1916); Northumberland Baptist Association, *Minutes*, 1900–1916; Swarthmore Monthly Meeting, Membership, 1893–1930 (Friends Historical Library); *Princeton College Bulletin* 1–16 (1889–1904); *Presbyterian and Reformed Review* 1–13 (1890–1902); *Reformed Quarterly Review* 36–43 (1890–96).

61. Swarthmore Monthly Meeting, Membership, 1893–1930; Philip S. Benjamin, *The Philadelphia Quakers in the Industrial Age, 1865–1920* (Philadelphia: Temple University Press, 1976), 17–47; John M. Moore, ed., *Friends in the Delaware Valley: Philadelphia Yearly Meeting, 1681–1981* (Haverford, Pa.: Friends Historical Association, 1981), 104–53.

declined at all four campuses among faculty hired after 1900, but the transition was slow.

Some bridged the old and new academic cultures. Henry Van Dyke of Princeton was a professor of English, an alumnus, and a Presbyterian minister who did graduate work at Princeton Theological Seminary and in Germany. His appointment symbolized the change from McCosh's evangelical Presbyterianism to the more genteel style of Patton and Wilson. Van Dyke wrote *The Story of the Other Wise Man*, a saccharine Christmas story still in print. A champion of liberal theology, he chaired the committee that modernized the Presbyterian *Book of Common Worship* in 1903. At the same time, he was a leading defender of literary idealism in professional circles.[62] Swarthmore's John Lowes traveled farther toward the new scholarship. He began his career as professor of ethics and Christian evidences at Hanover College in Indiana. He had English added to his title and eventually left for doctoral studies at Harvard, where he fell under the spell of philologically based criticism. Swain then hired Lowes as one of Swarthmore's new academic breed. Lowes later returned to Harvard and was elected president of the Modern Language Association.[63] Careers like these show that the old and new academic models are not dichotomous. There were many transitional figures.

By World War I all four campuses were bureaucratizing, progressively differentiating functions among presidents, faculties, and governing boards. Trustees, clerical and lay alike, increasingly left administration to the presidents and concerned themselves with policy and finances. Faculties reduced the time spent on duties other than teaching and research; they traded their former roles for autonomy. Presidents slowly acquired staffs to take over those duties and separated their lives and their salaries from those of faculty members. Energetic presidents consolidated considerable power and established themselves as the channel of communication among faculty, trustees, and other constituents.

62. Henry F. May, *The End of American Innocence* (Chicago: Quadrangle Paperbacks, 1964), 77–97; Hugh T. Kerr, ed., *Sons of the Prophets* (Princeton: Princeton University Press, 1963), 151–60; J. David Hoeveler, *James McCosh and the Scottish Intellectual Tradition: From Glasgow to Princeton* (Princeton: Princeton University Press, 1981), 333.

63. Michael Warner, "Professionalism and the Rewards of Literature," *Criticism* 27 (Winter 1985): 18.

The period between 1890 and 1917 has often been depicted as a golden age for faculty, the time when they escaped the limits of denominational colleges for the dynamism of universities. But the faculty experience at these four colleges defies such clear-cut dichotomization. It is even problematic that the academic revolution produced monetary and status gains for faculty. At these four colleges in the late nineteenth century they were part of a local elite and leaders of genteel culture. Faculty status and wealth apparently did not increase after the turn of the century, even at the two institutions participating in the academic marketplace. Instead, these case studies support Colin Burke's conclusion that there was an inverse relation between relative economic standing and professionalization.[64] As university-trained faculty formed a new academic profession and culture, they freed themselves from some social and intellectual limitations and established their place in the emerging national culture. Between 1890 and 1915 professorial life became a more specialized and professional calling, in which faculty achieved greater control over their work at the cost of greater isolation from the local society. They lost some of the benefits of a less exclusive academia, as did society.[65] Histories of academic professionalization have described the ultimate result well, but have often oversimplified the process.

64. Burke, 232–33.

65. See Lewis Perry, *Intellectual Life in America: A History* (New York: Franklin Watts, 1984), 290–314, for an insightful discussion of the changing relation of intellectuals and society.

8

Knowledge Fit for Protestant Gentlemen

The saga of the triumph of the elective system over the classical curriculum is well known. Simply stated, it contrasts exciting curricular experiments at universities with the classical curricula that supposedly stifled colleges until they finally accepted defeat, cast off the constraints of the prescribed curriculum, and embraced the elective system. However, as seen in Chapter 4, the curricular variety of these four colleges between 1865 and 1890 defied that image, suggesting that collegiate innovation has been underestimated. An examination of the curricula at these four colleges between 1890 and 1917 demonstrates that neither electives nor vocationalism triumphed. Instead, a new consensus emerged based on a definition of liberal education that incorporated breadth, electives, and specialization.

Contrary to the assumption that religious and curricular conservatism were synonymous, at Bucknell and Princeton two theologically traditional presidents, the Revs. John Harris and Francis Patton, championed electives and professional courses. Harris loosened Bucknell's requirements so that, by 1900, only freshmen followed a prescribed schedule. He established a bachelor of philosophy degree with no Greek requirement and expanded the science faculty. After the turn of the century, Bucknell added new degrees in the sciences, engineering, and jurisprudence. By 1917 its students could choose from ten parallel courses of study ranging from liberal arts to domestic science.[1]

1. J. Orin Oliphant, *The Rise of Bucknell University* (New York: Appleton-Century-Crofts, 1965), 215–26; John H. Harris, *Thirty Years as President of Bucknell with Bac-*

At Princeton, President Patton greatly extended the electives permitted under James McCosh. By 1900 only one-third of the junior courses and none of the senior courses were required. The School of Science continued to be a refuge for students hoping to avoid the classics, but it increasingly offered more technologically specialized programs for students truly interested in science. For instance, for the school's degree in civil engineering the only required nontechnical courses were one year of English and a foreign language. In Patton's years the proportion of students in the scientific curriculum doubled from one-sixth to about one-third. Toward the end of his presidency he considered making the senior year preprofessional. Patton's rejection of a faculty plan to restore structure to the curriculum precipitated his ouster.

Propelled into office by the faculty's desire for a new curricular structure and by alumni financial backing, Wilson used the opportunity to create a system of "distribution and concentration" that has become the dominant curricular model in twentieth-century colleges. There had been experiments with grouping courses for breadth and depth since Johns Hopkins did so in the 1870s, and Wilson may have derived some of his ideas from his former employer, Bryn Mawr. Wilson's timing and Princeton's prestige gave the approach national attention. It provided a rationale for upper-class course selection by focusing upon a majority (or "major") field of study. Upperclassmen chose three courses in their major department and two electives. Freshmen courses were prescribed (with a choice among modern languages); sophomores had three requirements and two electives. Thus, freshmen and sophomores, except those in civil engineering, followed a relatively common program until major studies began.[2]

Wilson's plan gave each degree program more integrity and equalized the admission requirements. Candidates for the B.A. could choose any major, while B.S. candidates were restricted to the sciences and those pursuing the new bachelor of literature degree had to major

calaureate and Other Addresses (Washington, D.C.: privately printed, 1926), 19; Bucknell University, *Catalogue*, 1885–86 to 1916–17.

2. Princeton University, *Catalogue*, 1887–88 to 1901–2; Kenneth W. Condit, *History of the Engineering School of Princeton University, 1875–1955* (Princeton: Princeton University Press, 1962), 68; Patricia Graham, *Community and Class in American Education, 1865–1918* (New York: John Wiley & Sons, 1974), 193–94; John M. Mulder, *Woodrow Wilson: The Years of Preparation* (Princeton: Princeton University Press, 1978), 134–35.

in the humanities or the social sciences. The new system also permitted a more distinctive and prestigious scientific curriculum. After Wilson's 1904 reorganization, the B.S., which had been an easy option for some students wanting to take less classics, added demanding scientific requirements.[3]

Of the four colleges only Franklin and Marshall retained a wholly prescribed classical curriculum after 1890. Entering classes attended courses as a group until 1893, when rising enrollment forced the division of classes into sections. The prescribed curriculum was preserved by requiring as many as ten courses per term and relegating others to the status of options. In 1894 the optional courses entered the regular curriculum; seniors were allowed to choose eight courses from a list of twelve. Since there was no substantive change in the courses offered, the actual effect of the elective system was that seniors could skip some of the old requirements in order to take the formerly optional courses.[4]

A petition from a delegation of juniors ended the classical monopoly in 1899. These young men, primarily premedical students, complained that the extensive classical language requirements prevented them from spending sufficient time on science. President Stahr temporarily removed the Greek requirement and reported his action to the board of trustees the following June, along with a resolution of support from the Potomac Synod, for a permanent reduction of the classics requirements for students interested in science. The board accepted that a modification was "called for by the demands of the age and the needs of the Church," clearing the way for a parallel curriculum.[5] The resulting bachelor of philosophy program allowed students to replace Greek with science and modern languages and offered some electives to seniors.

By 1912 Franklin and Marshall was the only college in Pennsylvania without a degree program in science. President Apple used this fact

3. Henry Wilkinson Bragdon, *Woodrow Wilson: The Academic Years* (Cambridge: Belknap Press of Harvard University Press, 1967), 288–94; Varnum L. Collins, *Princeton*, American College and University Series (New York: Oxford University Press, 1914), 328–29; Princeton University, *Annual Report of the President*, 1904.

4. Franklin and Marshall College, *Catalogue*, 1892–93 to 1901–2; Franklin and Marshall College, Board of Trustees, Minutes (Franklin and Marshall Archives), 13 June 1893.

5. Franklin and Marshall, Trustees, 17 June 1899, p. 32; H.M.J. Klein, *History of Franklin and Marshall College, 1787–1948* (Lancaster, Pa., 1952), 130.

to get trustee approval for a bachelor of science curriculum in which French and German were the only language requirements. Two years later the classical and philosophical programs were combined, enabling students to receive a B.A. without studying Greek. These programs provided neither a satisfactory sense of purpose nor an adequate depth of specialization. Finally, a major revision in 1915 established a prescribed freshman curriculum to be followed by a major of seven courses and three minor studies consisting of five courses each. Thus, Franklin and Marshall went directly from a heavily prescribed curriculum to a system of distribution and concentration without an intervening period of extensive electives. It maintained the most consistent vision of the liberal arts among the four colleges by hanging onto an outmoded curriculum until a new structure appeared.[6]

Swarthmore's curricular development contradicts normal expectations. In the late 1880s and early 1890s Swarthmore increased its classics requirements and reduced electives, bringing its curriculum closer to that offered by other colleges. But long-standing antipathy toward the classics undercut the reinforced classical course, and most students chose the bachelor of letters or bachelor of science degrees, which did not require classical languages. In the class of 1902 only eight of fifty-two graduates received a B.A., as opposed to twenty-seven B.L. and seventeen B.S. degrees. When President Swain took office the next fall he abolished the B.L., allowing students to receive the B.A. without classical languages.

Swain, who came to the presidency the same year that Wilson did, instituted in his first year a sweeping and innovative reform similar to the one that soon attracted national attention at Princeton. Although Swain implemented his program before Wilson started his, he received little publicity. Under Swain's plan, freshmen fulfilled distribution requirements in English, a foreign language, science, mathematics, history, economics, and Bible study. The major study dominated the next three years, with three courses per semester in the major or related departments and two electives. Students majoring in science were brought under the bachelor of arts umbrella,

6. H. H. Apple, *Report of the President of Franklin and Marshall College*, 1912, 1915. For complaints about the inadequacy of the science facilities, see Richard Schiedt, "The Natural Sciences Then and Now," *Reformed Church Review* 7 (April 1903): 196–213; Franklin and Marshall, *Catalogue*, 1901–2 to 1916–17.

while engineering students had a distinctive program. Previously, engineering students completed a variation of the B.S. curriculum and received an engineering degree after three years of employment in the profession. This remnant of apprenticeship was replaced by a new course of study leading directly to a bachelor of science in engineering degree that was almost wholly prescribed and technical. After 1908 Swarthmore offered only the B.A. and B.S.E.[7]

The 1890s was a decade of experimentation at Bucknell, Princeton, and Swarthmore. Each created programs parallel to the B.A., temporarily saving its traditional form by providing alternatives for students who would not study the classical languages. The alternative bachelor degrees in philosophy, letters, or literature preserved some of the ideals of liberal culture while permitting some specialization. Electives allowed students to sample the new academic areas but provided neither the depth nor the direction needed in a long-term solution. There was surprising curricular diversity within and among the colleges.

Between 1900 and World War I, a new curricular consensus emerged. The chaos caused by the widespread adoption of electives in the 1890s inspired attempts to find a new curricular structure. The most important solution was the major study, usually combined with distribution requirements or prescribed courses for freshman year. Several years before President Lawrence Lowell adopted distribution and concentration for post-Eliot Harvard, Swarthmore and Princeton had already instituted such programs. Franklin and Marshall followed suit in 1915. The distribution requirements preserved a version of the broad preparation that had been the hallmark of a liberal education. Only engineering students were exempt from cross-disciplinary distribution requirements. Concentration in a major discipline was the new ingredient that reflected the necessity of specialization in the face of the explosion of knowledge. Bucknell was the exception, continuing parallel curricula into the 1920s. The concept of major and minor studies, the common freshman curricula, and the standardization of high school preparations revived a sense of direction in curricular thinking, which had lost its way at the turn of the century.

A new curricular structure was necessitated by the expansion of

7. Swarthmore College, *Catalogue*, 1885–86 to 1919–20; Swarthmore College, *The Register of Swarthmore College, 1862–1914* (Swarthmore, Pa., 1914), 54–79; Swarthmore College, Faculty, Minutes (Friends Historical Library), 15 October 1902.

knowledge in the sciences and the social sciences. Before 1890 teaching in each branch of science was limited to a few courses taught by lecture and demonstration. But around 1890 the colleges started constructing laboratories, modernizing observatories, and hiring more university-trained scientists, all of which facilitated more specialized instruction. Areas of knowledge formerly covered by one instructor divided again and again as department offerings increased in number and depth. Typically, areas covered by a two- to four-term sequence in 1890 expanded to eight to ten courses by 1915. Bachelor of science programs became more distinctively scientific and ceased to be refuges from the classics. On the other hand, the vast majority of students now studied less science; complexity segregated the "two cultures" of arts and sciences.[8]

In the 1890s the social sciences gained academic respectability. Systematic attempts to cover the areas once contained in the broad mental and moral philosophy courses of senior year became regular academic courses and eventually developed into departments. For instance, after Anselm Hiester took a two-year leave from Franklin and Marshall to study political science at Columbia University, the college created a department for his specialty. Hiester replaced his traditional course in political economy with courses that reflected the more relativistic historical school of thought. Adding the scientific study of social phenomena to the rapidly expanding curricular order helped make a prescribed curriculum untenable. Social sciences became one of the areas that all nonengineering students sampled and in which some found a major.[9]

Between 1890 and 1920 the role of colleges in professional preparation was fundamentally reexamined. The desire to attract more upper-middle-class students tempted colleges to offer courses that applied more directly to professional careers. The classical curriculum had always been viewed as preparation for the professions, but

8. For specifics on building and hiring, see Harris, 19; Klein, 131–32; and Collins, 343. Homer D. Babbidge, Jr., "Swarthmore College in the Nineteenth Century: A Quaker Experience in Education" (Ph.D. diss., Yale University, 1953), 154–87. Catalogs chronicle additions to the physical plant and the faculties. Lewis Perry, *Intellectual Life in America: A History* (New York: Franklin Watts, 1984), 286–88.

9. Anselm Hiester, "Political Economy," *Reformed Church Review* 7 (April 1903): 226–42. For an excellent discussion of scientific social observation and professionalization in this period, see Peter Novick, *That Noble Dream: The "Objectivity Question" and the American Historical Profession* (New York: Cambridge University Press, 1988), chaps. 1–4.

the relationship was based on disciplining the mind for further study rather than providing professionally applicable content. As the old curricular models collapsed in the 1890s, the question of the relationship between colleges and professional preparation was reopened.

After dabbling with vocationalism, the colleges withdrew to a preprofessional role in medicine, law, and business. Colleges found themselves competing with proprietary medical schools for students. This competition for future doctors gave science professors a stronger voice in the fight for resources and curricular reform. Bucknell, Princeton, and Swarthmore experimented with separate premedical programs and certificates, but all three dropped them after the influential Flexner Report of 1910 criticized such programs. All four colleges modified their curricula for premedical students in line with Flexner's recommendations, stressing general academic preparation rather than vocationalism. Similarly, the rising demand for college-trained lawyers and businessmen encouraged growth in political science and economics departments rather than in vocationally designed curricula, except at Bucknell. Princeton declined an offer from the Wanamaker family to begin a business program, and Franklin and Marshall offered no business courses until the 1920s.[10]

Swarthmore, Princeton, and Franklin and Marshall were hesitant to offer explicitly technical or professional preparation except in their engineering programs. In the 1890s Swarthmore backed away from its earlier vocationalism and confirmed that direction by adopting Swain's proposals for a uniform freshman curriculum and major studies in 1902. Several years later Swarthmore resumed teacher training, two decades after abolishing a freestanding normal program. This time the work was to be done in an education department and was treated as an academic major within the liberal arts curriculum.[11] Franklin and Marshall continued to base "its claim for patronage and support on the advantages which it offers for obtaining a thorough liberal education."[12] At Princeton, President Patton was willing to allow the senior year to become virtually a year of professional school, but Wilson reemphasized liberal education.[13] Fearing

10. See Chapter 10 for full discussion of the colleges' changing role in professional training.

11. Babbidge, 184–88.

12. Franklin and Marshall, *Catalogue*, 1913–14, p. 23.

13. Princeton University, Board of Trustees, Minutes (Princeton University Archives), 8 June 1896; Woodrow Wilson, *College and State* (New York: Harper Bros., 1925), 1:491–98; Princeton, *Report*, 1904.

the narrowness that might stem from premature exposure to occupational concerns, he directed the School of Science away from applied science. At all three colleges, liberal arts rather than explicit professional or vocational work dominated by World War I, except in engineering.

But at Bucknell, President Harris designed more explicitly vocational courses of study, hoping to increase the size of the school and the wealth of the alumni body. For decades the university's stated purpose had been "to impart sound instruction in all non-professional studies" through "the established college curriculum."[14] Immediately after his inauguration in 1889, Harris began to change the orientation. A confidant complained to former President Hill that, in the next semester, "special instruction will be furnished at that time for all who will come here to receive it. . . . We have done a vast amount of advertising on these particular lines, some of which I have thought was far from being judicious."[15]

In 1901 the board of trustees approved Harris's plan to affiliate with professional schools. Using local lawyers to teach legal courses and regular professors for the political science and economics courses, his jurisprudence curriculum permitted a full year of legal studies to be applied to the B.A. As with the medical program, Harris hoped to attract sons of the profession's practitioners. He aggressively recruited normal school graduates and other prospective teachers, and courses were correlated with the certification requirements of New York, New Jersey, and Pennsylvania. An all-female home economics track, begun as a two-year course in 1914, became a four-year degree program in 1917. Engineering began on a rudimentary level in the 1890s. The first formal program, civil engineering, opened in 1902 and was soon followed by electrical, mechanical, and chemical engineering. About 40 percent of Bucknell graduates in the decade before World War I took their degrees in the jurisprudence, premedical, engineering, and home economics programs.

The traditional curriculum continued to attract many students, but Harris's vocationalism increasingly made Bucknell an exception among the four colleges. Bucknell advertised itself as "one of the most progressive of all colleges in recognizing and giving due place to the new

14. Quoted in Oliphant, 215; Bucknell, *Catalogue*, 1900–1901 and 1901–2.

15. Joseph Ashton to David Jayne Hill, 31 January 1889, Hill Papers, 1877–92 (University of Rochester Library Special Collections).

and important branches of Sociology, Economics, Finance, Banking, railroad transportation, Municipal Government and kindred subjects."[16] In the 1920s Harris's successor instituted distribution and concentration and reduced vocationalism, bringing Bucknell's curriculum closer to that of the other three colleges.

The colleges retained a small place in the curriculum for teaching about moral issues, especially from the perspective of their original constituencies. Some of the content of the traditional senior moral philosophy course was preserved long after the course formally disappeared. In 1899, Swarthmore created a Department of Biblical Literature and required every student to take one of its courses. Its departments of philosophy and history gave a pacifistic orientation to their teachings; in 1906, the history department initiated a course entitled "The Beginnings of Quakerism."[17] Franklin and Marshall retained a senior course composed of one term each of ethics and political economy. After the latter was absorbed into the new Department of Social and Political Science, it was replaced by a semester of Bible study on the rationale that knowledge of the Bible is "an essential element of all true culture."[18] At Princeton, a remnant of McCosh's courses survived in a required sophomore course on logic, psychology, and general philosophy.[19] At Bucknell, John Harris continued to teach a required senior ethics course until his retirement in 1919.[20]

Presidents and older professors made it clear that new standards of scholarship could not be allowed to threaten basic Christian beliefs. A senior professor at Princeton declared that the "pursuit of knowledge for its own sake shall not be held to imply that a culture that

16. Bucknell University, *Bucknell University Bulletin*, Announcements, ser. 7, no. 4 (1908–9), 4; Harris, 7–8, 20–24, 38–39, 81, 94; Bucknell, *Bulletin* (October 1909); Bucknell, *Catalogue*, 1889–90 to 1916–17; Oliphant, 221–22.

17. Babbidge, 188–200; Swarthmore College, Board of Managers, Minutes (Friends Historical Library), 6 December 1897; Swarthmore College, Committee on Instruction, Minutes (Friends Historical Library), 4 May 1906; Swarthmore, *Catalogue*, 1899–1900 to 1915–16.

18. Franklin and Marshall, *Catalogue*, 1890–91 to 1915–16; quote is from p. 53 of the 1915–16 issue.

19. Alexander T. Ormond, "The Aim of Philosophy Teaching in American Colleges," *Proceedings of the Middle States Association of Colleges and Secondary Schools* 13 (1899): 23–29.

20. Harris, 54, 77–79.

has been vitalized by religion is not the best thing for man."[21] President Patton asserted his belief in "university freedom" but defined it so that skepticism and atheism fell beyond freedom's pale.[22] President Harris swore that at Bucknell he "would have no instruction in any department indifferent to Him" and that Christianity should "pervade all instruction and every admonition."[23] Similar statements were made by representatives of Swarthmore and of Franklin and Marshall.[24] Younger faculty and later presidents usually settled for bland statements asserting the compatibility of scholarship with religiously and socially respectable positions. Over time, faculty delegated the burden of breeding moral gentlemen to campus life, rather than to the classroom.

The definition of mental discipline, central to the traditional conception of liberal education, was being challenged by the new subject areas. Whereas the humanities and mathematics were traditionally considered to be superior for developing intellectual power, after 1890 the sciences and social sciences gained equal places. President Harris reversed the classical approach and asserted that, of two subjects of similar disciplinary power, the one dealing with the most recent events was the most valuable.[25] Even a staunch classicist like Professor Andrew West of Princeton changed his views. In 1884 he vigorously asserted the classics' superiority, but by 1906 he accepted the claims of the social and physical sciences and merely argued against technical subjects.[26] A colleague in the Department of Biology

21. Alexander T. Ormond, "University Ideals at Princeton," *Journal of the Proceedings and Addresses of the National Education Association* 36 (1897): 355.

22. Princeton College, *Inauguration of Reverend F. L. Patton* (New York: Gray Bros., 1888), 28.

23. Harris, 104.

24. For instance, see William Birdsall's remarks in *Friends Intelligencer* 57 (1900): 613; Jefferson Kershner, "The Moral Value of College Work," *Reformed Church Review* 14 (October 1910): 429–49; Richard Schiedt, "The Attitude of Present-Day Scientists Toward Religion," *Reformed Church Review* 16 (January 1912): 46–70.

25. Harris, 101–2.

26. Andrew F. West, "Must the Classics Go?" *North American Review* 138 (February 1884): 151–62; Andrew F. West, "The Tutorial System in College," *Educational Review* 32 (December 1906): 500–514. For an approach by a well-known Princeton scientist that modernizes faculty psychology, see Henry Fairfield Osborn, "The Seven Factors of Education," *Educational Review* 32 (June 1906): 56–82. For a Princeton professor arguing for the equality of modern and classical languages in the formation of mental discipline, see William Vreeland, "Modern Languages in Secondary Schools and Colleges," *Proceedings of the Middle States Association of Colleges and Secondary Schools* 17 (1904): 30–40.

maintained that "a purely classical education and a purely scientific one are equally illiberal"; a broad and liberal training could only result from a combination of the two.[27] Within this broader definition of discipline, the new subjects and the elective system were reconciled in a modified definition of liberal education. Mental training was still central, but it now was acknowledged that a wider variety of subjects would teach students to think.

Thus the colleges solved the threat to their existence posed by the disintegration of the classical curriculum. With their traditional purpose discredited, the colleges were in danger of having no distinctive curricular role. After experimenting with various combinations of electives and professional courses around the turn of the century, a new consensus emerged on curricular structure and professional education. The distribution and concentration approach to liberal education retained the breadth of training that graduate schools could not give, while providing depth that was beyond the scope of high schools. As the high schools, graduate programs, and professional schools grew, colleges secured a curricular role as the intermediary between secondary schools and graduate or professional studies, a role without an equivalent in European higher education. Except for engineers, Franklin and Marshall, Princeton, and Swarthmore students had to delay specifically vocational preparation until after the baccalaureate degree. Bucknell was the exception, maintaining vocational options into the 1920s. Well before World War I, the colleges had regained a sense of direction in their academic programs after the period of confusion brought on by the explosion of knowledge.

Their experiences do not fit the picture of disarray and vocationalism presented in the most prominent account, Frederick Rudolph's *Curriculum.* The turn of the century certainly was a curricular watershed for these four colleges. Classical languages and literature declined, students gained more choice, and "faculty psychology" was abandoned for more flexible theories of learning. The confusion and experimentation as the prescribed curriculum broke down led quickly to the adoption of the structured choice of concentration and distribution. The colleges searched for and found a rationale that ac-

27. Edwin G. Conklin, "The Place of the Physical and Natural Sciences in the College Curriculum," in William H. Crawford, ed., *The American Colleges* (New York: Henry Holt, 1915), 75.

commodated the new disciplines and greater depth while maintaining a shared core. Rudolph asserts that "colleges that had once been so much alike . . . were no longer ideologically and stylistically on speaking terms."[28] To the contrary, these four colleges increasingly spoke the same curricular language after 1900.

28. Frederick Rudolph, *Curriculum: A History of the American Undergraduate Course of Study Since 1636* (San Francisco: Jossey-Bass, 1977), 191–236; quote is on 203. It was published by the Carnegie Council on Policy Studies in Higher Education in 1977 as the first of their influential series on curriculum.

9

"The Side Shows Have Swallowed Up the Circus"

Woodrow Wilson's famous lament that extracurricular "sideshows" were perverting college life reflected the potency of the new student subculture. An autonomous, and sometimes underground, student life developed in the 1870s and 1880s at all four colleges, most spectacularly at Princeton. After 1890 the new subculture became remarkably standardized and pervasive across the four campuses. Student organizations proliferated. Students developed a romanticized version of life in which peer-group prestige outweighed academic prowess. The dominant ethos was to devote one's emotional and physical strength to the organizations that constituted the "real" college world, and it devalued intellectual activity.[1] Complaints like Wilson's masked the extent to which adults and youths shared values and college authorities succeeded in co-opting the student culture.

Most student newspapers were cheerleaders for the student culture. With the founding of Bucknell's *Blue and Orange* in 1897, students at all four colleges had weeklies. Except in the late 1890s when Swarthmore's *Phoenix* was dominated by the administration, all four newspapers endorsed the emerging student culture and attacked attempts to regulate it. Students who failed to participate in activities were liable to criticism, sometimes by name. The mixed message was that students and campuses must be individualistic and competitive, but only within the accepted bounds of the student culture.

1. Wilson's statement, truncated here, was in his article "What Is College For?" *Scribner's Magazine* 46 (November 1909): 576. The actual passage is, "The side shows are so numerous, so diverting,—so important, if you will—that they have swallowed up the circus. . . ." The classic account of fin de siècle student life is Henry S. Canby, *Alma Mater: The Gothic Age of the American College* (New York: Farrar & Rinehart, 1936).

Coverage of formal student organizations constituted the bulk of reporting. These journals continued the same formats and themes that became popular in the 1880s. Stories on athletic contests dominated, and school spirit was the prevailing ethic. The four papers were remarkably similar in content and style throughout the period. Social and political issues were virtually ignored, even at the height of the Progressive Era.[2]

Intercollegiate athletics epitomized the fixation with highly organized extracurricular group activities and reinforced the male students' self-image as vigorous Christian gentlemen. In the 1890s and early 1900s, teams received financial support from young alumni, some of whom also acted as coaches. Successful teams no longer lived on a shoestring. Princeton's 1893 Thanksgiving Day football game with Yale, played in New York, attracted almost fifty thousand fans, while Swarthmore netted over thirteen hundred dollars from a game with the University of Pennsylvania.[3] Bucknell's alumni-backed athletic association built a track and underwrote its first basketball team in the mid-1890s. Franklin and Marshall had its first full football season in 1890, and the following year alumni financed its first gymnasium. Baseball, track, and basketball joined football as permanent fixtures on these campuses.

Previously run solely by students, in the 1890s teams received coaching as well as financial assistance from recent graduates. Soon they were prosperous enough to hire professional coaches and trainers and plan extensive schedules with frequent travel for the major sports teams. Alumni backing gave the athletic associations considerable autonomy from college authorities.

In the 1870s and 1880s college faculty and presidents occasionally opposed athletic activities, sometimes over the objections of younger faculty. In the 1890s the new generation of college officials almost unanimously praised the positive effect of athletics on morality and fully subscribed to the ethos of the active life. Even skeptics granted

2. *F&M Weekly* 1–25 (1891–1915); *Phoenix* 11–36 (1891–1917); *Orange and Blue* 1–18 (1896–1915); *Daily Princetonian* 15–40 (1890–1916). A similar apathy toward broader issues existed in the student press nationally according to Laurence R. Veysey, *The Emergence of the American University* (Chicago: University of Chicago Press, 1965), 278–79.

3. Wheaton J. Lane, *Pictorial History of Princeton* (Princeton: Princeton University Press, 1947), 159; Swarthmore College, Athletic Advisory Board, Minutes (Friends Historical Library), 20 October 1916.

Fig. 18. Robert "Tiny" Maxwell (under the arrow) playing football for Swarthmore.

that sports diverted animal spirits to relatively innocuous uses. But by the turn of the century even the most boosterish educators were convinced that they had to rein in this runaway enterprise. At Princeton, for instance, Professor William Scott avidly defended athletics against McCosh's criticisms only to discover decades later that many of the charges of cheating and professionalism had been true. An alarming number of gridiron deaths created nationwide demands for reform of that sport. Newspaper photographs of a bloodied Swarthmore player staggering off the field attracted national attention and convinced President Theodore Roosevelt to convene a conference to reform the game in 1905. The battered player, Robert "Tiny" Maxwell, played first for the University of Chicago. His Swarthmore tuition was paid by a wealthy young manager, Morris Clothier.[4]

At all four campuses, faculty standing committees were created to intervene in what had been initially a student and alumni arena. Princeton experimented with oversight committees in the 1880s; a permanent Committee on Outdoor Sports began regulating teams in the early 1890s. Bucknell's faculty followed suit at the turn of the

4. William Berryman Scott, "Some Memoirs of a Paleontologist" (ca. 1930, Princeton University Manuscript Collection, typescript), 571–78; Frederick Rudolph, *The American College and University* (New York: Vintage Books, 1962), 375–76; Richard J. Walton, *Swarthmore College: An Informal History* (Swarthmore, Pa.: Swarthmore College, 1986), 22–23. For the best account of the struggle for control of collegiate athletics as well as a chapter on Swarthmore, see Ronald A. Smith, *Sports and Freedom: The Rise of Big-Time College Athletics* (New York: Oxford University Press, 1988), esp. chaps. 14, 15.

century. By 1905 all four colleges had permanent faculty committees to oversee scheduling and other athletic matters that interfered with academic work. At Swarthmore, for instance, the athletic committee barred one of the stars from participating in the climactic game with Haverford due to academic deficiencies. President Swain had to defend the committee's action before angry alumni. The following year Swarthmore issued rules on athletic eligibility requiring full-time attendance and adequate academic performance by all team members. Similar eligibility rules were soon established at the other colleges. College officials shared the students' views on the value of athletics but were no longer willing to have it outside their oversight.[5]

Faculty committees were able to influence eligibility and scheduling because they impinged on academic life, but finances were more difficult to control. Purchasing equipment, arranging transportation, and hiring coaches were initially handled outside of college channels. The power of students and alumni in these areas had to be recognized and was eventually institutionalized through joint committees of faculty, alumni, and students. Princeton was the first to formalize this arrangement by creating the University Athletic Association in 1891. A general athletic treasurer replaced the student treasurer. At Bucknell the faculty was unable to control abuses until the board of trustees incorporated the fervent alumni into a reorganized athletic association, with an executive committee of three professors, two students, and two alumni, in 1911. In 1914 Franklin and Marshall created a Board of Control similar in composition and duties to those at Princeton and Bucknell. These groups hired the coaches, audited the financial records, and generally regulated athletics more closely than before.[6]

Intercollegiate athletics was institutionalized within a generally sup-

5. Joseph Swain to Morris Clothier, 10 November 1903, Swain Presidential Papers (Friends Historical Library); "Athletic Eligibility Rules of Swarthmore College 1904," Swain Presidential Papers; Arthur S. Link, ed., *The Papers of Woodrow Wilson* (Princeton: Princeton University Press, 1966–), vols. 7, 8. The faculty minutes are useful sources until regulation was delegated to committees. Only Swarthmore's athletic committee records seem to have survived. Swarthmore College, Athletic Committee (later Advisory Board), Minutes (Friends Historical Library), 1911–17.

6. Link, *Papers of Wilson*, 7:303n., 8:422–25; J. Orin Oliphant, *The Rise of Bucknell University* (New York: Appleton-Century-Crofts, 1965), 237–38. For an example of alumni fervor, see the "Bucknell edition" of G. J. Rosenn, *Intercollegiate Athletic Calendar, 1907–1908* (New York, 1907); H.M.J. Klein, *History of Franklin and Marshall College, 1787–1948* (Lancaster, Pa., 1952), 170.

portive atmosphere. The moral objections frequently raised in the 1870s and 1880s were rare after 1890. A few misgivings were uttered by the denominations. The Presbyterian *New York Observer* reminded Princetonians that the men who graduated "before the passion for athletic superiority set in were not physical invertebrates."[7] The *Messenger* criticized the emphasis on athletics at Reformed institutions like Franklin and Marshall. Other members of the denominations disagreed and supported intercollegiate athletics as a beneficial moral influence.[8] As the opponents aged and denominational influence waned, college officials paid less attention to the complaints.

In one instance, however, a denominational objection had a hearing. Traditional Quakers were especially offended by the sporting craze, and a nearby Quaker rival, Haverford College, banned football in 1905; the ban lasted nearly a decade. The same year, local Quakers unsuccessfully petitioned Swarthmore "against the professionalism, demoralizing practices and excitement which seemingly have become a part of accompaniment to the game [football], making of no avail the testimonies of our Society against wagering, the use of alcoholic liquors and the unfair and brutal treatment of fellow beings. It is unbecoming and improper on the part of any one, and especially of those claiming the name of Friend, to indulge in such practices."[9] But three years later the Jeanes bequest (see Chapter 6), which offered money in exchange for the abolition of intercollegiate athletics at Swarthmore, was taken seriously. Although the bequest was eventually declined, it led to reforms. The college banned all intercollegiate contests for a year and formed the Swarthmore Athletic Committee, composed of three faculty members, two alumni, and a student. The committee transferred powers from student managers to a professional physical director, took over the hiring of coaches, limited team trips, and audited the financial records.[10] The resolution of the Jeanes controversy was in line with the practices at the other three

7. *New York Observer*, 13 December 1894, p. 643.

8. The criticism was in *Reformed Church Messenger*, 17 June 1909. For support of athletics, see Samuel Ranck, "The Oxford Idea in Education," *Reformed Church Review* 7 (January 1903): 24–30.

9. Swarthmore College, Advisory Athletic Council, letter, 3 December 1905, Papers (Friends Historical Library); Philip S. Benjamin, *The Philadelphia Quakers in the Industrial Age, 1865–1920* (Philadelphia: Temple University Press, 1976), 45.

10. Swarthmore, Athletic Committee, Minutes (Friends Historical Library), 31 January 1912, 5 June 1912, 11 December 1912, 9 April 1913; Swarthmore College, Athletic Advisory Board, 26 September 1913–13 June 1917.

Fig. 19. Swarthmore students "off to Haverford" for the annual football rivalry.

campuses. Intercollegiate athletics was accepted as an integral part of higher education, but it was formally brought under institutional control.

Important as football and other sports were to the student culture, athletics was just the most prominent part of the newspapers' broader emphasis on activities. Campus journalism had a strong element of Babbittry; "joinerism" was rabidly promoted. Some articles promoted student activities in reverential tones. William Irvine personified the growing acceptance of student activities in religious circles. After graduating from Princeton he went to Lancaster Theological Seminary, where he captained Franklin and Marshall's first successful football team as well as founding the college's first weekly newspaper and glee club.[11]

11. John H. Brubaker III, *Hullabaloo Nevonia: An Anecdotal History of Student Life at Franklin and Marshall College* (Lancaster, Pa.: Franklin and Marshall College, 1987), 13. This is a unique and attractive volume devoted solely to student life. Klein, 122–23.

Like athletics, student religion developed formal organizations and intercollegiate connections. Religious groups at all four colleges affiliated with the YMCA. Bucknell's chapter, formed in 1882 to replace the old Society for Moral and Religious Inquiry, ran successful revivals in the late 1880s. It also participated actively in state YMCA activities, hosting the annual meeting of the collegiate division in 1903. The chapter sponsored speakers, Bible study groups, missionary and evangelistic campaigns, social events, and freshman orientation. In 1912 the YMCA was able to hire a full-time secretary. Cleverly, the organization printed cards with the schedule of football games on one side and prayer meetings on the other.[12]

Princeton's YMCA chapter, the Philadelphian Society, engaged in similar activities, particularly emphasizing foreign missions. Several Princeton graduates were national leaders in the Student Volunteer Movement, and Princeton sent large delegations to the annual meetings. In 1906 the Philadelphians established a permanent missionary school in Beijing, partially staffed by recent alumni. There was a noticeable increase in service activities in the latter years of the Progressive Era. In the 1910s the Philadelphians ran a night school for university employees, the Dorothea House for recent Italian immigrants, and a Town Club and two Boy Scout troops for area youth, as well as providing a Sunday school and speakers for local church groups. About twenty undergraduates also ran an annual summer camp for urban children at the New Jersey shore. In all, about 150 students annually participated in these activities.

About two-thirds of Princeton's students belonged to the Philadelphian Society. Weekly talks on religious and social issues by faculty and alumni were well attended. While few students embraced evangelical piety and formal church services were not popular, student-run religious organizations that fit the optimistic muscularity of the student culture did well. In 1891 the Philadelphians hired a full-time general secretary; by 1919 the administrative machinery included four professional full-time workers, a Graduate Advisory Committee of alumni, and a student committee with access to the university

12. Bucknell University, YMCA, Minutes (Bucknell University Archives), 1882–1916; Bucknell University, YMCA, Papers (Bucknell University Archives), 1901–8; John H. Harris, *Thirty Years as President of Bucknell with Baccalaureate and Other Addresses* (Washington, D.C., 1926), 74–75.

president.[13] Smaller groups engaged in similar activities at Franklin and Marshall and at Swarthmore. Religious enthusiasm had become a well-organized activity, often dominated by future ministers.

Literary societies enjoyed a brief renaissance in the 1890s and early 1900s before slipping permanently into a peripheral role. Theta Alpha at Bucknell added guest speakers and musical programs, and the annual debate with the rival Euepians was a major campus event. But by 1907 weekly attendance was down to fifteen, and both societies soon died out. Several students formed the competing Demosthean Club in 1899, using a literary format and meeting in a classroom. In 1905 they moved to a private room in Lewisburg, but within a year the social function overshadowed the literary, and the organization became the Delta Sigma fraternity. The *Mirror*, Bucknell's literary magazine, also faltered and published its last issue in May 1906, not to be replaced until the 1920s. Revivals of the literary societies in 1912 and 1916 were short-lived.[14]

At Princeton, intercollegiate debating briefly revived the Whig and Cliosophic societies. Annual debates with Harvard and Yale attracted large crowds in the 1890s, but these spectacles lost popularity after the turn of the century. As eating clubs became more popular enrollment in the societies dropped, despite the faculty's offer of prizes and academic credit for work done in them. Bringing outside speakers to the campus became their major function, and the halls barely survived, finally merging in the 1920s. One alternative literary activity was the *Nassau Literary Magazine*, which enjoyed some brilliant years under Edmund Wilson's editorship shortly before World War I.[15]

At Swarthmore the activities of the societies included the standard readings, speeches, and debates. For instance, on 17 March 1891 the future attorney general, A. Mitchell Palmer '91, presented the affirmative side of the resolution "that the American cabinet system is preferable to the English." The Delphics and the Eunomians contin-

13. *The Philadelphian Bulletin* 1—2 (1891–92); *Philadelphian*, n.s., 1 (1902); Philadelphian Society, *Report of the General Secretary, 1915–1916* (Princeton University Archives); Philadelphian Society, *One Hundred Years, 1825–1925* (Princeton, 1925).

14. Theta Alpha Literary Society, Minutes (Bucknell University Archives), 1891–1907; Oliphant, 233–34; Harry R. Warfel, *The Demies, 1899–1949* (Lewisburg, Pa., 1949), 1–17.

15. Jacob N. Beam, *American Whig Society* (Princeton: privately printed, 1933), 200–209; Wallace J. Williamson, *The Halls* (Princeton, 1947); Bliss Perry, *And Gladly Teach* (Cambridge, Mass.: Riverside Press, 1935), 135; Arthur Mizener, *The Far Side of Paradise* (Boston: Houghton Mifflin, 1949), 29–38.

Fig. 20. Eupeian Literary Society at Bucknell, 1896.

ued to function effectively for another decade, but after 1905 their meetings became sporadic and increasingly relied upon story-telling. Literary interests shifted to producing a literary supplement for the campus newspaper.[16]

The authorities at Franklin and Marshall made the most concerted effort to save the literary societies. The trustees were so distressed by decreasing student participation in the 1890s that they ordered the faculty to assign extra work to students who failed to join the societies, an order the faculty carried out for four years before begging for relief from the burden. Mock trials inspired a revival after the turn of the century. Even though the Goetheans and the Diagnothians retained their libraries and meeting rooms until 1919, they lost members to other activities and became small, selective groups. However, their monthly, the *College Student*, was revived after 1900. A faculty-dominated journal in the 1880s and a more typical student publication in the 1890s, it became a serious student literary magazine

16. Swarthmore College, Eunomian Literary Society, Minutes (Friends Historical Library), 1891–1910, esp. 17 March 1891, 27 September 1901; *Phoenix* 26–36 (1906–17).

in the 1900s.[17] Franklin and Marshall, Princeton, and Swarthmore each experienced a literary renaissance around 1910, with activities focusing on a specialized journal rather than the broad-based literary societies of the previous century.

In marked contrast to the plight of the literary societies, fraternities grew rapidly. Although such groups had existed since the 1860s, in the 1890s and 1900s they achieved a new affluence as wealthy alumni financed expensive houses and membership lists expanded. Fraternities (or eating clubs at Princeton) traditionally made arrangements with boardinghouses for meals, and rented meeting rooms. In the 1890s some fraternities purchased houses with alumni help. As the social and financial power of fraternities rose, college authorities sought more control over their actions. At Bucknell the faculty voted to prevent students from pledging until they had completed freshman year in good standing. At Swarthmore the faculty banned social functions on any night except Saturday, but the fraternities rented rooms in the village and carried on. Although Woodrow Wilson's bid to transform the eating clubs into a college system failed (see Chapter 6), the trustees allowed him to limit participation by freshmen and sophomores.[18] As with athletics, the faculties limited the most extreme abuses but could not make intellectual activities the center of student life.

Musical and dramatic groups also flourished, with glee clubs and mandolin clubs being particularly popular. The most visible group was the Princeton Triangle Club, whose forerunners had been squelched by Presbyterian sensitivities among trustees and faculty in the 1870s and 1880s. The club's musical farces prospered after a very successful 1893 production written by student Booth Tarkington. The faculty denied the club's request to go on tour in 1893 but relented in 1897, beginning a tradition of annual winter tours. In

17. Franklin and Marshall College, Board of Trustees, Minutes (Franklin and Marshall Archives), June 1896, June 1900; Brubaker, 52–53; Klein, 201; Henry J. Young, *Historical Account of the Goethean Literary Society, 1835–1940,* Franklin and Marshall College Studies, no. 3 (Lancaster, Pa., 1941), 55–56; Samuel Ranck, "The Literary Societies . . . ," *Reformed Church Review* 7 (1903): 243–54; *College Student* 11–36 (1890–1915); Franklin and Marshall College, Faculty, Minutes (Franklin and Marshall Archives), 1912–13, p. 152–74.

18. Oliphant, 234–40; Joseph Swain, "Utilization of the College Fraternity in Student Life," *Proceedings of the Middle States Association of Colleges and Secondary Schools* 23 (1909): 32–34; Benjamin, 45; Henry Wilkinson Bragdon, *Woodrow Wilson: The Academic Years* (Cambridge: Belknap Press of Harvard University Press, 1967), 332.

1900 the club opened its season in Carnegie Hall. The addition of a business staff increased organizational efficiency, and a graduate board institutionalized alumni support. At Franklin and Marshall, the glee club started by William Irvine regularly took to the road. At Bucknell, students started clubs in chess, French, German, and professional areas while a dramatic group, an orchestra, a glee club, and a band prospered.[19] Student yearbooks, which became popular publications in the 1890s, gave work to local photographers and memorialized the organizations.

College authorities, recognizing students' growing self-sufficiency and organizational proficiency, began to enlist their assistance in regulating college life. The committees for regulating athletics were the first manifestation of this strategy, which then was applied to other areas of student conduct. At Bucknell, President Harris appointed a Senior Council composed of seniors from the fraternities and two nonfraternity members to help govern the students, though he retained the ultimate power "to request the quiet withdrawal of any student he may regard, for moral reasons, undesirable."[20] At Franklin and Marshall, President Apple consulted with students before changing policies pertaining to campus social life and created several joint student-faculty-administration committees in the 1910s. Wilson regularly consulted a Senior Council at Princeton.[21] At Swarthmore, President Swain used fraternity leaders to improve discipline and impose peer pressure on errant students. The evolution of the school rule against the use of tobacco demonstrates the changing strategy. Every year until 1906 the catalog stated that students must abstain. With the creation of a student-faculty committee on smoking, this rule was dropped from the catalog. Yet the ban remained in practice, and student committee members militantly supported the ban.[22]

19. Donald Marsden, *The Long Kickline: A History of the Princeton Triangle Club* (Princeton, 1968), 3–43; Oliphant, 177–78, 240; Brubaker, 187–88; Lewis Edwin Theiss, *Centennial History of Bucknell University, 1846–1946* (Williamsport, Pa.: Grit Publishing Co., 1946), 222–26, 248–58.

20. Harris, *Thirty Years*, 526; John H. Harris, "The Responsibility of the College for the Moral Conduct of the Student," *Proceedings of the Middle States Association of Colleges and Secondary Schools* 20 (1906): 93–101; Oliphant, 240.

21. H. H. Apple, *Report of the President of Franklin and Marshall College*, 1915; Bragdon, 297.

22. Joseph Swain, "Utilization," 32–38; Swarthmore College, *Annual Catalogue*, 1905–

Honor systems were the strongest expression of the new trust in students. Princeton created one in 1893 when students decided that proctoring of examinations affronted their dignity and requested the right to regulate cheating. The faculty agreed to delegate primary responsibility to a student board. A decade later, Franklin and Marshall also instituted an honor system.[23]

Most students were more interested in having the freedom to devote themselves to activities than in participating actively in college governance. Once released from the most onerous restrictions of in loco parentis, most students accepted established values. Their sense of institutional pride and corporate effort also encouraged them to accept most rules.[24] The student press viciously attacked students who endangered the institution's name; students were apparently more concerned with their dignity than with replacing the value system. The student ethos demanded conformity. A student complained to Woodrow Wilson that, to be accepted socially, a student "can't be broad, or he will be thought queer; he can't entertain ideas much in advance of, or much different from those generally entertained by the student body, or his social aspirations will have vanished forever."[25]

One disciplinary problem, hazing, was intensified by the new student culture, which thrived on intense class loyalties. Princeton faculty, for instance, were confronted with protests from seniors whose honor was insulted by their having to sit with sophomores in chapel. At all four campuses more or less violent hazing vexed deans and faculties, but the student press consistently defended all except the most dangerous practices as a necessary and proper part of college life.[26]

---

6 and 1906–7; Swarthmore College, Executive Committee, Minutes (Friends Historical Library), 5 January 1905; Robert C. Brooks to Robinson, 16 February 1906, Faculty Papers (Friends Historical Library).

23. Varnum L. Collins, *Princeton*, American College and University Series (New York: Oxford University Press, 1914), 259; Franklin and Marshall College, *Catalogue*, 1903–4.

24. There was a similar fundamental conservatism among New England students. See George E. Peterson, *The New England College in the Age of the University* (Amherst, Mass.: Amherst College Press, 1964), 126–48.

25. Benjamin Chambers to Woodrow Wilson, 19 November 1907, Wilson Papers (Library of Congress Manuscript Division), box 36.

26. Link, *Papers of Wilson*, 8:51, 384–95, depicts the Princeton faculty dealing with a severe outbreak of hazing in 1893. Student newspapers are filled with accounts of

Although evangelical piety no longer set the campus tone after 1890, conventional religiosity was expected. Swarthmore's board of managers required all students to attend the campus Friends meeting on Sundays even after the proportion of Quakers in the student body had dipped below 40 percent. In 1906 the managers finally permitted students of other denominations to attend Sunday services at local churches, but they continued to require daily attendance at the morning campus services. Princeton, where a majority of students favored some compulsory chapel, halved its chapel requirements in 1912. Bucknell's chapel could not accommodate the expanding enrollment, so students were required to attend Sunday service in the local church of their choice. Required weekday-morning chapel services continued until 1919, but because all students could not be accommodated absences were not only overlooked but necessary. Only Franklin and Marshall remained small enough to require daily prayer meetings and on-campus Sunday chapel services for the whole student body.[27]

Enforcement of official regulations depended on the ability to house all students on campus. Only Swarthmore provided all students with dormitory rooms throughout the period. It continued a vestige of Quaker guarded education, admitting no more students than there were beds except for a few "townies" who lived at home. Required daily social hours and religious services guaranteed considerable faculty oversight of activities; they only escaped when fraternities and other social groups rented rooms in the village. When Bucknell expanded in the 1890s, the proportion of men in rooming houses and fraternities increased; women were required to live on campus or at home. As dormitories were constructed after the turn of the century, more men were drawn to campus by low prices. By 1910 only thirteen seniors lived off campus.

The all-male colleges were less concerned with providing housing. Construction of four neo-Gothic dormitories during Wilson's presidency still left some Princeton students off campus. In 1920 Princeton could only accommodate about two-thirds of its eighteen hundred students in the dormitories and dining halls. Franklin and Marshall tore down Harbaugh Hall, its only dormitory and dining hall, in

---

hazing and of faculty investigations. For a student newspaper defending the basic practice at Swarthmore, see *Phoenix* 36 (11 April 1916).

27. *Swarthmore College Bulletin* 3 (March 1906); *Nassau Herald*, 1895 and 1905; Harris, *Thirty Years*, 75–76; Oliphant, 239; Bucknell University, *Catalogue*, 1900–1901 to 1917–18; Franklin and Marshall, *Catalogue*, 1919–20, pp. 32–33.

1900, leaving the students to live in boardinghouses and dine in off-campus eating clubs until the 1920s.[28]

Conflicts between students and college authorities declined as rules enforcing Victorian life-styles were relaxed. As fraternities and athletics became popular, student tastes ended attempts to impose the "plain life" at Swarthmore and its less demanding equivalents at the other campuses. Student newspapers applauded administrators like Dean Bond at Swarthmore and President Wilson at Princeton when they eliminated restrictions on student life. At Bucknell, President Harris prohibited dances, but fraternities held them off campus. In 1919 Harris's successor liberalized the social rules. Off-campus clubs and fraternities at Princeton and at Franklin and Marshall enabled

Fig. 21. The "Jolly Bummers" eating club at Franklin and Marshall, 1893.

28. Pre–World War I catalogs usually listed student addresses as well as rooming policies. Marcia G. Synnott, *The Half-Opened Door: Discrimination and Admission at Harvard, Yale, and Princeton, 1900–1970* (Westport, Conn.: Greenwood Press, 1979), 189; Bragdon, 357; Brubaker, 84.

students to escape many of the rules that remained on the books.[29] The colleges were developing mechanisms to regulate student behavior more systematically within less Victorian guidelines. The requisite dormitories, dining halls, and administrators completed the system in the 1920s and made the remaining rules more enforceable.

"Democracy" was a common rhetorical theme in college writing. Democracy existed in the sense that success in extracurricular activities could offset parental wealth in establishing student prestige. A Princeton student's complaint that "democracy applied, with but few exceptions, only to athletics" suggests one limit on collegiate democracy.[30] Another was that collegiate democracy existed within institutions that did not reflect the ethnoreligious, racial, gender, or class heterogeneity of American society.

Class pictures reveal no black faces and class rosters contain few names indicative of the "new immigration." There is little firm evidence that the homogeneity was enforced by overt prejudice rather than by social customs and expectations. Only the extensive records of Woodrow Wilson's presidency at Princeton reveal active discrimination. Wilson could usually rely on African-Americans not applying. When one tried, Wilson advised him that it was "inadvisable for a colored man to enter Princeton."[31] Edwin Slosson, in his 1910 classic *Great American Universities*, accused Princeton of being the only major university that excluded blacks. In reference to Asian students, Slosson sarcastically noted that "the Princeton students, I believe, support some of their graduates as missionaries among the Chinese, but apparently they do not like to have them around."[32] An earlier president, James McCosh had been more tolerant, defending the right of a black Princeton Theological Seminary student to attend his psychology course against undergraduate protests.[33]

Few records of student religious affiliation have survived. Those

29. Homer D. Babbidge, Jr., "Swarthmore College in the Nineteenth Century: A Quaker Experience in Education" (Ph.D. diss., Yale University, 1953), 189–200; Warfel, 6–35; Franklin and Marshall, *Catalogue*, 1911–12; *Phoenix* 23 (1902–3).

30. Chambers to Wilson, Wilson Papers.

31. John M. Mulder, *Woodrow Wilson: The Years of Preparation* (Princeton: Princeton University Press, 1978), 168–74.

32. Edwin E. Slosson, *Great American Universities* (New York: Macmillan, 1910), 104–5.

33. Synnott, 174–76.

Fig. 22. Bucknell students on candid camera, ca. 1906.

that were kept were rarely made public. To judge from the names, it appears that few Catholics and Jews were enrolled at any of the four campuses. Princeton yearbooks recorded Catholic enrollment rising from 2 percent to 6 percent between 1900 and 1915, with Jewish enrollment remaining at 1 percent. Again, only the extensive records of Wilson's administration provide firm evidence of anti-Semitism. Although Wilson did not share the common prejudice against Jews, Princeton's homogeneity was consciously cultivated by others. Policies at other campuses are not revealed in the surviving records.[34] Scattered evidence suggests that many, probably most, students shared the standard Protestant prejudices toward non-Protestants and nonwhites. There is no evidence that students were concerned with denominational differences among Protestants. Even ardently religious students channeled much of their energy into YMCAs and other interdenominational Protestant groups.

The students were also drawn from a limited geographic range. Even Princeton was surprisingly regional. From 1890 to World War

34. Ibid., 177–89; Slosson, 105; J. Ridgway Wright to Woodrow Wilson, 16 September 1904, Wilson Papers, box 32; *Nassau Herald*, 1905, p. 94, and 1915, pp. 45–290.

I, about two-thirds of its students came from the Middle Atlantic states, a higher proportion than in antebellum days. Swarthmore, with a large contingent from the border states and the Midwest, was only slightly more dependent on the region. It drew about three-quarters of its students from the Middle Atlantic states in the 1890s, a proportion that increased to over 80 percent by World War I. Well over 80 percent of Bucknell students and 90 percent of Franklin and Marshall students were Pennsylvanians. The regionalism of the student bodies remained surprisingly stable throughout the period. None of the colleges broadened its geographical distribution, and Swarthmore became more parochial.[35] Neither improved transportation nor the decline of regionally distinct culture translated into a broader geographic appeal.

The age range also narrowed. The elimination of academies at Bucknell and Swarthmore left only Franklin and Marshall with that clientele on campus by 1917. Young collegiate students in their mid-teens and "mature" students in their late twenties also largely disappeared from the campuses. The increasingly age-specific transitions on the road to adulthood sharpened student sensitivity to having younger or older students in their midst.[36]

The colleges' approaches to coeducation of the sexes differed dramatically. Swarthmore was founded as a coeducational college, and its status was never an issue. The only controversy was over how strictly to monitor contact between the genders. Bucknell, which had a female institute for several decades, admitted women into college classes in 1884. President Harris eagerly promoted coeducation. He lauded the women's academic conscientiousness and created some sex-specific curricula to attract more female students. Both Franklin and Marshall and Princeton remained all-male after some ambivalence. In 1894 the Franklin and Marshall faculty urged that the college accept women; the trustees rejected the idea. Princeton shared its library and some faculty with newly founded, nearby Evelyn College for women for a decade but rejected formal affiliation; Evelyn

35. I have defined the Middle Atlantic states as New Jersey, New York, and Pennsylvania. Slosson, 105.

36. On the timing of growing up, see John Modell et al., "Social Change and Transitions to Adulthood in Historical Perspective," *Journal of Family History* 1 (1976): 7–32; and David L. Macleod, *Building Character in the American Boy* (Madison: University of Wisconsin Press, 1983), chap. 1. Ironically, today's "nontraditional students" were a tradition rejected by fin de siècle student culture.

College collapsed in 1897. Woodrow Wilson believed that coeducation "*vulgarizes* the whole relationship of men and women" and as president made no effort to revive the experiment.[37]

Prudes like Wilson would have been comforted by the fact that male student life, at least as reflected in student publications, did not differ significantly between the coeducational and single-sex institutions. At Swarthmore and Bucknell athletics and fraternities provided a male-centered social life. Men held most offices in major organizations. For instance, no woman was president of Swarthmore's senior class until the wartime absence of males enabled Mary Wilson to lead the class of 1919. The appointment of deans of women institutionalized the separate spheres. The presence of women at Swarthmore and Bucknell neither "feminized" student culture as much as critics of coeducation feared nor civilized it as much as supporters hoped. Wilson spoke for many in a national backlash against coeducation in the "Progressive" Era.[38]

Collegiate rhetoric about democracy carried the same connotations of homogeneity and conformity in college life as it did in the dominant group in American society. College records provide no systematic evidence of student class origins, but it is clear that almost all students were white Protestants of northern European descent. Most students did not share their parents' strong identification with ethnoreligious groups within Protestantism. Instead, the student culture reflected the breadth and the prejudices of the emerging, broadly Protestant upper-middle-class culture. Rhetoric about collegiate democracy disguised more than it revealed.

37. Woodrow Wilson to Charles Kent, 29 May 1894, in Link, *Papers of Wilson*, 8:583–84; Walton, 28; Babbidge, 144–53, 197–200; Harris, 35–37; Oliphant, 154–56; Franklin and Marshall, Trustees, 18 June 1894. Evelyn College's short life is very well chronicled in Francis P. Healey, "A History of Evelyn College, Princeton, New Jersey, 1891–1894" (Ph.D. diss., Ohio State University, 1967). There is an excellent short account in Patricia Graham, *Community and Class in American Education, 1865–1918* (New York: John Wiley & Sons, 1974), 194–97.

38. On the reactions against coeducation and the renewed emphasis on separation of the sexes where it already existed, see Rosalind Rosenberg, "Limits of Access: The History of Coeducation in America," in John Faragher and Florence Howe, eds., *Women and Higher Education in American History* (New York: W. W. Norton, 1988), 116–18; Lynn D. Gordon, *Gender and Higher Education in the Progressive Era* (New Haven: Yale University Press, 1990); David Potts, "Road to Repute: Church, Coeducation, and Campus at Turn-of-the-Century Wesleyan" (Paper presented at the annual meeting of the History of Education Society, Atlanta, Ga., November 1990).

Unlike in preceding decades, in the 1890s college authorities essentially shared students' belief in the active life. Although after 1900 they worried more about the frivolous and anti-intellectual side of this life and attempted to regulate the abuses, most still looked positively on activities. Intercollegiate athletics particularly attracted praise from alumni and the presidents, although some faculty dissented. John Harris of Bucknell was undoubtedly the most sanguine; he said that his heart never failed "to warm to the young giants who risk life and limb on the field of strife for the glory of alma mater. This intense struggle for glory other than their own cannot fail to have a beneficial effect upon those who take part in the game."[39]

Most agreed that athletics lessened the attractiveness of drinking, smoking, and other sensual vices. In the age of Teddy Roosevelt vigor was the order of the day. President Swain told a conference of Friends that there was "as much evil wrought in the world from weakness as from wickedness," and that without vigor life's affairs did not "look roseate and hopeful as they should."[40] At Franklin and Marshall, President Stahr attributed improved discipline to football victories and a successful glee club.[41] At Princeton a number of professors attended football practices, and guests at the team's annual banquet included professors, trustees, and influential alumni. President Patton opined that "out of these brawny contests some of the very best elements of manhood may emerge."[42] Woodrow Wilson defended football in public debate against a University of Pennsylvania professor and frequently stressed its contributions to building moral character, manliness, and self-denial.[43]

A few, such as Franklin and Marshall professor Jefferson Kershner, rejected such hyperbole. He maintained that "moral training comes from the serious things of life and not from play and sport." Kershner pointed to the paradox that intellectual work was more like the work of later life, yet in comparison with athletics it was disparaged as of little use in preparation for "real life." Such dissent failed to deflate

39. Harris, *Thirty Years*, 523.

40. Joseph Swain, "The Educated Man," *Proceedings of the General Conference of the Society of Friends* (1904): 173.

41. Franklin and Marshall, Trustees, 17 June 1890.

42. Francis L. Patton, *Speech: March 1, 1888* (New York: Princeton Club of New York, 1888). For signs of faculty interest, see Link, *Papers of Wilson*, 8:204, 415.

43. Link, *Papers of Wilson*, 8:449–50, 482–84.

the romanticism of colleagues like President Apple, who had played on the college's first football team and who believed strongly in the "making of the man" through active participation in student organizations.[44] Swarthmore's President Swain even said that the social graces cultivated by fraternities "should be the possession of every cultivated man or woman, even if secured at the expense of somewhat lower marks in classroom work."[45]

The presidents became more ambivalent by about 1910. President Apple reported to the Franklin and Marshall trustees that students' behavior had improved greatly, but that they were insufficiently studious and that a student who was successful in the extracurriculum was "likely to lose his head."[46] Swarthmore's President Swain urged fellow presidents "to emphasize more standards of scholarship and curtail outside activities."[47] Woodrow Wilson's lamentations about "sideshows" and his attack on the eating clubs were prominent examples of a widespread reconsideration of student life. Between 1870 and 1917, college authorities had gone from concern about the spreading contagion of vice, to naive faith in student organizations as reform agents, to a revised in loco parentis based on administrative control of student organizations and residential life.

The prevailing student ethic was that a college was a community that had a moral and a social as well as an intellectual side, and that the organized expressions of this community took primacy over the concerns of individuals. At the end of this period and on the eve of the 1920s, a decade in which student culture received national attention, Franklin and Marshall's *Student Weekly* expressed (with some hyperbole) the spirit of muscular Christianity. If you did not feel ashamed to miss a mass meeting or to fail to be in the cheering section, the *Weekly* asserted, then you were a "plain, ordinary *slacker and you don't belong here*."[48]

44. Jefferson Kershner, "The Moral Value of College Work," *Reformed Church Review* 14 (October 1910): 429–49; quote is on 443. For the opposite view in the same journal by an active alumnus, see Samuel Ranck, "The Oxford Idea in Education," *Reformed Church Review* 7 (January 1903): 24–30.

45. Swain, "Utilization," 34.

46. Apple, 1915, 11.

47. Middle States Association of Colleges and Secondary Schools, *Proceedings* (1909): 39.

48. *Student Weekly* 4 (5 November 1919): 2. For an intriguing impressionistic analysis of students outside this culture, see Helen L. Horowitz, *Campus Life: Undergraduate Cultures from the End of the Eighteenth Century to the Present* (New York: Knopf, 1987), chaps. 3 and 4.

Underneath this dominant ethos there were ironies and dissent. The rhetoric of "real life" and "democracy" hid virtually the opposite: many students reveled in the frivolous and isolated themselves from the heterogeneity of American society. They lived on campuses with Gothic architecture and medieval ceremonies that denied the modernity of the society in which they were going to have leading roles.[49] Conformity to the dominant style was enforced in the name of rugged individualism. Not all students conformed to the dominant ethos; college life was not "this side of paradise" for everyone. But for those within the charmed circle, it was a heady experience. Students at these campuses were among the first to experience a privileged and romantic college life-style that attracted affluent Americans by seeming to preserve traditional values while participating in their destruction.

49. For astute analyses of the contradictions of collegiate traditions and modernity, see Joseph Kett, *Rites of Passage: Adolescence in America, 1790 to the Present* (New York: Basic Books, 1977), 174–89; Jackson Lears, *No Place of Grace: Anti-Modernism and the Transformation of American Culture, 1880–1920* (New York: Pantheon Books, 1981), 181–82; and Paula Fass, *The Damned and the Beautiful: American Youth in the 1920s* (New York: Oxford University Press, 1977), esp. 130–39.

Part Three

EMERGENCE OF THE MODERN AMERICAN COLLEGE

10

The Age of the College

In higher education the period between the Civil War and World War I is conventionally dubbed "the age of the university." The label has obvious justifications. Remarkable developments in universities established the patterns of modern academic life. Graduate school training became the sine qua non for college teaching. The new academic profession's standards were determined by journals and organizations dominated by university faculty. Professional schools within universities became the gatekeepers for the most prestigious professions. Academic research was revolutionized and dominated by a small number of universities. But for most students, donors, and the public, these developments were dimly perceived; it was the colleges and the collegiate aspects of higher education that were visible and attractive. There was a structural reality to this perception; during a period of educational ferment, the American college achieved an important new social and intellectual role.

Parts One and Two presented four case studies. Part Three places them in the context of the educational and social system taking shape in the United States in the early twentieth century. This chapter explains how colleges assumed their unique role as advanced American education was systematized.

The American college traces its intellectual history from colonial, and even medieval, predecessors. However, its modern condition as a freestanding institution operating in a clearly articulated system was a post–Civil War development. In 1870 most colleges were parts of multifunctional institutions; many colleges survived only by offering secondary education.[1] None of the four colleges in this study stood alone for the entire period, and two maintained secondary schools throughout. Frequently noncollegiate students outnumbered collegians (Table 10).

The preparatory branches were not just feeders. They served other educational roles highly valued by denominational sponsors and local citizens. Unfortunately, few left records; Franklin and Marshall Academy is an exception. Formally controlled by the German Reformed church, the college was part of a Reformed educational ladder extending from elementary instruction through advanced theological studies. The academy potentially linked the church's common schools to the college, but initially most students ended their educations at the academy. After 1890 the academy gradually eliminated terminal students and replaced them with college preparatory students recruited from Reformed congregations throughout Pennsylvania. As a result the academy, which furnished about one-third of the college's freshmen in the 1870s and 1880s, produced about 50 percent of the freshmen between 1895 and 1910, hitting a peak in 1909 with forty academy graduates in a freshman class of sixty-eight.[2]

Table 10. Collegiate and Institutional Enrollments, 1869–1910

	Princeton	F&M	Bucknell	Swarthmore
1869–70	328	72	64	26
		{83}	{151}	{173}
1889–90	653	136	71	163
		{137}	{214}	{80}
	[118]			[30]
1909–10	1,266	223	411	359
		{256}	{236}	
	[134]	[18]	[116]	[ca. 5]

SOURCE: The figures were compiled from catalogs and other college publications.
NOTE: Unbracketed numbers indicate undergraduate enrollments. { } = secondary and other subcollegiate enrollments. [ ] = graduate and other postbaccalaureate enrollments. Colleges conventionally included "specials" in undergraduate enrollments, but their work was somewhere between secondary and higher education. Franklin and Marshall figures do not include the theological seminary.

1. According to Frederick Rudolph, *Curriculum: A History of the American Undergraduate Course of Study Since 1636* (San Francisco: Jossey-Bass, 1977), 160, only twenty-six colleges, mostly in the East, operated in 1870 without secondary branches.

2. Of 269 freshmen entering Franklin and Marshall College from 1872 through

After 1910 the academy's links to the college and the denomination loosened. For years the administration held down tuition to make the academy accessible to the average Pennsylvania German Reformed church member. Continued low tuition depended upon an increased endowment, but members did not respond with sufficient funds. At the same time, Pennsylvania significantly increased its support for public schools, creating free alternatives to the academy. Eventually tuition more than doubled and the fee reduction for Reformed students was eliminated, resulting in a sharp decline in the percentage of Reformed students in the academy (from 73 percent in 1908 to 35 percent in 1920). Increasingly, academy graduates went to other colleges, and Franklin and Marshall recruited from other preparatory schools. The college president tried to eliminate the academy in 1916, but it survived until World War II, annually providing about twenty freshmen to the college.[3]

Princeton briefly maintained a preparatory department, but the college's access to wealth soon provided other sources of students. McCosh's dreams for Princeton required more well-prepared students. The dependence of rivals like Harvard on exclusive private schools disturbed him, but New Jersey's weak secondary schools offered little alternative. He urged the New Jersey legislature to provide Scottish-style extensive free secondary education for the middle class, but his ambitions for Princeton demanded an immediate solution. With a donation from a wealthy alumnus he created a preparatory department, which functioned from 1873 to 1880 and supplied seventy-five students to the college.

Princeton soon moved into the prep school movement despite McCosh's ambivalence about its aristocratic and Episcopalian traditions. In 1875 John Blair, a devout Presbyterian of Scottish descent, underwrote the revival of what became Blair Academy as a feeder for Princeton. Even more significant was the creation of Lawrenceville School with a bequest from another Presbyterian, John C. Green, Princeton's greatest benefactor in the McCosh years. All of Law-

---

1885, 102 were academy graduates. Charles Stahr Hartman, "Franklin and Marshall Academy, 1872–1943" (master's essay, Johns Hopkins University, 1948), 13–117, is a rare and excellent history of a preparatory department.

3. Ibid., 45–72. Also see Franklin and Marshall College, Trustees, Minutes (Franklin and Marshall Archives), 16 June 1877, for an insightful view on the relationship of the academy to the high schools.

renceville's trustees were connected to Princeton, and McCosh personally selected the first headmaster, a Scottish Presbyterian immigrant who designed it along the lines of the most prestigious New England prep schools. With its ample endowment and grounds laid out by Frederick Law Olmsted, Lawrenceville was an instant success. By 1890 it was sending about thirty freshmen a year to Princeton. McCosh's successors had no ambivalence about the aristocratic ambiance of prep schools, and Princeton cultivated relationships with them so ardently that it enrolled one of the highest proportions of their graduates of any college in the country by 1900.[4]

Whereas Princeton's short-lived preparatory department was viewed as an unfortunate necessity, Swarthmore's early experience was the opposite. Many early managers and stockholders were primarily interested in secondary education and were suspicious of higher education. Few students in the preparatory classes intended to continue to the collegiate program. From Swarthmore's founding in 1869 until 1886, the secondary (and briefly primary) students outnumbered the collegiate. The preparatory department supplied nineteen of fifty-one freshmen in 1878 and thirteen of fifty-nine in 1888. After a bitter fight (see Chapter 2) the preparatory classes were phased out in the early 1890s. While the faculty, college students, and some managers wanted a totally collegiate institution, secondary schools were a higher priority for most Hicksites. The collegiate faction won because, unlike the German Reformed church, Hicksite Quakers developed an adequate network of academies to provide a guarded secondary education and prepare candidates for the college.[5]

Bucknell University included at various times a theological seminary, a male academy, a female institute, and an institute of music. In 1865, only 99 of the 268 Bucknell students were in the collegiate

4. Princeton University, *Catalogue*, 1873–74 to 1879–80; James McLachlan, *American Boarding Schools: A Historical Study* (New York: Charles Scribner's Sons, 1970), 193–207; J. David Hoeveler, *James McCosh and the Scottish Intellectual Tradition: From Glasgow to Princeton* (Princeton: Princeton University Press, 1981), 300–306, 347–48; Patricia Graham, *Community and Class in American Education, 1865–1918* (New York: John Wiley & Sons, 1974), 189–90; Frederick Rudolph, *The American College and University* (New York: Vintage Books, 1962), 285.

5. Statistics compiled from Swarthmore College, *Annual Catalogue*, 1877–78, 1878–79, 1887 –88, 1888-89; Allen C. Thomas and Richard Henry Thomas, *A History of the Society of Friends*, American Church History Series, vol. 12 (New York: Christian Literature Co., 1894), 278; Edward H. Magill, *Sixty-Five Years in the Life of a Teacher, 1841–1906* (Boston: Houghton Mifflin, 1907), 149–50.

department; in 1889–90, only 71 of 286. Collegians did not become a majority until the period of rapid growth under President Harris in the 1890s. By 1899–1900, collegians accounted for 315 in a total enrollment of 487. The academy continued to send most of its graduates to the university, preparing about 20 percent of the freshman classes for many years. But the proportion eventually declined while the college grew: in 1914 the academy supplied only seven of the 140 male freshmen. With public high schools providing secondary education to the Lewisburg area and freshmen to Bucknell, the trustees abolished the academy in 1917, although they retained a subfreshman class.[6] Most presidents and faculty resented preparatory work, but colleges were a luxury in the 1870s. The development of freestanding, or at least clearly distinguished colleges by World War I was a victory for their professional ambitions and for the systemization of American education.

The lack of a true educational "system" in the late nineteenth century was evident in the unsystematic nature of the admissions process before 1900. Antebellum applicants took oral exams from the faculty; after the Civil War, written exams became standard. Prospective students were examined on campus during commencement week or early September on classical authors, mathematics textbooks, and other materials stipulated by that college. Until the early 1900s each college set individual admission requirements. By setting very specific measures of achievement, such as four books of the Aeneid or 137 pages of Gage's physics textbook, and requiring different combinations of supplementary subjects such as geography, history, and English literature, there were almost as many combinations of requirements as there were colleges.[7]

All qualified students were admitted; there was no danger of an oversupply. Underprepared students were sent to the preparatory department or given "special" standing in the college. Financial ne-

6. In 1902 Bucknell Academy and the female institute prepared 28 of the 137 new students in the university. Bucknell University, Requirements for Admission, 1902–3 (notebook in Bucknell University Archives). Catalogs show similar ratios in other years. Bucknell University, Board of Trustees, Minutes (Bucknell University Archives), 11 January 1917.

7. The example is from Franklin and Marshall College, *Catalogue*, 1903–4, p. 17. Much of the information in the following discussion is drawn from the catalogs and faculty minutes of the four colleges.

cessity encouraged flexible standards, especially in hard times; the few surviving records suggest that most candidates were accepted. The faculty admitted some students who had not precisely fulfilled the admission requirements with "conditions," deficiencies to be corrected. Faculty minutes reveal widespread use of this alternative. For instance, the Princeton faculty "conditioned" 83 of 208 freshmen admitted in 1898 and an astonishing 230 of 328 in 1907 during Wilson's campaign to raise standards.[8]

In the nineteenth century, presidents personally administered admissions, corresponding endlessly with parents, headmasters, and candidates about entrance requirements and finances. David Jayne Hill spent his last summer at Bucknell processing admissions letters. President Magill wrote five letters in the summer of 1875 to one student's parents, trying to arrange financial assistance. Even at a larger college like Princeton every new student reported directly to President McCosh. In the 1890s the trustees assigned a faculty member to assist McCosh's successor; presidents at the other three colleges were allocated assistants in the 1900s. Presidents continued to oversee admissions into the 1920s and occasionally intervened, as when President Swain asked an alumnus to influence a star athlete to choose Swarthmore over Princeton. "I would be glad if thee would have a talk with Pfeiffer and see if thee cannot turn him this way."[9]

More than secretarial assistance was needed. Admissions was outgrowing the old practices, and the presidents spent much of their time around the turn of the century trying to systematize the process. The colleges' growth could make the work overwhelming. In addition, the colleges were increasingly dealing with institutions unconnected with their local or denominational communities. Admission of students from the colleges' preparatory divisions provided an early shortcut in the admissions process. Other preparatory schools soon developed similar arrangements with colleges, usually those affiliated

8. Princeton University, Faculty, Minutes (Princeton University Archives), 19 October 1898; Princeton University, *Annual Report of the President*, 1907. See also Bucknell, Requirements, for liberal use of "conditions."

9. Joseph Swain to James Lippincott, Swain Presidential Papers (Friends Historical Library), 14 January 1904. Magill's correspondence on admissions, which he handled for both the college and the preparatory department, is voluminous; Edward Magill, Presidential Papers (Friends Historical Library). Presidential papers at all four colleges show that great attention was paid to admissions. Bucknell, Trustees, 26 June 1888. Varnum L. Collins, *Princeton*, American College and University Series (New York: Oxford University Press, 1914), 294.

with the same denomination. At first this certificate system operated informally, as reflected in a letter in 1886 to President Apple at Franklin and Marshall College from the principal of a Reformed church academy describing a group of his students whom he wanted admitted to the freshman class without examination: "They are pretty well prepared except in German. Of course they can get along with [the] class by reason of their knowledge of Pa. German, but for their sake I would suggest that the Faculty condition them in German Grammar. They can study up before the opening of the fall term."[10] The author was a former professor at the college whose ability to get students admitted on his recommendation stemmed from personal ties. A year later the Franklin and Marshall faculty established a formal certificate system whereby students from approved schools were admitted on the principals' recommendations.[11] Bucknell admitted students informally on principals' recommendations for twenty years before officially offering admission by certificate in 1896 to graduates of all Pennsylvania normal schools and selected academies and high schools.[12]

Swarthmore, the first to establish a list of certified schools, sent faculty members to investigate each institution and by 1884 granted the privilege to nine Friends schools. The faculty slowly expanded the list in the 1890s, examining each request carefully and eventually including non-Friends schools. With the arrival of Joseph Swain from the Midwest where the certificate system was prevalent, Swarthmore considerably expanded its list.[13] A large number of students were admitted by certificate at all of the colleges except Princeton.

10. Principal Nathan Schaeffer to Theodore Apple, 9 June 1886 (Franklin and Marshall Archives).

11. Franklin and Marshall College, Faculty, Minutes (Franklin and Marshall Archives), 4 May 1887. The assertion that eastern colleges did not use certificates is partially incorrect. Although no state or regional system existed in the East these colleges developed certification systems based primarily on denominational relationships. Two works mistaken on this point are Joseph L. Henderson, *Admission to College by Certificate*, Teachers College Contributions to Education, no. 50 (New York: Teachers College Press, 1912), and Edward A. Krug, *The Shaping of the American High School, 1880–1920* (Madison: University of Wisconsin Press, 1969).

12. Bucknell University, Faculty, Minutes (Bucknell University Archives), e.g., 6 September 1878 and 23 June 1879; J. Orin Oliphant, *The Rise of Bucknell University* (New York: Appleton-Century-Crofts, 1965), 230–31; Bucknell University, *Catalogue*, 1896–97.

13. Swarthmore College, Faculty, Minutes, 5 and 12 October 1882, 22 January

Princeton's broader geographic constituency made certificates less feasible. The system depended upon personal contact between the faculties and principals, many of whom had previous connections with the particular college. These relationships sufficed for the three colleges that drew their students primarily from Pennsylvania but were inadequate for Princeton's national ambitions. In the 1870s Princeton began giving its admission examinations in midwestern and southern cities. McCosh wrote to one alumnus who volunteered to administer the examinations that, if "there is a fair chance of getting even a few students from Louisville," he should begin to advertise immediately, with Princeton paying the cost. In the 1880s Bucknell also began holding off-campus examinations within Pennsylvania.[14]

Even when geography was not a problem, Princeton did not cooperate with public high schools. Its social prestige and connections with the elite prep schools eventually enabled Princeton to draw upon them for three-quarters of its students. Despite criticism in the *Educational Review* and by a prominent alumnus-educator, Wilson Ferrand, as late as 1912 the faculty still rejected the certificate system and accepted the New York regents examinations only if reread by Princeton faculty.[15]

Even the certificate system left out many new public high schools that objected to adjusting their curricula to individual colleges. The first instance of intercollegiate cooperation came when nine New England colleges synchronized their entrance requirements for English in 1879. Six years later the formation of the New England Association of Colleges and Preparatory Schools created a permanent

---

1894; Swarthmore College, Stockholders, *Minutes of the Annual Meeting of the Stockholders*, 1884, pp. 12–13. A good example of the system at work in Magill's correspondence is Principal Fannie Pyle (Friends High School, West Chester, Pa.) to Edward Magill, 26 August 1884, Magill Presidential Papers. For an example of a school seeking to be placed on the certificate list, see George Megangee to Charles De Garmo, 2 and 14 March 1896, De Garmo Presidential Papers (Friends Historical Library). Joseph Swain, "Remarks," *Proceedings of the Middle States Association of Colleges and Secondary Schools* 16 (1902): 42.

14. James McCosh to Logan Murray, 26 March 1877, James McCosh Papers (Princeton University Archives). The correspondence continued the next year (11 and 22 May, 2 December). Hoeveler, 305–6; Bucknell, *Catalogue*, 1885–86, p. 14; Oliphant, 230–31.

15. "Editorial," *Educational Review* 5 (January 1893): 90–91; Francis L. Patton to Wilson Ferrand, Patton Papers (Princeton University Archives), 11 December 1901; Princeton University, School of Science Faculty, Minutes (Princeton University Archives), 26 February 1902; Princeton, Faculty, 19 February and 13 May 1912.

organization to coordinate articulation. In the Middle Atlantic states, a group of Pennsylvania colleges met in 1887 on the initiative of Swarthmore's President Magill. They formed the College Association of Pennsylvania and elected President Apple of Franklin and Marshall as the first president. Although formed to deal with the relationship of private colleges to the state government, by 1893 its focus shifted to articulation and its geographic scope broadened as it became the Association of Colleges and Preparatory Schools of the Middle States and Maryland. In 1894 the New England and Middle Atlantic associations agreed upon uniform English entrance examinations for colleges from Maine to Maryland. This led to a National Conference on Uniform Entrance Requirements in English that set national standards in the late 1890s. High schools and academies were told which literary works would be covered in tests for the next few years so they could satisfy all colleges' requirements with a single curriculum.[16]

The work of the Middle States group led to the creation of the College Entrance Examination Board (CEEB).[17] In 1899, Columbia's President Nicholas Murray Butler persuaded the Middle States Association to form committees to consider establishing such an agency. In 1900 they reported favorably, and a year later the CEEB administered its first tests to 973 students. Twelve colleges including Swarthmore were represented on the first board, and a thirteenth, Princeton, participated in its development. Bucknell joined the CEEB in its second year, and Franklin and Marshall, although not a member until after World War I, accepted the results of the board's examinations from the beginning.[18]

At first the CEEB was merely one of several options. In 1913 only one-seventh of Princeton applicants took the board's tests; the remainder took Princeton's own entrance examinations. An even smaller

16. Herbert Malick, "An Historical Study of Admission Practices in Four-Year Undergraduate Colleges of the U.S.: 1870–1915" (Ph.D. diss., Boston College, 1966), 189–90; Krug, 125–29, 363–65. The catalogs list the entrance requirements. For the official action by the Middle States Association, which all four joined, see the *Proceedings* 1 (1894): 61–63.

17. Charles Eliot's Committee of Ten, the Committee on College Entrance Requirements, and the National Conference on Uniform Entrance Requirements in English dealt with the problem in the 1890s. Educational journals such as the *Educational Record* also focused their attention on this issue.

18. Malick, 209–13; College Entrance Examination Board, *Annual Report of the Secretary*, 1901–13.

percentage chose the CEEB tests at the other three colleges. However, the precedent set by Columbia, Barnard, and New York University in 1901 of abolishing their own tests and requiring all applicants to take the board's examinations eventually prevailed. In 1915 Princeton, Harvard, and Yale took the same step. Swarthmore followed suit but retained a certificate system for Friends schools. Both Bucknell and Franklin and Marshall continued holding their own examinations until the 1920s as well as accepting certificates and the CEEB examinations.[19]

Entrance requirements came to be expressed in nationally recognized quantitative measures, an idea suggested by the National Education Association (NEA) in 1899. It proposed that colleges set their requirements in "units" indicating the years spent studying a subject rather than specifying textbooks and areas of coverage.[20] In 1901 Swarthmore followed the NEA recommendation, requiring applicants to have taken a basic core of high school courses and to choose the others from a list of electives. Bucknell, Franklin and Marshall, and Princeton adopted similar plans over the next twelve years. By 1913 colleges almost universally expressed their requirements in units and permitted a choice of exams rather than examining all subjects. When the CEEB developed comprehensive examinations in 1916, students gained even greater choice. Under this plan the colleges accepted high school certificates for most units, and students chose four subjects for extensive examination.[21]

Educational reformers hoped to rationalize the whole system. Not only would courses become measurable units, but there would be a uniform, nationally recognized boundary between secondary and higher education. Graduation from a secondary school was not the only path to college admission until well after 1900. Since admission was based on work completed, colleges sometimes accepted students before they graduated from secondary school or on the recommendation of private tutors. Graduates of normal schools, collegiate institutes, and less prestigious colleges entered at various levels. Among the students entering Franklin and Marshall in September 1913 were

19. Malick, 240–41, 288; CEEB, 1902–16.

20. Malick, 196–298, 313. The term "unit" was in use prior to the Carnegie Foundation's adoption of it.

21. See the catalogs of each college. Also, Collins, 328–29; Harry C. McKown, *The Trend of College Entrance Requirements, 1913–1922*, Bureau of Education Bulletin, no. 35, 1924 (Washington D.C.: U.S. Government Printing Office, 1925), 53–54.

two graduates of Elizabethtown College admitted to the senior class and three graduates of Millersville Normal School admitted to the junior class; the sophomore class included graduates of Kutztown Normal School, Williamsport-Dickinson Seminary, Schuykill Academy, and Massanutten Academy.[22] On the other hand, early graduates of Swarthmore were admitted to Harvard's junior class. After Swarthmore raised its standards by holding back most students in 1881, Harvard accepted its graduates into the senior class. In the late 1880s over 10 percent of Swarthmore's graduates went on for a second bachelor's degree, entering the senior class of more prestigious institutions. Princeton admitted graduates of other colleges into its senior class.[23]

Setting admission standards in units of work rather than specific levels of knowledge in effect defined the length of secondary education. The Carnegie Foundation, needing a definition to determine which institutions qualified for its college faculty pension fund, adopted the NEA's approach. It defined colleges as institutions that require "four years of academic or high school preparation or its equivalent in addition to preacademic or grammar schools."[24] The foundation sought to clarify the two levels of education further by urging abolition of collegiate preparatory departments and of the admission of students before high school graduation. Between 1890 and 1915 the line between higher and secondary education became more distinct. Institutions that originated in small-town America—academies, normal schools, and collegiate preparatory departments—had to adjust to a more bureaucratic system demanded by an urbanizing society.

The modern era of selective admissions at prestigious private colleges was a few years off. Princeton hired its first admissions director in 1922 to administer the beginning of selective admissions. Except

22. Krug, 159–63; H. H. Apple, *Report of the President of Franklin and Marshall College*, 1913–14, p. 6.

23. Swarthmore, Stockholders, 1877; *Phoenix* 6 (1886). "Alumni Notes" lists several such cases; Homer D. Babbidge, Jr., "Swarthmore College in the Nineteenth Century: A Quaker Experience in Education" (Ph.D. diss., Yale University, 1953), 180. For a discussion at Princeton of whether to admit two graduates of other colleges into the senior class, see Francis L. Patton to S. R. Winans, 21 November 1901, and Patton to Robert D. Williams, 30 November 1901, Patton Papers. For Bucknell, see Bucknell, Requirements.

24. Krug, 160, quoting the foundation's *First Annual Report* of 1906. Ellen C. Lagemann, *Private Power for the Public Good* (Middletown, Conn.: Wesleyan University Press, 1983), 94–95.

for a few students turned away due to lack of dormitory space, the four colleges admitted all qualified students before World War I. Those not qualified were usually admitted as "specials" or sent to a preparatory school for further training. The trauma of outright rejection originated when some private colleges decided to limit enrollments in the early 1920s. Princeton and Swarthmore did so primarily for "reasons of space rather than race," though prejudice, especially anti-Semitism, encouraged selective admissions.[25] The confidence to reject qualified students stemmed from the colleges' newly secured role in educating the professions.

The colleges' ambitions intersected with those of powerful members of the professions, transforming professional training and turning liberal arts colleges into influential gatekeepers. In colonial and early republic America, the learned professions were dominated by those with a college degree followed by professional apprenticeship. Evangelicalism and the Jacksonian political spirit of the antebellum United States reduced the educational requirements for admission into the professions. Some professionals, mainly those in elite urban positions, continued to be college educated, but colleges educated only a small proportion of future doctors and lawyers—and not even all ministers. The trend was reversed by a resurgence of professional self-consciousness and a growing public acceptance of the claims of expertise that encouraged stricter licensing procedures. In the mid-1890s Johns Hopkins Medical School, Harvard Divinity School, and Harvard Law School became the first institutions in their fields to require baccalaureate degrees for admission. Increasingly, the best positions went to those who attended the professional schools that required baccalaureate degrees.[26]

25. Marcia G. Synnott, *The Half-Opened Door: Discrimination and Admissions at Harvard, Yale, and Princeton, 1900–1970* (Westport, Conn.: Greenwood Press, 1979), 189–93; quote is on 189. Richard J. Walton, *Swarthmore College: An Informal History* (Swarthmore, Pa.: Swarthmore College, 1986), 43. The development of selective admissions has been carefully analyzed in Harold Wechsler, *The Qualified Student: A History of Selective College Admission in America* (New York: John Wiley & Sons, 1977).

26. For a study of the professions before the Civil War, see Daniel H. Calhoun, *Professional Lives in America* (Cambridge: Harvard University Press, 1965), esp. 178–97; Colin Burke, *American Collegiate Populations: A Test of the Traditional View* (New York: New York University Press, 1982), 249–62. For the broader context, see Robert H. Wiebe, *The Search for Order, 1877–1920* (New York: Hill and Wang, 1967), 111–23.

The conflict over training was especially acute in medicine, where training in proprietary schools was rapidly replacing apprenticeship in the 1890s and 1900s. The role of colleges was precarious because they competed directly with medical schools for students. Colleges responded by offering courses that qualified students for advanced standing in the professional schools. In the early 1890s the College of Physicians and Surgeons agreed to accept Princeton's B.S. degree in place of the first six months of study. Princeton also issued special certificates to graduates who took advanced courses in biology and chemistry, recommending them for advanced standing in medical schools. In the mid-1890s Bucknell recruited students who wanted one or two years of college before going to medical school. In 1901 Bucknell opened a Department of Medicine purporting to offer most of the nonclinical studies of the first two years of medical college. Swarthmore pledged that its preparatory medical course would lead to admission in the second year of Philadelphia's leading medical colleges. Franklin and Marshall created a bachelor of philosophy degree in 1899 to enable future physicians to study more science and enter the second year of medical school. Even some Franklin and Marshall Academy graduates bypassed the college to go directly into medical colleges.[27]

The pressure from leading medical educators that culminated in Abraham Flexner's famous indictment of American medical schools in 1910 revolutionized medical education. Liberal arts colleges gave up any pretense of professional training. Princeton ceased to list its program in 1905. The Flexner Report led to the abolition of Bucknell's Department of Medicine and Swarthmore's preparatory medical course. In turn, all four colleges increased their offerings in biology and other sciences along the lines Flexner suggested. Flexner went further than even the AMA contemplated and recommended two years of college as a minimum requirement for medical school admission. As none of the eight medical schools in Pennsylvania had previously required any college study, the colleges stood to benefit from the report. Science was to be left to colleges, and professional training to medical schools. Since the medical reforms effectively favored native-born, affluent, Protestant, white males, these four col-

27. Princeton, *Catalogue*, 1892–93 to 1900–1901; Bucknell, *Catalogue*, 1896–97, insert; Oliphant, 218–22; Swarthmore, *Catalogue*, 1900–1901; Franklin and Marshall, Trustees, 17 June 1899; Hartman, 45.

leges were particularly well positioned to provide the kind of gentlemen that the AMA wanted in medicine. The notice in the *Daily Princetonian* that read, "After 1908 candidates for admission to the Cornell University Medical College must be graduates of approved colleges or scientific schools," reflected a major victory for liberal arts colleges. By World War I some college science, if not a baccalaureate degree, was required by most medical schools.[28]

The colleges' relationship to the law profession evolved along parallel lines. As in medicine, college control over the profession declined in the face of Jacksonian hostility. Bucknell, Franklin and Marshall, and Princeton made abortive attempts to start law schools before the Civil War. After the Civil War, law schools (many of them proprietary) replaced law office apprenticeship as the most common form of training. Between 1870 and 1910 the proportion of those admitted to the bar who were law school graduates jumped from one-quarter to two-thirds.

In 1893, when Harvard Law School became the first to require a baccalaureate degree for admission, it heralded a greater role for colleges in educating lawyers. As in medicine, educators at leading professional schools led the campaign for higher educational standards. The Association of American Law Schools, founded in 1900, was dominated by prestigious law schools and championed full-time attendance in three-year law programs that required at least a high school diploma for entrance. The four colleges in this study worked as feeders within this system; none of them made a serious attempt to found a law school after the Civil War. Instead, they developed curricula designed either to attract future lawyers for one or two years or to give their graduates advanced placement in existing law schools. In the 1890s Woodrow Wilson developed a pre-law program

28. *Daily Princetonian* 23 (29 April 1908); John Winter Rice, *A History of the Teaching of Biology at Bucknell University* (Lewisburg, Pa., 1952), 3–5; Oliphant, 218–22; John H. Harris, *Thirty Years as President of Bucknell with Baccalaureate and Other Addresses* (Washington, D.C., 1926), 40–42, 81–94; Swarthmore, *Catalogue*, 1900–1901 to 1910–11; Franklin and Marshall, *Catalogue*, 1911–12 and 1912–13; Abraham Flexner, *Medical Education in the United States and Canada* (New York: Carnegie Foundation for the Advancement of Teaching, 1910); Lagemann, 61–74; Kenneth M. Ludmerer, *Learning to Heal: The Development of American Medical Education* (New York: Basic Books, 1985), 72–122, 166–90; Paul Starr, *The Social Transformation of American Medicine* (New York: Basic Books, 1982), 116–27; Princeton, *Catalogue*, 1904–5 and 1905–6; Gerald Markowitz and David Rosner, "Doctors in Crisis," *American Quarterly* 25 (March 1973): 83–107.

based on political science courses after failing to interest President Patton or donors in establishing a law school at Princeton. Bucknell created the most vocational program, which, in addition to political science and economics courses, offered applied courses taught by local lawyers and promised advanced standing in affiliated law schools. A Pennsylvania Supreme Court decree that a college diploma was grounds for waiving the preliminary law exam considerably enhanced these colleges' position.[29]

Reform took place more gradually in legal education than in medical training. A transformation of the magnitude of that following the Flexner Report did not occur until well after World War I. But colleges, especially in the East, benefited from both custom and entrance requirements that made college degrees advantageous for entering the most prestigious law schools and firms. As in medicine, educational reform was intertwined with racial and ethnoreligious predilections. Night schools and other less socially prestigious law schools continued to supply lawyers for the lower end of the profession to serve upwardly mobile new immigrants and African Americans. The four colleges in this study provided students who met the standards for education and "character" desired by the dominant members of the legal profession.

Colleges had much less competition in the third traditional learned profession. Theology had the highest educational standards among the professions. In 1900 most seminaries required a year of college, and almost half required a college degree; in the East the proportions were much higher. Since many seminaries were connected to colleges, their curricula developed naturally in sequence with baccalaureate work. Crozer Theological Seminary, the Theological Seminary of the Reformed Church, and Princeton Theological Seminary were clearly graduate institutions and did not compete with the colleges. Theological seminaries pioneered the professional model that eventually prevailed in the other learned professions and in academia.[30]

29. Jerold Auerbach, *Unequal Justice: Lawyers and Social Change in Modern America* (New York: Oxford University Press, 1976), 74–129; William R. Johnson, *Schooled Lawyers: A Study in the Clash of Professional Cultures* (New York: New York University Press, 1978), 58–164; Arthur S. Link, ed., *The Papers of Woodrow Wilson* (Princeton: Princeton University Press, 1966–), 7:63–68, 8:381–83; John M. Mulder, *Woodrow Wilson: The Years of Preparation* (Princeton: Princeton University Press, 1978), 133–34; Harris, 94.

30. Rudolph, *Curriculum*, 179; Natalie A. Naylor, "The Theological Seminary in

A different model developed in engineering, the one area in which most of these colleges offered vocational training. Princeton, Swarthmore, and Bucknell established engineering programs at considerable cost. Civil engineering was the least expensive and most popular. These programs were natural extensions of the science curriculum, but the willingness to spend large sums on them suggests their importance in attracting students and donors.

The approach to business training was quite different. Although a college diploma rapidly gained currency as an appropriate credential for executives in the new corporations, there were relatively few formal business programs before World War I. Economics departments particularly benefited from the growing relationship, but even vocationally minded President Harris of Bucknell did not create a business program. Princeton turned down an offer from Philadelphia's Wanamaker family to underwrite a business program.[31] Liberal education or engineering training combined with the right social credentials sufficiently prepared graduates to enter corporate life.

These colleges, however, were ambivalent about competing for a role in training for another growing profession, public school teaching. State normal schools overlapped the last years of high school and the first years of college. Colleges convinced a few normal school graduates to enter their junior or senior classes. But as long as a college degree was neither required nor expected, they remained a small minority. Early normal school leaders hoped that their graduates would continue to college, but by the 1890s the two institutions were competitors.

Swarthmore's flirtation with becoming a normal school in the mid-1880s was the only venture in explicitly vocational teacher training by these colleges. President Magill wanted to train teachers through the baccalaureate program, but, having saved Swarthmore from be-

---

the Configuration of American Higher Education," *History of Education Quarterly* 17 (Spring 1977): 17–30.

31. Selected correspondence of 1916 and 1917, John Grier Hibben Papers (Princeton University Manuscript Collection); Princeton, *Catalogue*, 1916–17. The university especially objected to Rodman Wanamaker's desire to have businessmen teach these courses. Kenneth W. Condit, *History of the Engineering School of Princeton University, 1875–1955* (Princeton: Princeton University Press, 1962), 75–96; Princeton University, *Annual Report of the President*, 1916, pp. 9, 31–32. The relationship of colleges and business training has been neglected and needs the same careful scholarship that has recently been devoted to the professionalization of law and medicine.

coming a normal school, he refused to consider subcollegiate teacher training. No new teacher training programs were created at Swarthmore until a grant from the Friends General Conference and the college's alumni association underwrote an education department in 1906. James McCosh envisioned Princeton training high school teachers as Scottish universities did, but he made little progress and his successors had little interest in teacher training. A number of graduates from both Bucknell and Franklin and Marshall became teachers, but neither college offered formal training through education departments until the 1910s. The colleges continued to produce teachers, especially for schools in their denomination and for prep schools, but that was a modest market. The job of preparing teachers for the mushrooming public schools remained primarily in the hands of state normal schools.[32] As these colleges secured roles in educating students for more highly paid and prestigious professions, they had little incentive to make special efforts to attract future teachers.

In contrast to normal schools, which overlapped the freshman and sophomore years, graduate study raised new questions about colleges' upper limits. The explosion of knowledge beyond the bounds of theological seminaries and amateur science created the problem of organizing postbaccalaureate studies in the new subject areas. Bucknell, Franklin and Marshall, and Swarthmore responded ambivalently. Each offered the traditional M.A. "in course" after three years of vaguely defined studies, good citizenship, and a small fee. Over the next few decades they experimented with various types of advanced work. In 1872 the *Mercersburg Review* called on the Reformed church to underwrite graduate studies at Franklin and Marshall. Swarthmore had a few "resident graduates" in the 1870s. In the 1880s and 1890s each college offered a few graduate courses, primarily for their own graduates. In addition to offering on-campus graduate courses, the colleges experimented with credit for courses taken by their graduates at universities or for off-campus work, and with giving degrees by examination.

By 1910 such programs and the M.A. "in course" were disappearing in the face of a consensus that master's degrees required at least a year of study. Franklin and Marshall, perhaps because the

32. Paul M. Mattingly, *The Classless Profession: American Schoolmen in the Nineteenth Century* (New York: New York University Press, 1975), 162–64; Swarthmore, *Catalogue*, 1906–7 to 1914–15; Hoeveler, 305–6; Apple, 1912 and 1919.

theological seminary was across the street, offered only a handful of master's degrees and abolished its graduate program in 1924. Bucknell's graduate student body reached 114 in 1906 before declining to forty-five in 1915 and five in 1920. Swarthmore's small program peaked with six master's degrees in 1908. After awarding a flurry of honorary doctorates to bolster their staffs' credentials in the 1880s and 1890s, none of the three colleges gave serious thought to offering doctoral work. By 1917 graduate work had been standardized, and the three institutions were willing to leave most graduate study to the universities.[33]

Princeton, after decades of ambivalence, developed a medium-sized, prestigious graduate program by World War I. James McCosh arrived at Princeton determined to establish European-style university studies. He urged the establishment of graduate fellowships and badgered the trustees to compete with Harvard. In 1877 he established graduate studies and awarded the first fellowship. Two years later Princeton awarded its first doctorates. But few full-time students matriculated, and only twelve doctorates were awarded, all to Princeton graduates, during McCosh's presidency. He had more luck endowing fellowships to send Princeton graduates to other graduate schools. The trustees refused to underwrite McCosh's desire to compete with the research universities.[34]

In the late 1890s Princeton brought its degrees into line with policies at the leading universities. The perfunctory M.A. "in course" was abolished, and requirements were standardized for master's degrees and doctorates. Even so, when the College of New Jersey was officially renamed Princeton University in 1896, the graduate program remained modest. In 1905 Bucknell had as many graduate students as Princeton, yet the latter became a founding member of the American Association of Universities in 1900. Apparently Prince-

33. Bucknell, *Catalogue*, 1889–90 to 1919–20; Franklin and Marshall, *Catalogue*, 1893–94 to 1923–24; Swarthmore, *Catalogue*, 1883–84 to 1919–20; Franklin and Marshall College, Alumni Association, *Report*, 1905; "Editorial," *Mercersburg Review* 19 (January 1872): 153–57.

34. McCosh urged the creation of fellowships in his inaugural. Princeton College, *Inauguration of James McCosh* (New York: Carter & Bros., 1868), 82–87; Princeton University, Trustees, Minutes (Princeton University Archives), 22 December 1875; *Princeton College Bulletin* 1 (March 1889): 42–52; Princeton College, *Alumni Directory* (Princeton, 1888), 73–78; Hoeveler, 286–93; Roger L. Geiger, *To Advance Knowledge: The Growth of American Research Universities, 1900–1940* (New York: Oxford University Press, 1986), 1–18.

ton's wealth and social prestige enabled it to join that group and be considered a "university" when its curriculum hardly justified the term. Princeton enrolled only sixty-seven full-time and seventy-six part-time graduate students in 1911. On the eve of World War I, Princeton enrolled eighty-nine full-time graduate students, most supported by fellowships, and forty-eight part-time students.

Unlike most universities, Princeton made no provision for professional preparation; all graduate work was in the disciplines. The two plans for the graduate college over which Wilson and West locked horns both envisioned residential life in Gothic dormitories. They disagreed only about whether to isolate graduate students from undergraduates. Princeton's wealth enabled it to develop top-notch libraries and to provide university-level research facilities for its graduate students and faculty by 1917. Building its graduate college a mile from the main campus guaranteed that the tone of undergraduate life remained very collegiate.[35] As American higher education bifurcated into colleges and universities, Princeton moved into the latter category as a total institution, but for most students and alumni it remained a college.

Speeches and magazine articles by presidents and other college spokesmen at the turn of the century suggested that colleges were on the verge of demotion, if not extinction. Yet these four colleges were all stable or growing. These jeremiads became rhetorical commonplaces, particularly useful for soliciting support from alumni. But there were also honest fears. While the likelihood of fundamental change seems, in hindsight, to have been minimal, collegiate spokesmen may be excused for their concern that the dramatic changes in the role and image of college might not turn out to their benefit.

The clearest perceived threat was movement toward the "university," by which supporters meant not merely adding graduate schools

35. Princeton, *Annual Report*, 1907; Princeton, Trustees, 13 January 1916. In 1906–7 full-time enrollment was only thirty-eight; in 1915–16 it was 126. Collins, 255–86. For two statements on Princeton's approach, see Alexander T. Ormond, "University Ideals at Princeton," *Journal of the Proceedings and Addresses of the National Education Association* 36 (1897): 346–57; and Andrew F. West, *The Graduate College of Princeton* (Princeton: Princeton University Press, 1913). The first professional graduate program was a master's degree course in engineering begun in 1921. Condit, 89; Princeton University, *Report of the Librarian* (Princeton, 1921), 1–13. For a sense of a faculty member who was committed to Princeton becoming a research university, see the Edwin G. Conklin Papers (Princeton University Archives).

onto existing colleges but adopting a European-style educational system. Admiration for German academic life led some to agree with John Burgess's declaration that he was "unable to divine what is to be ultimately the position of Colleges which cannot become Universities and which will not be Gymnasia."[36] In Germany students progressed from a restrictive secondary education directly to the social freedom and academic specialization of the university without an intervening collegiate experience. Although the dissimilarity between gymnasia and American high schools made transplanting the German system unlikely, some university reformers adopted it as a model and proposed eliminating or shortening baccalaureate studies. Reducing college work to three years or less was possible, particularly as students going to medical or law school were already doing so de facto by leaving without a degree. Although attacks on the college received considerable publicity, the spirited defenses probably tell more about the insecurity of college leaders than about the reality of the threat.

Most university presidents spoke in favor of preserving the college's role in American education. Daniel Gilman, first president of Johns Hopkins University and founder of the first American graduate school, strongly defended the liberal arts colleges and expected all Johns Hopkins graduate students to have a baccalaureate degree. He maintained that colleges provided intellectual discipline, which had to precede the intellectual freedom of university work. Gilman believed that colleges provided an essential moral as well as intellectual preparation and that, with the growth of universities, colleges "will be recognized as more important than ever, because they lead to higher work."[37] President Jacob Schurman of Cornell wanted to shorten secondary education but retain the four-year college course. His only concern was that colleges might try to do university work and abandon the disciplinary work they did best. The preponderance of discussion in the *Educational Review* and the Association of American Universities shared these positive evaluations of colleges.[38] Even William Rainey Harper, who experimented with

36. Rudolph, *American College*, 330, quoting Burgess's *American University of 1884*.

37. Daniel C. Gilman, "The Idea of a University," *North American Review* 133 (October 1881): 353–67; quote is from 359.

38. Jacob Schurman, "The Ideal College Education," *Proceedings of the Annual Convention of the College Association of the Middle States and Maryland* 3 (1891): 64–73. A similar worry was expressed in "Editorial," *Educational Review* 1 (1891): 387–88. The debate over the role of the colleges was particularly well recorded in the forty volumes of *Educational Review* (1891–1910). Rudolph, *American College*, 443–49.

a Germanic structure at the University of Chicago, spoke warmly of college life at President Swain's inauguration at Swarthmore.[39] The college was to be a distinctive part of the emerging American system. Vive la différence!

Representatives of all four colleges stressed the need for a broadening and disciplinary experience preceding students' entry into their vocations and, naturally, nominated the college as the appropriate institution to provide it. As President Stahr said of Franklin and Marshall, "It does not claim to be a university. It lays stress on college education as liberal culture fitted to make men, preparatory to their taking up the study of a profession."[40] In 1913 Stahr's successor, President Apple, affirmed that Franklin and Marshall still believed that "the ideal of a college education is mastery of fundamental principles, training toward specific professional education being secondary and incidental."[41]

College and university presidents shared a desire to clarify the line between collegiate and university studies. Former President Edward Magill of Swarthmore wrote to Daniel Gilman that the ideal to be aimed for was "the separate existence of our various grades of Institutions each doing the very best work possible in our own field without aspiring to be more than it really is, or to do more than belongs to its particular grade." Only with a "good solid four-year College course, kept intact between our secondary Schools and universities," would order be restored in the educational system.[42] The withdrawal by 1917 of all except Franklin and Marshall from

39. See, for instance, papers by Stanford's David Starr Jordan and Yale's Arthur Hadley in Association of American Universities, *Journal of Proceedings* 4 (1904): 21–33. Harper's surprising remarks were quoted in *Friends Intelligencer* 59 (22 November 1902): 739.

40. John Stahr, "Remarks," in College Association of the Middle States and Maryland, *Proceedings* 22 (1908): 9.

41. Apple's remarks are quoted in H.M.J. Klein, *History of Franklin and Marshall College, 1787–1948* (Lancaster, Pa., 1952), 160. See also Woodrow Wilson, "Should an Antecedent Liberal Education Be Required of Students in Law, Medicine, and Theology?" *Proceedings of the National Education Association* 32 (1893): 112–17; Andrew F. West, *American Liberal Education* (New York: Charles Scribner's Sons, 1907), 65–77; John Stahr, "President's Report: 1907," in Franklin and Marshall, Trustees, 10 June 1907.

42. Edward Magill to Daniel C. Gilman, 12 December 1894 (Gilman Collection, Johns Hopkins University Archives). Also, Richard Schiedt, "College-Need and College Needs," *Reformed Quarterly Review* 41 (January 1894): 117–28.

preparatory work and all but Princeton from substantial graduate work structurally fulfilled the rhetorical commitment.

The distinction between professional and liberal education was more difficult to establish. Although the rhetoric of the time and historians ever since have often counterposed the college and the university, the professional schools outside of universities posed a rarely acknowledged but greater threat. Many potential students bypassed or shortened their college educations in order to attend proprietary medical and law schools. It was probably the increasing numbers of students going into business who were responsible for rising enrollments in four-year college courses. Since graduate business schools were almost nonexistent there was little incentive to leave without a degree.[43] Once the more prominent medical and law schools began requiring college degrees, the four-year program was safe.

In the 1890s colleges experimented with balancing liberal and applied studies. In that decade Swarthmore made its last major effort at teacher training, President Patton at Princeton considered making senior year preprofessional, and John Harris rapidly expanded undergraduate professional curricula at Bucknell.[44] But with the ascendancy of Presidents Swain and Wilson in 1902, Swarthmore and Princeton moved clearly to what Laurence Veysey has labeled "liberal culture." Franklin and Marshall was the most consistent defender of the liberal arts. President Thomas Apple told the College Association of Pennsylvania in 1888 that "the college should preserve its character as ministering first and foremost to high liberal culture, and should keep itself carefully distinguished from the professional school, the technic school, etc."[45] Liberal education, amended to allow some student choice and specialization, was clearly dominant at three of the colleges in the 1900s. Only students in engineering programs and in some of Bucknell's vocational tracks did not share a common liberal arts curriculum in the underclass years. At all four colleges a majority "majored" in a discipline.

The emerging consensus on the educational role of colleges was reinforced by their considerable success in convincing the public of

43. Andrew West, "Remarks," *Proceedings of the Annual Convention of the College Association of the Middle States and Maryland* 17 (1903): 53–60. See also Stahr, "President's Report," for another attack on medical school admissions.

44. Patton's report to the Princeton trustees, 8 June 1896.

45. Thomas G. Apple, "The Idea of a Liberal Education," in College Association of Pennsylvania, *Proceedings* 1 (1887): 13–14.

their unique social and moral atmosphere. The collegiate spirit appealed to the popular mind, an attraction reinforced by collegiate novels and athletics. For most students and parents the social rewards of college life overshadowed the intellectual pursuits. Presidents repeatedly asserted the social and moral superiority of private colleges in terms that appealed to the values of upper-middle-class parents. College publicity stressed smallness, gentle and personal oversight, healthy activities, and desirable peers. The rapidly growing eastern and midwestern universities, many with enrollments reaching the five thousand range by 1910, could not convincingly make the same claims.

Presidential rhetoric at the four colleges became more confident after 1900.[46] In 1903 Swarthmore President Joseph Swain still portrayed dangers but surmised that colleges would survive if they improved their academic facilities while continuing to provide more contact between students and faculty and closer moral and social oversight than universities. President John Harris of Bucknell more expansively asserted that colleges would soon be deluged with students. Princeton's Dean West proclaimed renewed faith that the four-year college course would endure in 1903, having been convinced a few years earlier that shortening it to three years was unavoidable. President John Stahr told Franklin and Marshall's trustees in 1907 that "the fear which many have entertained as to the future of the denominational colleges and the smaller institutions of learning is really groundless."[47] The educational system that President Magill proposed when he organized the College Association of Pennsylvania had come about; college had become the preferred institution for more privileged youths seeking access to the most prestigious professions. In 1893 Woodrow Wilson defensively pleaded for making a bachelor's degree a prerequisite for professional training in order to return law, medicine, and theology to the status of "learned professions." By contrast, in 1909 the *Reformed Church Messenger* confidently

46. Laurence R. Veysey, *The Emergence of the American University* (Chicago: University of Chicago Press, 1965), 264–83, 441–44, and Rudolph, *American College*, 440–61, find a similar national trend.

47. Stahr's "President's Report"; Joseph Swain, "Remarks," *Friends Intelligencer* 60 (20 June 1903): 393; John Harris, "Remarks," Middle States Association of Colleges and Secondary Schools, *Proceedings* 7 (1903): 79–81; Andrew F. West, "What Should Be the Length of the College Course?" ibid., 53–60; Edward Magill, "The Proper Relation of Colleges to the Educational Institutions of the State," in College Association of Pennsylvania, *Proceedings* 1 (1887): 11.

asserted that "in law and medicine as well as in theology the tendency is to insist that students for these professions shall have a college course as a preparation."[48] By World War I an American educational ladder had been built and colleges occupied a secure rung. Clear distinctions between secondary, collegiate, and graduate or professional studies were gaining acceptance, distinctions that have characterized American education ever since. The ambitions of college authorities intersected with those of the new professional and business classes. The presidents' confident pronouncements suggest that the "age of the university" was also an "age of the college."

The college's intellectual role in transmitting a tradition with classical and medieval origins makes the college appear more venerable than it is. Institutionally, the American college is relatively modern. Although its form derives partially from colonial models, much of it is a twentieth-century development. Historians must be careful not to read history backward and view the college as an ideal type emerging into a predestined future perceived by the wisest educators. Its form was hardly predestined, and its relationship to other types of education was uncertain at the beginning of the century.

The development of the college was one part of the rationalization of a system of education in the United States. The relationship of baccalaureate work to other levels of education changed dramatically between the Civil War and World War I. While the outlines of an educational system were evident in the 1860s, much was not systematized. The relationships of colleges to high schools, normal schools, professional training, and graduate study were neither rationalized nor static. Different configurations of institutions might well have occurred if the colleges' interests had not intersected with those of crucial members of the professions in favor of the freestanding four-year baccalaureate college. Threatened by two emerging giants, the high school and the research university, the college not only survived, but prospered. As the American educational system crystallized, the colleges carved out a major role without parallel in Europe.

48. "Editorial," *Reformed Church Messenger*, 4 March 1909, p. 1; Woodrow Wilson, *College and State* (New York: Harper Bros., 1925), 1:223–31.

11

The College in the Social Order

By definition education transmits culture to the next generation, a fundamentally conserving duty. The first fund-raising effort for an American college, "New England's First Fruits," explained that after providing for the basic economic, political, and religious needs, "one of the next things we longed for, and looked after was to advance *Learning* and perpetuate it to Posterity; dreading to leave an illiterate Ministery to the Churches, when our present Ministers shall lie in the Dust."[1]

The "First Fruits" embodied the tensions that have characterized American education ever since. Perpetuating learning to posterity potentially conflicts with new learning and a new generation. For educational institutions to prosper, the culture being passed on must be acceptable to the donors to whom the appeal is addressed. Operating an expansive educational system requires considerable financial backing, making it unlikely that American education would ever radically challenge the fundamental centers of power and wealth. On the other hand, the tradition of decentralized, locally controlled institutions that developed in the early republic made it unlikely that any group would be able to perpetuate its version of culture and to control higher learning unchallenged. Thus, the college can be a center of contention for groups with wealth or for different generations within powerful groups that seek to modify the version of culture being perpetuated.

Between the Civil War and World War I the institution begun in

1. Richard Hofstadter and Wilson Smith, *American Higher Education: A Documentary History* (Chicago: University of Chicago Press, 1961), 1:6.

Massachusetts Bay Colony, the American college, underwent fundamental change. During this period, much of our modern conception of the college was created by institutions such as the four studied here. Rapid social and economic change intersected with the ambitions and ideals of college authorities. The interaction was complex. The institutional changes, analyzed in Chapter 10, can be established more concretely than the social and economic consequences. The colleges were neither centers of radical change nor islands of stasis. In the half-century studied here, these colleges remained the province of affluent, white, Protestant Americans of northern European descent. But within that broad constituency there were competing interests and conflicting visions of American culture that sought to use the college. In turn, they would be shaped and used by the colleges.

These four colleges grew dramatically (Table 11). The three antebellum colleges grew from six to twelve times between the end of the Civil War and World War I, while the American population tripled. There were 381 students at those three in 1867, and over 3,000 at the four in 1917.

Determining the social meaning of the growing college enrollments requires knowledge of the social and economic status of students' families. Unfortunately, the records at the four colleges provide little information about class origins. Admissions forms were brief, and few survived. Financial aid was neither extensive nor systematically administered. Presidents personally awarded the small number of scholarships, and their correspondence gives only fragmentary glimpses of the process. Class reunion publications record graduates' occupations, but only Princeton published them regularly before World War I.

Table 11. Total Collegiate and Graduate Enrollments, 1867–1917

	Bucknell	F&M	Princeton	Swarthmore
1867–68	60	57	267	—
1890–91	103	114	760	165
1909–10	527	241	1,311	359
1916–17	715	319	1,555	484 (1917–18)

SOURCE: The figures were compiled from catalogs and other college publications.

The cost of education provides inferential evidence about the accessibility of these colleges. In 1869 the more extravagant Princeton students spent the most (ca. $400), though more frugal Princeton students spent less (ca. $300) than boarding students paid ($350) for a "guarded education" at Swarthmore. Bucknell and Franklin and Marshall were much less expensive: students spent an average of about $200. In the 1870s and 1880s the differential increased. Costs at Bucknell and Franklin and Marshall declined slightly to about $180 by 1890, while at Swarthmore they rose to $450. Princeton estimated that its students' expenses in 1890 ranged from $311 to $650, depending on room and board arrangements. Because there was deflation of about one-third over these two decades, real costs rose at all four.

Expenses rose in real and absolute dollars at all four colleges during the quarter-century after 1890. By World War I, expenses approximately doubled at Bucknell and Franklin and Marshall to about $350 to $400. Swarthmore calculated $568 as a reasonable student budget, although it reported that one-quarter of the students spent over $800. Princeton projected "necessary expenses" ranging from $570 to $775, depending on the type of room and board and not including books and personal expenses.

The pattern is consistent. Princeton was the most expensive and Swarthmore was second throughout, costing one and one-half to two times as much as the other two colleges. That this was true before 1900 is striking because Swarthmore had little prestige outside a small social circle and was not even fully committed to collegiate work. But the attraction of guarded education to some wealthy Quakers and other Philadelphians provided sufficient students. Bucknell and Franklin and Marshall, even though they were more clearly collegiate than Swarthmore before 1900, charged significantly lower fees. Seemingly, support by an elite urban group was more important than curriculum for institutional prosperity.

Rising enrollments at these colleges must not have included many children from the working or even clerical middle classes. In 1910 the average salary for American clerical workers was under $1,200, and industrial workers averaged less than $700. Relatively little financial aid was available to meet the rising costs. In the 1870s and 1880s the colleges offered reductions or tuition waivers for ministerial candidates and children of ministers or, at Swarthmore, for children of Friends. These dispensations either covered a decreasing proportion of costs or were eliminated in later years. There is no evidence that financial aid kept pace with rising enrollments. The proportion of students assisted and the percentage of student costs covered by financial aid probably declined after 1890. Over a half-century in which deflation and inflation approximately balanced each other, the higher expenses were real increases. Costs were making these four colleges less accessible.

The expense of the gentlemanly student life-style that dominated campuses after 1890 caused much of the increase. The relatively high cost of Swarthmore's guarded education, even when it had little prestige, suggests that as colleges became more residential the costs rose and potential students were squeezed out. The costs of joining campus organizations, maintaining a respectable wardrobe, and participating in the social life added to the expenses of all but the most iconoclastic students. Presumably enrollment growth resulted primarily from an increase in upper-middle- and upper-class students at these colleges. As Colin Burke postulated, accessibility to private colleges probably declined after the Civil War, and students were drawn increasingly from wealthier families.[2]

Although the economic class of students' families can only be estimated, the changing social characteristics can be established more precisely. These colleges reflected the shift from an ethnically and denominationally conscious Protestantism to one that was relatively accepting of all Protestants of northern European descent. In the 1860s each college was the vehicle of a denomination, three with distinctive ethnic or cultural styles. The governing boards and most faculty identified with these groups and expected the college to perpetuate those identities by influencing the students and training future teachers, ministers, and lay leaders. These colleges were open to outsiders, especially local residents of other Protestant denomi-

2. The figures for expenses were compiled from the catalogs. Since each college reported expenses differently and because so many students lived off campus, these are useful approximations rather than precise figures. The late nineteenth century was a deflationary period. Prices dropped by about one-third between 1870 and 1900 and then slowly returned to earlier levels by World War I. See Series E 52–63, Wholesale Price Indexes (Warren and Pearson), Bureau of the Census, *Historical Statistics of the United States: Colonial Times to 1970* (Washington, D.C., 1975), 1:200–201; Colin Burke, *American Collegiate Populations: A Test of the Traditional View* (New York: New York University Press, 1982), 226–30.

nations. But the authorities and the principal donors at each institution saw themselves as preserving a distinct denominational identity within Protestant America.

Over the next five decades the colleges' social contexts converged. Ethnicity was subsumed within denominationalism. The Scotch-Irish Presbyterians and the German Reformed eschewed behavioral distinctiveness. The Hicksite Quakers made the most enduring attempt to maintain a distinct life-style, based on denominationalism rather than ethnicity. Denominational differences were muted as theological differences declined and the non-Protestant "new" immigration increased the sense of commonality among Protestants.

Students were the first to reject distinctiveness and embrace a common collegiate culture. By the 1880s many students at each college were conscious of developments on other campuses, and most conformed to the general ideals of the emerging student culture. Later, members of that generation, as faculty and alumni, replaced their elders' version of the colleges' missions. By the 1910s virtually no ethnic or life-style distinctiveness remained on the campuses. Each retained a connection to a Protestant denomination, but that did little to differentiate day-to-day behavior at the four colleges. Each campus was dominated by a Protestantism that neither challenged privilege nor required a distinctive life-style. This was not secularism; rather, it was a decline in distinctiveness and piety. Observance of conventional Protestant practices continued to be expected of students and faculty in the 1910s. A demanding and restrictive pietistic Protestantism had been replaced by a more exuberant and permissive muscular Christianity.

The students of the 1870s and 1880s and the faculty and trustees of later decades substituted new lines of social demarcation. They saw themselves as the authentic Americans, an ideal type that plastered over most of the denominational and ethnic divisions of earlier nineteenth-century Protestant America. Other groups remained largely outside the pale. The clearest exclusion was racial. Only one black appears to have attended any of these colleges. Only one case of overt racial discrimination survived in the records (committed by a future president of the United States!), so the exact mixture of discrimination, custom, and accumulated disadvantage is unclear. Catholics and Jews were rare on the campuses. Again, records leave little indication of the mixture of discrimination and custom. It was not until the 1920s that the beginning of selective admissions made ethnoreligious discrimination overt and traceable.[3]

Gender has been downplayed in this study as a variable "held constant" while examining the creation of the archetypal college model by the dominant groups. The all-male and the coeducational campuses shared a basically similar student culture. Subtle distinctions were lost, and the contribution of female students to campus life was underreported in student publications, which featured male activities at the coeducational colleges (see Chapter 9). The shift from piety to muscular Christianity was a triumph for a style that favored separate activities and masculine leadership. Victorian convention obscures the more intimate contacts between the genders.[4]

Generation is a particularly important social category for analyzing higher education. In this study, three identifiable generations were evident: (1) the governing board, president, and senior faculty; (2) the junior faculty; and (3) the students. Policies planned principally by one generation often had unexpected outcomes in another. The ethnic and denominational commitment of donors in the 1860s and 1870s financed campuses that spawned a student culture which largely ignored those distinctions. Donations designed to promote mid-Victorian pietistic Protestantism wound up supporting a somewhat hedonistic, "muscular Christian" student life. Debates over student life and curricula that were expressed in the rhetoric of democracy and social mobility were often disputes among different generations with similar economic and social status. Debates within the colleges were primarily over life-style and cultural identity rather than more fundamental economic or social divides.

This study was designed to isolate the factors that determined institutional size and material success. The case studies were selected from

3. On the relationship of cultural prejudices and selective admissions, see two excellent works: Harold Wechsler, *The Qualified Student: A History of Selective College Admission in America* (New York: John Wiley & Sons, 1977), and Marcia G. Synnott, *The Half-Opened Door: Discrimination and Admissions at Harvard, Yale, and Princeton, 1900–1970* (Westport, Conn.: Greenwood Press, 1979).

4. The long-standing inattention to women's higher education is being corrected by a recent flurry of excellent scholarship. There is an excellent synthesis: Barbara M. Solomon, *In the Company of Educated Women* (New Haven: Yale University Press, 1985). For an excellent multiple case study of women's collegiate experience at five colleges in the same period, see Lynn D. Gordon, *Gender and Higher Education in the Progressive Era* (New Haven: Yale University Press, 1990).

among colleges in the 1860s without regard to their form in 1917 or today, in an attempt to avoid the anachronism of grouping institutions by their modern category.[5] Thus, Princeton was included even though it is a university and the other three are colleges; the distinction between college and university was not relevant in 1865. All four had nonbaccalaureate departments before taking their modern form as solely institutions of higher education. Curriculum was not what differentiated the colleges from the nascent universities. Bucknell and Franklin and Marshall had curricula very similar to Princeton's in the 1860s and 1870s, while Swarthmore, the early curricular rebel, came closest to Princeton's prestige and wealth by 1917. Franklin and Marshall, which shared considerable religious and intellectual heritage with Princeton, wound up the smallest and poorest institution. Curriculum proved to be a poor predictor of later material success.

Access to wealth explains much more. Princeton had an endowment in 1869 of over $500,000, a figure not matched by the other three colleges until the twentieth century. James McCosh raised $3 million in twenty years by parlaying reputation and ethnoreligious connections into an entrée to fortunes being made in New York, Philadelphia, and Pittsburgh. Under McCosh and his successors Princeton was able to build an impressive campus and hire a large faculty, including some academic stars from research universities.

The other colleges started with more modest endowments and social connections. Swarthmore was run as frugally as possible until the turn of the century; the expenses remained stable from 1878 to 1902. Its annual deficits, ranging from $15,000 to $20,000, were made up by contributions from wealthy managers. In 1880 its endowment was a mere $75,000. Once traditional Quakers capitulated to champions of the new collegiate culture, Swarthmore expanded its connections to broader Philadelphia society and to Carnegie and Rockefeller philanthropy. By 1917 its endowment had soared to $1 million.[6]

5. Some anachronism remained because I perforce chose colleges that survive today. In addition, choosing colleges on the basis of archival sources probably biased the selection toward wealthier colleges.

6. Homer D. Babbidge, Jr., "Swarthmore College in the Nineteenth Century: A Quaker Experience in Education" (Ph.D. diss., Yale University, 1953), 230; Swarthmore College, *Annual Catalogue*, 1879–80; General Education Board, *Report of the Secretary*, 1916–17, p. 23.

Under President Hill in the 1880s, Bucknell's student body remained stable while the endowment jumped from $121,000 to $350,000, mainly due to William Bucknell's generosity. In the 1890s Harris took the opposite strategy, using donations to enlarge facilities while the endowment grew only slightly to $400,000. Bucknell's student body grew rapidly under Harris, but by 1910 his fixation with growth was hurting Bucknell's reputation and undermining its fund-raising. A campaign to enlarge the endowment by $1 million begun in 1903 initially raised about $300,000 but then stalled, leaving the endowment at about $800,000 in 1917. Long-term health was sacrificed for short-term growth.

Franklin and Marshall, partially due to its formal denominational tie, remained closest to its mid-nineteenth-century traditions and penury. The college lived modestly throughout the period, experiencing neither crisis nor entrepreneurial success. An endowment of $121,000 in 1875 rose marginally to $170,000 by 1910; then, aided by the General Education Board, it grew quickly to $550,000 by 1916.[7]

The differences in wealth among the colleges was considerable. In 1917 Swarthmore's endowment was at the level of Princeton in the 1880s, Bucknell was at the level of Princeton in the 1870s, and Franklin and Marshall was at the level of Princeton in the 1860s. An institution like Princeton that had the prestige to attract plutocrats like J. P. Morgan and Henry Clay Frick to a presidential inauguration had very different opportunities than did the other three. In turn, an institution like Harvard with several times Princeton's endowment had further opportunities.

Colleges obviously were neither forced to court wealthy sponsors nor accept their offers. But failing to do so reduced colleges' options. They could decline to solicit some sources of support, as did Swarthmore before 1902 and Franklin and Marshall throughout the period, but the "opportunity cost" of distinctiveness increased. If colleges sought to compete for academic and social prestige in the emerging national system of higher education, they became dependent on those who could finance their expansive and expensive ambitions—increasingly, urban donors. William Bucknell's takeover at Bucknell was the most dramatic example of rising urban power. Princeton

7. Most figures for Bucknell and for Franklin and Marshall were derived from catalogs. Also, H.M.J. Klein, *The History of the Eastern Synod of the Reformed Church in the United States* (Lancaster, Pa.: Rudisill & Smith Co., 1943), 309, 355–59.

drew on the elites of New York and Philadelphia, and later extended its drawing power to Pittsburgh and farther west. Swarthmore's increasing affluence resulted from support by urban Hicksites. Franklin and Marshall's access to Lancaster maintained it modestly, but its failure to tap the elite of Philadelphia or Pittsburgh more fully left it the least affluent of the four. The old reliance on rural, small-town, and small-city money inspired by denominational loyalty no longer sufficed.

The sizable denominationally inspired urban donations lacked predictability. Alumni in the urban elites increasingly offered dependable sources, especially when induced by foundations' matching grants. This also broadened the base of support, drawing in smaller gifts from the upper-middle class to supplement upper-class philanthropy. Committed alumni were often enthusiastic champions of the new collegiate culture who were usually rebuffed in their fight for positions on the governing boards in the 1880s and 1890s. As long as there were periodic contributions from rich members of the denominations and the colleges' needs remained simple, alumni power was limited. But as budgets increased and wealthy alumni proved willing and able to make regular contributions, the penalty for ignoring them grew. Alumni supported their alma mater's competition with other campuses—not to be different, but to do the same things better, from the football team to the chapel. Vocal alumni shared similar values and styles across the four campuses by World War I.

As Laurence Veysey has pointed out, the motives of the donors, students, and faculty might differ, but their relationship was symbiotic.[8] There was certainly a mutually beneficial relationship between the students' ambitions and those of the colleges. The colleges' prosperity was insured by their success in making the baccalaureate degree a valued credential for the most prestigious and well-paid professions. The subsequent occupations of their graduates cannot be traced precisely, as evidence on alumni careers was not collected systematically until offices for alumni affairs and fund-raising were created after World War I. But general patterns can be ascertained.

In a sample of Franklin and Marshall graduates in the classes from 1867 to 1885, 30 percent were lawyers and 26 percent were ministers.

8. Lawrence R. Veysey, *The Emergence of the American University* (Chicago: University of Chicago Press, 1965), 263–380.

The remainder was divided among teaching (13 percent), medical (13 percent), business (11 percent), and scientific and engineering careers (7 percent).[9] A striking number changed professions during their lives, some having tried one or two before coming to Franklin and Marshall.

The figures are quite similar to Princeton's, using its classes of 1868 and 1881 as a sample. Law was also the first choice (35 percent). Business was second (19 percent), ahead of the ministry (15 percent), medicine (11 percent), and teaching (10 percent). There were 5 percent in scientific and engineering careers and 5 percent in a variety of others. Business was slightly more popular and the ministry slightly less popular at Princeton than at Franklin and Marshall.

Over one-third of Bucknell's graduates in the 1870s and 1880s entered the ministry. Other professional choices do not seem to have been recorded. Quaker Swarthmore naturally produced no ministers. Of its male graduates in the classes from 1873 to 1892, about one-quarter (26 percent) entered business, 21 percent went into teaching, 16 percent were engineers, 11 percent in law, 10 percent in medicine, and 16 percent in other fields.

After 1890 the number of Princeton students entering business rose sharply. In the class of 1899, almost half (49 percent) of the graduates entered business, while law (16 percent), the ministry (9 percent), and teaching (5 percent) declined. Medicine (9 percent), science and engineering (3 percent), and others (9 percent) remained fairly stable. Later classes followed similar patterns.[10]

Unfortunately, comparable data for alumni who graduated from the other three colleges after 1890 could not be located. Scattered evidence suggests trends similar to Princeton's at the other three colleges, except that teaching was a more common choice at them. At the three colleges that traditionally prepared ministers, the proportion of graduates entering the ministry declined; the absolute number remained constant.

Princeton seems to have drawn students from the wealthiest fam-

9. Franklin and Marshall College, Alumni Association, *Obituary Record*, 1897–1909.

10. Data compiled from reunion books published by the classes of 1868 (in 1869), 1881 (in 1901), 1899 (in 1909), and 1912 (in 1922). Since categories were not consistent only general impressions are warranted.

ilies, and, in turn, many of them moved into positions of power and wealth. Swarthmore was the next most prosperous, especially after 1902. Bucknell and Franklin and Marshall were much less expensive and seem to have drawn and produced fewer elite students. But all four attracted the children of well-off parents, and most of their graduates entered relatively lucrative and prestigious careers.

Colleges had always been attended and supported primarily by the upper and middle classes. But the nature of those classes was changing with urbanization and industrialization. In the 1880s and 1890s upper-class culture was institutionalized through "blue books," country clubs, elite resort areas, and educational institutions. Residential collegiate prep schools were created to provide the ultimate class, religious, and age segregation for upper-class youth. Certain colleges—primarily older, private Protestant ones—acquired the mantle of social acceptability. Princeton and, later, Swarthmore were among those most favored. Such colleges received the offspring of the upper class and, more important, its benevolence. Possibly because the American elite lacked the titles and estates of the British aristocracy that it emulated, colleges became an important source of identity and a primary recipient of elite wealth.

The managerial and professional upper-middle class increasingly separated itself not just from the working class but from the clerical and small-business middle class as well. College education was one way to demarcate and perpetuate that distinction for one's children. High school, which had become a necessity for most nonmanual jobs, created the expectation that youths would spend twelve years in age-segregated institutions among their peers. Success depended on negotiating age-specific obstacles: the next step was college at about the age of eighteen. The concept of generation was being fine-tuned, and parents and students came to expect that the latter's next four years would be spent with peers their own age.

The urban environment came to be viewed as socially and physically unhealthy. Much of the upper-middle class moved to streetcar suburbs if not farther out to railroad suburbs. These neighborhoods were homogeneously affluent and beyond the range of most Catholics and Jews. Upper-middle-class youths were kept in age-segregated institutions for longer periods of time, preferably in nonurban settings far from immigrant and working-class neighborhoods.[11] The emerging upper-middle class contributed many of the students and some of the funds for college expansion.

These four colleges increasingly adopted styles that fit upper- and upper-middle-class educational needs and cultural expectations. In addition to becoming a prerequisite for professional success, colleges successfully convinced affluent parents of the social and moral superiority of private colleges. College publicity featured small and bucolic campuses, gentle and personal oversight, healthy activities, and desirable peers. The rapidly growing eastern and midwestern universities could not convincingly make the same claims. The collegiate spirit had broad appeal, reinforced by collegiate novels and athletics. For most students and parents the sense of community and the social rewards of college life no doubt overshadowed the intellectual attractions.

These four institutions adapted to the increasingly age-specific youth culture expected by secondary school graduates by shedding other functions and becoming primarily collegiate institutions populated by eighteen- to twenty-two-year-olds. Most secondary and normal programs were dropped. Franklin and Marshall Academy survived but was increasingly separated from the college. Three of the colleges abandoned graduate programs. Princeton eventually added a graduate school, but the main campus maintained an essentially collegiate atmosphere for the undergraduates.

Colleges helped form the new upper and upper-middle classes, which, in turn, were willing to support elite colleges in a style to which they wanted to grow accustomed. All four beautified their campuses. In 1917 even the least affluent, Franklin and Marshall, offered an attractive 58-acre campus with ten buildings as well as athletic fields and tennis courts in a leafy area on the outskirts of Lancaster. Bucknell occupied a scenic site in the Susquehanna River valley and could boast of a recent Carnegie library among other new buildings.

11. On the evolution of the middle class and the separation of the upper-middle class, see Stuart M. Blumin, *The Emergence of the Middle Class: Social Experience in the American City, 1760–1900* (New York: Cambridge University Press, 1989), chap. 8. On changing middle-class family strategies, see Paula Fass, *The Damned and the Beautiful: American Youth in the 1920s* (New York: Oxford University Press, 1977), chap. 2. On spatial segregation and suburbanization, see Kenneth Jackson, *Crabgrass Frontier: The Suburbanization of America* (New York: Oxford University Press, 1985), chaps. 4–9.

Swarthmore added new science buildings in the early 1900s and also received a library from Andrew Carnegie. New gardens and other horticultural additions created Quaker quietude at Swarthmore within the Philadelphia metropolitan area. Princeton students no doubt preferred getting a lake instead of a library from Carnegie; their campus became a showpiece featuring "collegiate gothic" buildings designed by the style's leading proponent, Ralph Adams Cram.

The four colleges increasingly fulfilled the ideal of the college that was attractive to the upper and upper-middle classes, especially in the East. College life was to be a residential experience on a relatively tranquil campus small enough to provide a sense of community. Only Swarthmore provided room and board for all students, but Bucknell and Princeton were moving toward that by 1917 and Franklin and Marshall eventually would follow. The desire to have residential campuses raised questions of size. Soaring numbers of high school graduates and college applicants meant that continuing to accept every qualified student would create large institutions, delay becoming an all-residential campus, and change the social makeup of the student bodies. These four campuses provided an attractive, stable community in an increasingly urban and crowded society. They also offered a socially homogeneous community for Protestants of northeastern European ancestry at the height of the new Catholic and Jewish immigration. This atmosphere, so valued by the Eastern upper and upper-middle classes, would be threatened by further enrollment growth.[12] The colleges did not erect formal barriers until the 1920s, when the exclusiveness of these colleges as implied by their definitions of character and community was explicitly enforced through selective admissions.

12. See Roger L. Geiger, *To Advance Knowledge: The Growth of American Research Universities, 1900–1940* (New York: Oxford University Press, 1986), 129–39, for an insightful discussion of the relationship and implications of selective admissions for collegiate and university ideals.

Conclusion

On 2 April 1917, former college professor and president Woodrow Wilson declared war. The four colleges' enthusiastic response to American entry into World War I exemplified their cultural convergence. So many students volunteered that all four colleges were strained financially. When the government established the Student Army Training Corps (SATC) program, the authorities at all four colleges eagerly applied to host branches on their campuses.

Princeton leapt into the war effort with particular enthusiasm. President John G. Hibben, former intimate and colleague of Wilson, fervently promoted "preparedness." As a member of the Advisory Committee of University Presidents, he became a national spokesman for the Plattsburg System and established courses in military training at Princeton in 1915. Several of his faculty served on national committees supporting the war effort. History professor Robert McElroy chaired the National Security League Committee on Patriotism, leading an unscholarly attack on the University of Wisconsin's loyalty.[1] At Bucknell, so many male students joined the armed forces in the nine months before it established a branch of the SATC that faculty had to be retrenched.[2]

More ambivalence toward the war might have been expected at the other two campuses. Franklin and Marshall's affiliation with the German Reformed church and its German heritage might have

1. Carole S. Gruber, *Mars and Minerva: World War I and the Uses of the Higher Learning in America* (Baton Rouge: Louisiana State University Press, 1975), 84, 104–5, 120–21, 148, 220–22.

2. J. Orin Oliphant, *The Rise of Bucknell University* (New York: Appleton-Century-Crofts, 1965), 212.

Fig. 23. The Student Army Training Corps at Franklin and Marshall.

dampened enthusiasm. Instead, enrollment plummeted from 319 in September 1916 to about 200 the following fall and to 50 in September 1918 due to military service. Since the draft age was twenty-one, most departing students must have been volunteers. The surnames of Franklin and Marshall's casualties indicate an even mixture of Anglo and Germanic descendants. The ambivalence of a few students is suggested by President Apple's announcement that "students who left for the army or to work on farms" would be promoted to the next class. But in all other ways Franklin and Marshall authorities actively promoted the patriotic reputation of their German Reformed college. They boasted that Franklin and Marshall was making the highest per capita contribution to the armed forces of any college in Pennsylvania. The only faculty member who publicly questioned American intervention was dismissed (see Chapter 7). Count Bernstorff, the former German ambassador, was stripped of his honorary doctor of laws degree in absentia. Establishing a branch of the SATC enhanced the image of loyalty and prevented further erosion of enrollments and finances.[3]

Swarthmore's Quaker heritage presumably should have ruled out military training. Pacifist sentiments dominated the campus until the

3. H.M.J. Klein, *History of Franklin and Marshall College, 1787–1948* (Lancaster, Pa.: 1952), 159, 174–98.

American entry into the war. Then, while some faculty and alumni continued to oppose military training, President Swain and most students turned into ardent supporters. In the spring of 1918 most male undergraduates signed a petition demanding compulsory military training on campus. After debate, the divided board of managers agreed to voluntary training and allowed Swain to apply for a SATC branch (see Chapter 6), although the board held out against permitting arms on the campus until a few days before the armistice.[4]

When 140,000 students on 516 campuses were inducted into the first SATC units on 1 October 1918, Woodrow Wilson told them that they had "ceased to be merely individuals . . . [and had joined] with the entire manhood of the country."[5] It would have been more accurate if Wilson had said that college students were part of an elite subculture. The way these colleges embraced the war, sometimes with unseemly haste, suggested the extent to which they had converged on a national, Anglo-Protestant culture and had abandoned the identities that separated them half a century earlier. Their homogeneity undercut the basis for independent inquiry that might have enabled faculty and students to avoid rushing to judgment. Instead, these colleges led the stampede.[6]

After World War I, all four colleges enhanced their social and educational reputations. With the departure of President John Harris in 1919, Bucknell dispensed with his autocratic procedures, strict discipline, and vocational curricular tracks. Bucknell quickly adopted a curriculum and a campus style more like the other three. Harris had greatly expanded the college, but his fixation with growth and vocationalism eventually sullied Bucknell's reputation. Exclusivity, selectivity, stability, and liberal arts were becoming the hallmarks of elite colleges. Franklin and Marshall gained more autonomy from the German Reformed church and created alumni trustees, broadening its fund-raising base and improving its finances. Both Bucknell and Franklin and Marshall solidified their regional reputations.

Princeton and Swarthmore enjoyed national prominence and the attention of the elite. Swarthmore moved into the national spotlight

4. Richard J. Walton, *Swarthmore College: An Informal History* (Swarthmore, Pa.: Swarthmore College, 1986), 26–28.

5. Quoted in Gruber, 213. See also 231 n. 40 on Haverford.

6. Gruber, 81–212; David M. Kennedy, *Over Here: The First World War and American Society* (New York: Oxford University Press, 1980), 57–59, 73–75.

in the 1920s with the implementation of President Aydelotte's pioneering "honors program." This combined with its growing social reputation among the eastern elite to make Swarthmore one of the most prestigious colleges in the country. Princeton's doctoral programs and research, especially in science and mathematics, established its reputation in academia as a leading research university, an achievement that differentiated its faculty from those of the other three colleges. For undergraduates and alumni Princeton remained a college, truly a "university college," and augmented its collegiate reputation with winning football teams and completion of a handsome Gothic campus.[7]

New dormitories, chapels, stadiums, gymnasiums, and dining halls made all four into residential colleges on picturesque, bucolic campuses. Enrollments were limited to assure residential facilities for all students and to preserve the social homogeneity of the campus. Limits on both size and heterogeneity distinguished them from urban colleges and state universities. Each further loosened its denominational tie while remaining respectably Protestant and observing religious formalities.

Movies, novels, and athletic events spread the romantic image of the residential college broadly across American society. At the same time as the comprehensive high school was starting to provide an all-embracing social as well as educational life for adolescents, some colleges were offering an almost complete "life" to a privileged minority. These four colleges were among the institutions that helped shape this archetype and, in turn, were poised to benefit from personifying it.[8]

These four private, Protestant, white, dominantly male, eastern colleges represent a numerically small but very influential segment of American higher education. Limiting the study within these parameters focused attention on the formation of an institution by the

7. Roger L. Geiger, *To Advance Knowledge: The Growth of American Research Universities, 1900–1940* (New York: Oxford University Press, 1986), 200–203, 236–38.

8. The leading book on interwar American higher education is David O. Levine, *The American College and the Culture of Aspiration, 1915–1940* (Ithaca: Cornell University Press, 1986). Levine shares the prevailing stereotype of pre–World War I colleges and thus exaggerates the war as a watershed for colleges. But he does an excellent job of analyzing the increasing social distinctions among colleges in the 1920s.

dominant cultural group of the period. Examining four institutions avoided the limitations of a case study while permitting institutional comparisons built on careful analysis of the interaction of collegiate interests. But these boundaries limit generalizing from the findings to a national context.

Fortunately, there have been multiple case studies of New England, midwestern, and southern colleges that provide some basis for comparison.[9] These studies suggest similar patterns of development along a regional continuum following economic maturation. Many changes detailed in this study had occurred in New England colleges about a decade earlier. In turn, developments in these four colleges in the Middle Atlantic states preceded those in similar midwestern institutions. This order may have been determined by the pace of the decline of agricultural communities and the rise of urban professional and corporate cultures that enabled college authorities to finance their desires to eliminate secondary and normal programs and develop their campuses around collegiate work stressing liberal arts. There was one noticeable gender difference: the liberal arts curriculum was less popular among men in the Midwest, where it had a feminine connotation.

In the South, colleges faced a tenacious evangelical denominationalism as well as economic underdevelopment. Ira Read found a number of underfunded colleges that were legally bound to denominations which provided little financial support. Their situation mirrored that at Franklin and Marshall and at early Swarthmore; but the southern colleges were poorer, and their denominational connections persisted well after World War I. They depended on individual gifts from members of their denominations. Few qualified for money from Rockefeller's General Education Board and the Carnegie Foundation. Even Vanderbilt had to fight until 1914 to break free from the control of Methodist bishops. Governing boards often passed up potential funds to remain true to their traditional religious mission.[10]

9. George E. Peterson, *The New England College in the Age of the University* (Amherst, Mass.: Amherst College Press, 1964); Timothy Smith, "The Religious Foundations of Higher Education in Illinois" (Unpublished manuscript, ca. 1969); Joan G. Zimmerman, "College Culture in the Midwest, 1890–1930" (Ph.D. diss., University of Virginia, 1978).

10. Ira Read, "Church and College in the South" (Paper presented at the annual meeting of the History of Education Society, Atlanta, Ga., November 1990); Paul K. Conkin, *Gone with the Ivy: A Biography of Vanderbilt University* (Knoxville: University of Tennessee Press, 1985), chaps. 8 and 9.

All of these multiple case studies find considerable intellectual liveliness in late nineteenth- and early twentieth-century colleges. These were not the intellectual backwaters often invoked as straw men by university spokesmen and later by historians. Most colleges interacted intelligently with their communities, often experimenting with a variety of responses to new social and intellectual developments, and had strong local and regional roots.

Some colleges in these studies (especially those in the South) later developed more formal denominational ties, but the fundamentalism of the 1920s should not be read back upon the earlier period. Protestant evangelicalism was relatively optimistic and open to new ideas in the late nineteenth century. It perpetuated some prejudices that limited inquiry, but those were generally held by the majority of Americans. Some colleges resisted the siren calls of urban wealth and modernism, or found pockets of wealth willing to underwrite an alternative vision; but they did not become militantly defensive institutions until the 1920s. Most colleges adopted mainstream Protestantism and jockeyed for prestige among the Protestant professional and business class like the four in this study.

All of the studies found college spokesmen juxtaposing "college" and "university" as they sought a role for their institutions. Their emerging self-definition invariably stressed the "whole man," liberal arts, and a moral environment as the colleges' unique attraction. The rhetoric exaggerated the universities' threat to their existence but successfully created an image that socially well-connected colleges could use to gain support. George Peterson reported that New England colleges had found secure roles by 1900. The colleges in this study took a little longer. Joan Zimmerman detected midwestern private colleges reaching the same level of confidence in the 1920s. A new generation of college case studies that are much more sensitive to social context than most existing "house histories" promises to enrich our understanding of colleges in the next few years.[11]

This study is part of a growing body of literature that is molding a new understanding of the social and educational role of higher ed-

11. Three of the most impressive are David M. Stameshkin, *The Town's College: Middlebury College, 1800–1915* (Middlebury, Vt.: Middlebury College Press, 1985); David Potts, *Wesleyan University, 1831–1910* (New Haven: Yale University Press, 1992); and Patricia Palmieri, "In 'Adamless Eden': The Women's Intellectual Community at Wellesley" (Unpublished manuscript).

ucation, and particularly of colleges, between the Civil War and World War I. My work supports the general direction of revisionist scholarship of the 1980s, especially that of Colin Burke and Louise Stevenson.[12] This study suggests five guidelines for revising older interpretations of the subject and integrating recent and future research into a broader conceptual framework.

First, colleges were actors in their own destinies. The colleges did not merely react to demand; college authorities actively sought sponsorship to promote their institutions and visions, while clients sought the status, identity, and credentials that colleges could offer. The reflexive vocabulary that talks of colleges "responding to society" should be replaced with a more interactive language.

Second, the dysfunctions within institutions of higher education need to be kept in mind. Generational issues in particular need more attention as a source of competing interests and unintended outcomes. Parents were attracted by different visions of the college experience than their children. Younger faculty in the late 1800s often collaborated with students against college presidents and governing boards. In the 1900s faculty, especially younger ones, started living in a world shaped by "university" training and values, while students and alumni were shaping a "collegiate" culture. We must avoid the functionalist assumption that institutions always act rationally, and be more sensitive to contradictions.

Third, we must resist the temptation to anachronistically read later social and economic conditions backward, assuming that "modernization" was inevitable and overdue. For decades historians believed that colleges should have responded to a presumed demand for education pent up by conservative curricula and repressive social rules. This study finds that such demand largely did not exist before 1900. Most communities and denominations were more interested in secondary and vocational programs than in collegiate work, let alone the intellectual freedom and specialization of universities. The university reformers, too often quoted as omniscient observers, had little to offer most educational consumers of the nineteenth or early twentieth centuries. Most colleges were not discrete institutions until the

12. Colin Burke, *American Collegiate Populations: A Test of the Traditional View* (New York: New York University Press, 1982); Louise L. Stevenson, *Scholarly Means to Evangelical Ends: The New Haven Scholars and the Transformation of Higher Learning in America, 1830–1890* (Baltimore: Johns Hopkins University Press, 1986).

twentieth century. Not until after the turn of the century did college study become a common requirement for the professions and business management. Colleges could only take their modern form as patterns of coming of age, ethnoreligious identity, class formation, and professionalization changed. Reforming curricula and campus rules alone would not have attracted many more youths.

Fourth, we should examine institutions within their actual communities and not impose later definitions of "society." If higher education is judged solely from a national perspective, localism and regionalism are obscured and nineteenth-century colleges are inevitably judged failures. A national perspective misses a fundamental point: colleges served local, denominational, and regional communities created by agrarian and early industrial economies. Colleges had not "endured in increasing isolation and obscurity," in Lewis Perry's words;[13] rather, they related quite closely to their own communities—as opposed to universities, which were often quite isolated from their immediate communities and regions while participating in a national and international scholarly community.

Finally, higher education between the Civil War and World War I needs to be understood not only in terms of the triumph of modern ideas but also in the context of the ascendancy of a national corporate economy and accompanying changes in the upper and upper-middle classes. Especially in the East, the residential private college became a functional and romantic tool that helped separate affluent Protestant youths from those in other ethnoreligious groups, races, genders, and classes. The academic values that characterize the word "university" defined the subculture of professional academics and the small minority of students who went on to graduate school. The universities sponsored research that has come to have momentous economic, military, social, and cultural impacts. But for most upper- and upper-middle-class Americans, higher education meant a college education and a collegiate social life.

The American college is unique. No European educational system has a similar institution. Even Britain and Germany, the two societies from which Americans have drawn most heavily for educational practices, organize higher education quite differently. Events after the

13. Lewis Perry, *Intellectual Life in America: A History* (New York: Franklin Watts, 1984), 281.

Civil War might have fashioned a system in the United States more similar to that of other Western societies. The small, private liberal arts college could have been reduced to a minor institution by high schools, large universities, urban commuter colleges, normal schools, and professional schools. Instead, certain colleges and university colleges emerged as social arbiters serving the winners of the early rounds of industrialization.

The significance of the four colleges in this study lies less in their typicality than in their roles as leaders in the development of an important institution in higher education—one that brokers considerable power in this country, especially in the East. Outside the Northeast, private colleges have been less prominent, but the model influenced public colleges and universities across the country as intercollegiate athletics, collegiate Gothic architecture, fraternities and sororities, and other collegiate trappings spread west. Thus, this study analyzes the forging of a model that has accrued substantial social power.

Once institutionalized by the most powerful social groups in industrializing America, the collegiate model was adopted by others. An important sign of "making it" in the United States has been access to such colleges. Affluent Americans excluded on racial, religious, ethnic, or gender lines either sought access to the established colleges or created colleges based on a similar model. Jewish families concentrated on gaining access to the Protestant institutions, while Catholics and African Americans tended to build parallel institutions. Women did both. Since World War II religious and racial barriers have been lowered, and traditionally female, Catholic, and African-American colleges increasingly participate in a monolithic prestige structure topped by many of the older, formerly Protestant colleges.

Whereas the college helped homogenize Protestant denominations at the turn of the century, in the late twentieth century it has become a homogenizer across the Protestant-Catholic-Jewish "triple melting pot" and even across racial lines. Its main gatekeeping role has shifted to separating youth by their class origins and destinations. Broadening application pools have further increased the selectivity, and thus the prestige, of colleges like these four. In the late twentieth century, their names remain near the top of academic and social rankings of American colleges.

The accessibility of American colleges, their commitment to a broad education, and their personal attention to students are admirable. Their numbers have helped create unprecedented accessibility to higher education and a public sense of involvement. The private liberal arts colleges have become more meritocratic since World War I, mixing the most academic offspring of the affluent with the most academically successful from less affluent families. The most prestigious colleges have maintained their social and academic reputations by severely limiting their enrollments, thus accentuating their power as gatekeepers.

Colleges play a paradoxical role in American education. They created a popular image of higher education that has encouraged a proportion of youths unmatched in any other country to continue their education. But the most desirable colleges regulate and dispense privilege. As when Daniel Webster defended private privilege through sentimental attachment, for each college "there are those who love it."

Bibliography

General Sources

Adelman, Melvin L. *A Sporting Time: New York City and the Rise of Modern Athletics, 1820–1870*. Urbana: University of Illinois Press, 1986.

Allmendinger, David F. *Paupers and Scholars: The Transformation of Student Life in Nineteenth-Century New England*. New York: St. Martin's Press, 1975.

Angelo, Richard. "A House Is Not a Home." *History of Education Quarterly* 24 (Winter 1984): 609–18.

Association of American Colleges. *Bulletin*. Vols. 1–2 (1915–16).

Association of American Universities. *Journal of Proceedings*. Vols. 1–17 (1901–17).

Association of American University Professors. *Bulletin*. Vols. 1–6 (1915–20).

Auerbach, Jerold. *Unequal Justice: Lawyers and Social Change in Modern America*. New York: Oxford University Press, 1976.

Baltzall, E. Digby. *An American Business Aristocracy*. New York: Collier Books, 1962.

———. *The Protestant Establishment*. New York: Vintage Books, 1964.

Barnes, Sherman B. "The Entry of Science and History into the College Curriculum, 1865–1914." *History of Education Quarterly* 4 (1964): 44–58.

———. "Learning and Piety in Ohio Colleges." *Ohio Historical Quarterly* 69 (October 1960): 327–52.

Bishop, Charles. "Teaching at Johns Hopkins." *History of Education Quarterly* 27 (Winter 1987): 499–515.

Bledstein, Burton J. *The Culture of Professionalism*. New York: W. W. Norton, 1976.

Blumin, Stuart M. *The Emergence of the Middle Class: Social Experience in the American City, 1760–1900*. New York: Cambridge University Press, 1989.

Broome, Edwin C. *A Historical and Critical Discussion of College Admission Requirements*. New York, 1902.

Brubacher, John S., and Willis Rudy. *Higher Education in Transition*. New York: Harper & Row, 1968.

Bruce, Robert V. *The Launching of Modern American Science, 1846–1876*. New York: Knopf, 1987.

Buck, Paul H. *Social Sciences at Harvard, 1860–1920.* Cambridge: Harvard University Press, 1965.

Buckley, William. *God and Man at Yale.* Chicago: Henry Regner, 1951.

Bureau of the Census. *Historical Statistics of the United States.* Washington, D.C.: U.S. Government Printing Office, 1975.

Bureau of the Census. Decennial Census. 1860–1910.

Burke, Colin. *American Collegiate Populations: A Test of the Traditional View.* New York: New York University Press, 1982.

Butts, R. Freeman. *The College Charts Its Course.* New York: McGraw-Hill, 1939.

Calhoun, Daniel H. *Professional Lives in America.* Cambridge: Harvard University Press, 1965.

Canby, Henry S. *Alma Mater: The Gothic Age of the American College.* New York: Farrar & Rinehart, 1936.

Carnegie Foundation for the Advancement of Teaching. *Reports.* Vols. 1–17 (1906–20).

College Association of Pennsylvania. *Proceedings.* Vols. 1–2 (1887–88).

College Association of the Middle States and Maryland. *Proceedings.* Vols. 1–4 (1889–92).

College Entrance Examination Board. *Annual Report of the Secretary.* Vols. 1–13 (1901–13).

Conkin, Paul K. *Gone with the Ivy: A Biography of Vanderbilt University.* Knoxville: University of Tennessee Press, 1985.

Crawford, William H., ed. *The American Colleges.* New York: Henry Holt and Co., 1915.

Cremin, Lawrence A. *American Education: The Metropolitan Experience, 1876–1980.* New York: Harper & Row, 1987.

———. *American Education: The National Experience, 1783–1876.* New York: Harper & Row, 1980.

Curti, Merle. *American Scholarship in the Twentieth Century.* Cambridge: Harvard University Press, 1953.

Curti, Merle, and Roderick Nash. *Philanthropy in the Shaping of American Higher Education.* New Brunswick, N.J.: Rutgers University Press, 1965.

Current, Richard N. *American History.* New York: Knopf, 1987.

DeVane, William C. *Higher Education in Twentieth-Century America.* Cambridge: Harvard University Press, 1965.

Dictionary of American Biography. New York: Scribner's, 1934.

"Editorial." *Educational Review* 5 (January 1893): 90–91.

Education. Vols. 14–27 (1893–97).

Educational Review. Vols. 1–57 (1891–1919).

Fass, Paula. *The Damned and the Beautiful: American Youth in the 1920s.* New York: Oxford University Press, 1977.

Findlay, James F., Jr. *Dwight L. Moody: American Evangelist, 1837–1899.* Chicago: University of Chicago Press, 1969.

Flexner, Abraham. *Medical Education in the United States and Canada.* New York: Carnegie Foundation for the Advancement of Education, 1910.

Garraty, John A., and Robert A. McCaughey. *The American Nation.* New York: Harper & Row, 1987.

Geiger, Roger L. *To Advance Knowledge: The Growth of American Research Universities, 1900–1940.* New York: Oxford University Press, 1986.

General Education Board. *General Education Board: An Account of Its Activities, 1902–1914.* New York, 1915.

———. *Report of the Secretary.* (1914/15–1916/17).
———. *Review and Final Report, 1902–1964.* New York, 1964.
Gilman, Daniel C. *Collection.* Johns Hopkins University Manuscript Collection.
———. "The Idea of a University." *North American Review* 133 (October 1881): 353–67.
Goodchild, John, and Irene Huk. "The American College History." In *Higher Education: Handbook of Theory and Research,* edited by John Smart, 6:201–90. New York: Agathon Press, 1990.
Gordon, Lynn D. *Gender and Higher Education in the Progressive Era.* New Haven: Yale University Press, 1990.
Graham, Patricia. *Community and Class in American Education, 1865–1918.* New York: John Wiley & Sons, 1974.
Gruber, Carole S. *Mars and Minerva: World War I and the Uses of the Higher Learning in America.* Baton Rouge: Louisiana State University Press, 1975.
Guralnick, Stanley M. *Science and the Ante-Bellum American College.* Philadelphia: American Philosophical Society, 1975.
Hall, Peter D. *The Organization of American Culture, 1700–1900.* New York: New York University Press, 1984.
Handlin, Oscar, and Mary Handlin. *The American College and American Culture.* New York: McGraw-Hill, 1970.
Handy, Robert T. *A History of the Churches in the United States and Canada.* New York: Oxford University Press, 1977.
Hatch, Nathan O., ed. *The Professions in American History.* Notre Dame, Ind.: University of Notre Dame Press, 1988.
Heilbroner, Robert L., and Aaron Singer. *The Economic Transformation of America.* New York: Harcourt Brace Jovanovich, 1984.
Henderson, Joseph L. *Admission to College by Certificate.* Teachers College Contributions to Education, no. 50. New York: Teachers College Press, 1912.
Herbst, Jurgen. *From Crisis to Crisis: American College Government, 1636–1819.* Cambridge: Harvard University Press, 1982.
———. *German Historical School in American Scholarship.* Ithaca: Cornell University Press, 1965.
Hofstadter, Richard, and C. DeWitt Hardy. *The Development and Scope of Higher Education in the United States.* New York: Columbia University Press, 1952.
Hofstadter, Richard, and Walter Metzger. *The Development of Academic Freedom in the United States.* New York: Columbia University Press, 1955.
Hofstadter, Richard, and Wilson Smith. *American Higher Education: A Documentary History.* Chicago: University of Chicago Press, 1961.
Hopkins, Charles H. *History of the YMCA in North America.* New York: Association Press, 1951.
Horowitz, Helen L. *Campus Life: Undergraduate Cultures from the End of the Eighteenth Century to the Present.* New York: Knopf, 1987.
Hudson, Winthrop S. *American Protestantism.* Chicago: University of Chicago Press, 1961.
Ingham, John N. *The Iron Barons: A Social Analysis of an American Urban Elite, 1874–1965.* Westport, Conn.: Greenwood Press, 1978.
———. "Masters of the Mill: Innovation and Social Class in the Nineteenth-Century Iron and Steel Industry." Unpublished manuscript, 1986.
Jackson, Kenneth. *Crabgrass Frontier: The Suburbanization of America.* New York: Oxford University Press, 1985.

Jarausch, Konrad H., ed. *The Transformation of Higher Learning, 1860–1930.* Chicago: University of Chicago Press, 1983.

Jencks, Christopher, and David Riesman. *The Academic Revolution.* Chicago: University of Chicago Press, 1968.

Johnson, Rossiter. "College Endowments." *North American Review* 136 (May 1883): 490–96.

Johnson, William R. *Schooled Lawyers: A Study in the Clash of Professional Cultures.* New York: New York University Press, 1978.

Kennedy, David. *Over Here: The First World War and American Society.* New York: Oxford University Press, 1980.

Kett, Joseph. *Rites of Passage: Adolescence in America, 1790 to the Present.* New York: Basic Books, 1977.

Kitzhaber, Albert R. "Rhetoric in American Colleges, 1850–1900." Ph.D. diss., University of Michigan, 1953.

Krug, Edward A. *The Shaping of the American High School, 1880–1920.* Madison: University of Wisconsin Press, 1969.

Lagemann, Ellen Condliffe. *Private Power for the Public Good.* Middletown, Conn.: Wesleyan University Press, 1983.

Lears, Jackson. *No Place of Grace: Antimodernism and the Transformation of American Culture, 1880–1920.* New York: Pantheon Books, 1981.

Leslie, W. Bruce. "The Response of Four Colleges to the Rise of Intercollegiate Athletics, 1865–1915." *Journal of Sport History* 3 (Winter 1976): 213–22.

———. "When Professors Had Servants: Prestige, Pay, and Professionalization, 1860–1917." *History of Higher Education Annual* (1990): 19–30.

Levine, David O. *The American College and the Culture of Aspiration, 1915–1940.* Ithaca: Cornell University Press, 1986.

Limbert, Paul M. *Denominational Policies in Higher Education.* Teachers College Contributions to Education, no. 378. New York: Teachers College Press, 1929.

Long, Clarence D. *Wages and Earnings in the United States, 1860–1890.* Princeton: Princeton University Press, 1960.

Ludmerer, Kenneth M. *Learning to Heal: The Development of American Medical Education.* New York: Basic Books, 1985.

Malick, Herbert. "An Historical Study of Admission Practices in Four-Year Undergraduate Colleges of the U.S.: 1870–1915." Ph.D. diss., Boston College, 1966.

Markowitz, Gerald, and David Rosner. "Doctors in Crisis." *American Quarterly* 25 (March 1973): 83–107.

Marsden, George M. *The Evangelical Mind and the New School Presbyterian Experience.* New Haven: Yale University Press, 1970.

Mattingly, Paul M. *The Classless Profession: American Schoolmen in the Nineteenth Century.* New York: New York University Press, 1975.

May, Henry F. *The End of American Innocence.* Chicago: Quadrangle Paperbacks, 1964.

McGrath, Earl J. "The Control of Higher Education in America." *Educational Record* 18 (April 1936): 259–72.

McKown, Harry C. *The Trend of College Entrance Requirements, 1913–1922.* Bureau of Education Bulletin, no. 35, 1924. Washington, D.C.: U.S. Government Printing Office, 1925.

McLachlan, James. *American Boarding Schools: A Historical Study.* New York: Charles Scribner's Sons, 1970.

———. "The American Colleges in the Nineteenth Century: Toward a Reappraisal." *Teachers College Record* 80 (December 1978): 287–306.

Merritt, Raymond H. *Engineering in American Society, 1850–1875.* Lexington: University of Kentucky Press, 1969.

Middle States Association of Colleges and Secondary Schools. *Proceedings.* Vols. 1–27 (1894–1920).

Modell, John, et al. "Social Change and Transitions to Adulthood in Historical Perspective." *Journal of Family History* 1 (1976): 7–32.

Modell, John, and Tamara Hareven. "Urbanization and the Malleable Household." *Journal of Marriage and Family* 35 (August 1973): 467–79.

Nation. Vols. 1–105 (1870–1917).

National Bureau of Economic Research. *Income in the United States: Its Amount and Distribution, 1909–1919.* New York: Harcourt, Brace, & Co., 1921; reprint, New York: Arno Press, 1975, 102–3.

National Education Association. *Journal of the Proceedings and Addresses.* Vols. 23–58 (1884–1920).

Naylor, Natalie A. "The Theological Seminary in the Configuration of American Higher Education." *History of Education Quarterly* 17 (Spring 1977): 17–30.

New York Observer. Vols. 72 and 73 (1894 and 1895).

North American Review. Vols. 176–83 (1903–6).

Norton, Fred L. *A College of Colleges.* New York: Fleming B. Revell, 1889.

Norton, Mary B., et al. *A People and a Nation.* Vol. 2, 2d ed. Boston: Houghton Mifflin, 1986.

Novick, Peter. *That Noble Dream: The "Objectivity Question" and the American Historical Profession.* New York: Cambridge University Press, 1988.

Oleson, Alexandra, and Sanborn C. Brown, eds. *The Pursuit of Knowledge in the Early American Republic.* Baltimore: Johns Hopkins University Press, 1976.

Oren, Dan A. *Joining the Club: A History of Jews and Yale.* New Haven: Yale University Press, 1985.

Palmieri, Patricia. "In 'Adamless Eden': The Women's Intellectual Community at Wellesley." Unpublished manuscript.

Perry, Lewis. *Intellectual Life in America: A History.* New York: Franklin Watts, 1984.

Peterson, George E. *The New England College in the Age of the University.* Amherst, Mass.: Amherst College Press, 1964.

Pfinster, Allan O. "The Role of the Liberal Arts College." *Journal of Higher Education* 55 (March/April 1984): 145–70.

Porter, Noah. *American Colleges and the American Public.* New York: Charles Scribner, 1878.

Potts, David. *Baptist Colleges in the Development of American Society, 1812–1861.* New York: Garland, 1988.

———. "Curriculum and Enrollments." *History of Higher Education Annual* 1 (1981): 88–109.

———. "Road to Repute: Church, Coeducation, and Campus at Turn-of-the-Century Wesleyan." Paper presented at the Annual Meeting of the History of Education Society, Atlanta, Ga., November 1990.

———. *Wesleyan University, 1831–1910.* New Haven: Yale University Press, 1992.

Pritchett, Henry. "The Policy of the Carnegie Foundation." *Educational Review* 32 (June 1906): 83–93.

Read, Ira. "Church and College in the South." Paper presented at the Annual

Meeting of the History of Education Society, Atlanta, Ga., November 1990.

Ringer, Fritz K. *Education and Society in Modern Europe*. Bloomington: Indiana University Press, 1979.

Rosenberg, Rosalind. "The Limits of Access: The History of Coeducation in America." In *Women and Higher Education in American History*, edited by John Faragher and Florence Howe, 107–29. New York: W. W. Norton, 1988.

Rudolph, Frederick. *The American College and University*. New York: Vintage Books, 1962.

———. *Curriculum: A History of the American Undergraduate Course of Study Since 1636*. San Francisco: Jossey-Bass, 1977.

Schmidt, George P. *Liberal Arts College*. New Brunswick, N.J.: Rutgers University Press, 1957.

Schurman, Jacob. "The Ideal College Education." *Proceedings of the Annual Convention of the College Association of the Middle States and Maryland* 3 (1891): 64–73.

Scott, Donald M. *From Office to Profession: The New England Ministry, 1750–1850*. Philadelphia: University of Pennsylvania Press, 1978.

Sharpless, Isaac. *The American College*. The American Book Series. Garden City, N.Y.: Doubleday, Page, 1915.

Silva, Edward T., and Sheila A. Slaughter. "Against the Grain: Toward an Alternative Interpretation of Academic Professionalization." *History of Higher Education Annual* 2 (1982): 128–70.

———. *Serving Power: The Making of the Academic Social Science Expert*. Westport, Conn.: Greenwood Press, 1984.

Slosson, Edwin E. *Great American Universities*. New York: Macmillan, 1910.

Smith, Ronald A. *Sports and Freedom: The Rise of Big-Time College Athletics*. New York: Oxford University Press, 1988.

Smith, Timothy L. "The Religious Foundations of Higher Education in Illinois." Unpublished paper, ca. 1969.

Solberg, Winton U. *The University of Illinois, 1867–1894*. Urbana: University of Illinois Press, 1968.

Solomon, Barbara M. *In the Company of Educated Women*. New Haven: Yale University Press, 1985.

Soltow, Lee. *Men and Wealth in the United States, 1850–1870*. New Haven: Yale University Press, 1975.

Stameshkin, David M. *The Town's College: Middlebury College, 1800–1915*. Middlebury, Vt.: Middlebury College Press, 1985.

Starr, Paul. *The Social Transformation of American Medicine*. New York: Basic Books, 1987.

Stevenson, Louise L. "Between the Old-Time College and the Modern University: Noah Porter and the New Haven Scholars." *History of Higher Education Annual* 3 (1983): 39–57.

———. "Preparing for Public Life: The Collegiate Students at New York University, 1832–1881." In *The University and the City*, edited by Thomas Bender. New York: Oxford University Press, 1988.

———. *Scholarly Means to Evangelical Ends: The New Haven Scholars and the Transformation of Higher Learning in America, 1830–1890*. Baltimore: Johns Hopkins University Press, 1986.

Storr, Richard J. *Beginning of Graduate Education in America.* Chicago: University of Chicago Press, 1953.

Stricker, Frank. "American Professors in the Progressive Era: Incomes, Aspirations, and Professionalism." *Journal of Interdisciplinary History* 19 (Autumn 1988): 231–57.

Synnott, Marcia G. *The Half-Opened Door: Discrimination and Admissions at Harvard, Yale, and Princeton, 1900–1970.* Westport, Conn.: Greenwood Press, 1979.

Tewksbury, Donald G. *The Founding of American Colleges and Universities Before the Civil War.* New York: Teachers College Bureau of Publications, 1932.

Thelin, John R. *Higher Education and Its Useful Past.* Cambridge: Schenckman Publishing Co., 1982.

Thomas, Russell Brown. *The Search for a Common Learning: General Education, 1800–1960.* The Carnegie Series in American Education. New York: McGraw-Hill, 1962.

Thornburg, Opal. *Earlham: The Story of the College, 1847–1962.* Richmond, Ind.: Earlham College Press, 1963.

Tobias, Marilyn. *Old Dartmouth on Trial: The Transformation of the Academic Community in Nineteenth-Century America.* New York: New York University Press, 1982.

United States Bureau of Education. *A History of Higher Education in Pennsylvania.* Contributions to American Educational History. Washington, D.C.: U.S. Government Printing Office, 1902.

Veysey, Laurence R. *The Emergence of the American University.* Chicago: University of Chicago Press, 1965.

———. "The History of Higher Education." *Reviews in American History* 10 (December 1982): 281–91.

———. Review of *Glimpses of the Harvard Past. History of Education Quarterly* 27 (Summer 1987): 272–75.

Warner, Michael. "Professionalization and the Rewards of Literature." *Criticism* 27 (Winter 1985): 1–28.

Webster, David S. "The Bureau of Education's Suppressed Rating of Colleges, 1911–1912." *History of Education Quarterly* 24 (Winter 1964): 499–511.

Wechsler, Harold. *The Qualified Student: A History of Selective College Admission in America.* New York: John Wiley & Sons, 1977.

Wiebe, Robert H. *The Search for Order, 1877–1920.* The Making of America Series. New York: Hill and Wang, 1967.

Zimmerman, Joan G. "College Culture in the Midwest, 1890–1930." Ph.D. diss., University of Virginia, 1978.

Zunz, Olivier. *Making America Corporate, 1870–1920.* Chicago: University of Chicago Press, 1990.

Bucknell University

American Baptist Education Society. *Annual Meeting.* New York, 1896.

American Baptist Education Society. Correspondence, 1898–1903. American Baptist Historical Society, Rochester, N.Y.

The Bucknellians. "Publicity Letters" (1908–9). Bucknell University Archives.

Bucknell University. *Alumni Catalogue.* Lewisburg, Pa., 1915, 1921, 1926.

———. *Bucknell University Bulletin.* (1901–19).

———. *Catalogue* (formerly *Catalogue of the University of Lewisburg*, until 1887; 1870–1923).
———. *Charter and By-Laws.* Lewisburg, Pa., 1956.
———. *John Howard Harris: An Appreciation.* Lewisburg, Pa., 1924.
———. *Memorials of Bucknell University, 1846–1896.* Lewisburg, Pa., 1896.
———. *Memorials of Bucknell University, 1919–1931.* Lewisburg, Pa., 1931.
———. "Notebook of Applicants, 1902–1903." Bucknell University Archives.
———. *Quinquennial Catalogue.* Lewisburg, Pa., 1900.
Bucknell University, Board of Trustees. Minutes, 1866–1917. Bucknell University Archives.
Bucknell University, Faculty. Minutes, 1874–1917. Bucknell University Archives.
Bucknell University, YMCA. Minutes, 1882–1916. Bucknell University Archives.
———. Papers, 1901–8. Bucknell University Archives.
College Herald. Vols. 1–9 (1870–80). Lewisburg, Pa.: Theta-Alpha and Euepia Literary Societies.
Decker, John O. *Alpha-Phi Chapter of the Kappa Sigma Fraternity, 1896–1911.* Williamsport, Pa.: Grit Publishing Co., 1911.
Fleming, Sanford. "American Baptists and Higher Education." Unpublished manuscript, American Baptist Historical Association, Rochester, N.Y., 1965.
Harris, John H. Papers. Bucknell University Archives.
———. "Remarks." *Proceedings of the Middle States Association of Colleges and Secondary Schools* 17 (1903): 79–81.
———. "The Responsibility of the College for the Moral Conduct of the Student." In Middle States Association of Colleges and Secondary Schools, *Proceedings* 20 (1906): 93–101.
———. *Thirty Years as President of Bucknell with Baccalaureate and Other Addresses.* Washington, D.C., 1926.
Hill, David Jayne. As It Seemed to Me. Ca. 1930. University of Rochester Library Special Collections. Typescript.
———. *Lecture Notes on Economics and Politics.* Lewisburg, Pa., 1884.
———. Letters to Daniel C. Gilman, 26 March, 20 June, and 10 July 1888. Johns Hopkins University Manuscript Collection.
———. Papers. Bucknell University Archives.
———. Papers, 1877–92. University of Rochester Library Special Collections.
———. Scrapbook, 1850–80. Bucknell University Archives.
Kalp, Lois. *A Town on the Susquehanna, 1769–1975.* Lewisburg, Pa.: Colonial Printing Co., 1980.
Loomis, Justin R. "Address." In National Baptist Educational Convention, *Proceedings* (1870): 51–56.
———. Papers. Bucknell University Archives.
Morehouse, H. L. Letter to President John H. Harris, 10 May 1899. Bucknell University Archives.
National Baptist. Vols. 5–19 (1869–83).
National Baptist Educational Convention. *Proceedings* (1870 and 1872).
Newman, Albert H. *A History of the Baptist Churches in the United States.* The American Church History Series, vol. 2. New York: Christian Literature Co., 1894.
Northumberland Baptist Association. *Minutes* (1881–1916).

Oliphant, J. Orin. *Beginnings of Bucknell University: A Sampling of the Documents*. Lewisburg, Pa.: Bucknell University Press, 1954.

———. *The Library of Bucknell University*. Lewisburg, Pa.: Bucknell University Press, 1962.

———. *The Rise of Bucknell University*. New York: Appleton-Century-Crofts, 1965.

Orange and Blue. Vols. 1–19 (1897–1916).

Parkman, Aubrey. "David Jayne Hill." Ph.D. diss., University of Rochester, 1961.

———. *David Jayne Hill and the Problem of World Peace*. Lewisburg, Pa.: Bucknell University Press, 1975.

Potts, David B. *Baptist Colleges in the Development of American Society, 1812–1861*. New York: Garland Press, 1988.

Rice, John Winter. *A History of the Teaching of Biology at Bucknell University*. Lewisburg, Pa., 1952.

Rosenn, G. J. *Intercollegiate Athletic Calendar, 1907–1908*. Bucknell ed. New York, 1907.

Snyder, Charles M. *Union County, Pennsylvania: A Bicentennial History*. Lewisburg, Pa.: Colonial Printing House, 1976.

Theiss, Lewis Edwin. *Centennial History of Bucknell University, 1846–1946*. Williamsport, Pa.: Grit Publishing Co., 1946.

Theta Alpha Literary Society. Minutes, 1871–1907. Bucknell University Archives.

Torbet, Robert G. *A Social History of the Philadelphia Baptist Association, 1707–1740*. Philadelphia, 1944.

University Mirror. Vols. 1–7 (1882–90).

University of Lewisburg, Board of Curators. Minutes, 1871–81. Bucknell University Archives.

Warfel, Harry R. *The Demies, 1899–1949*. Lewisburg, Pa., 1949.

Franklin and Marshall College

Appel, Theodore. "Creation and Cosmogony." *Mercersburg Review* 24 (January 1877): 123–38.

———. *The Life and Work of John Williamson Nevin*. Philadelphia: Reformed Church Publication House, 1889.

Apple, Henry H. *Report of the Board of Trustees of Franklin and Marshall College to the Eastern, Potomac, and Pittsburgh Synods*. Lancaster, Pa., 1916.

———. *Report of the President of Franklin and Marshall College*. (1910–22).

Apple, Thomas G. "The Idea of a Liberal Education." In College Association of Pennsylvania, *Proceedings* 1 (1887): 12–14.

Brubaker, John H., III. *Hullabaloo Nevonia: An Anecdotal History of Student Life at Franklin and Marshall College*. Lancaster, Pa.: Franklin and Marshall College, 1987.

College Days. Vols. 1–5 (1873–79).

Dubbs, Joseph Henry. *History of Franklin and Marshall College*. Lancaster, Pa.: Franklin and Marshall Alumni Association, 1903.

———. *A History of the Reformed Church German*. The American Church History Series. New York: Christian Literature Co., 1895.

The F and M Weekly. Vol. 1–25 (1891–1915).

Franklin and Marshall College. *Catalogue* (1873–1922).

———. *Catalogue of Officers and Students, 1787–1903*. Lancaster, Pa., 1903.

———. *Charters and Acts of Assembly Relating to Franklin and Marshall College*. Compiled in Lancaster, Pa., 1934.

Franklin and Marshall College, Alumni Association. Letter to Hon. John Cessna, President of the Board of Trustees, 24 January 1866. Franklin and Marshall Archives.

———. *List of Graduates*. Lancaster, Pa., 1900.

———. *Obituary Record* (1897–1909).

———. *Report* (1902–5).

Franklin and Marshall College, Board of Trustees. Minutes, 1866–1922. Franklin and Marshall Archives and President's Office.

Franklin and Marshall College, Class of 1872. "Petition to the Faculty of Franklin and Marshall College." 21 May 1872. Franklin and Marshall Archives.

Franklin and Marshall College, Diagnothian and Goethean Literary Societies. *The College Student: A Monthly Magazine* (1881–1915).

Franklin and Marshall College, Faculty. Minutes, 1872–1922. Franklin and Marshall Archives.

Franklin and Marshall College, Junior Class. *Oriflamme* (1883–1916).

Franklin and Marshall Paper. Lancaster, Pa., 1936.

Girvin, J. Barry. "The Life of William U. Hensel." *Journal of the Lancaster County Historical Society* 70 (1966): 186–248.

Good, Rev. James I. *History of the Reformed Church in the U.S. in the Nineteenth Century*. New York: Board of Publications of the Reformed Church in America, 1911.

Hartman, Charles Stahr. "Franklin and Marshall Academy, 1872–1943." Master's essay, Johns Hopkins University, 1948.

Hensel, William. *A Message to the Friends of Franklin and Marshall in the Reformed Church*. Philadelphia, 1914.

Hiester, Anselm. "Political Economy." *Reformed Church Review* 7 (April 1903): 226–42.

Ireland, Owen S. "The Crux of Politics: Religion and Party in Pennsylvania, 1778–1789." *William and Mary Quarterly* 42 (October 1985): 453–75.

Kershner, Jefferson. "The Moral Value of College Work." *Reformed Church Review* 14 (December 1910): 429–49.

Klein, Frederic S. *Since 1887, Franklin and Marshall College Story*. Lancaster, Pa.: Commercial Printing House, 1968.

———. *Spiritual and Education Background of Franklin and Marshall College*. Lancaster, Pa.: Commercial Printing House, 1939.

Klein, H.M.J. *History of Franklin and Marshall College, 1787–1948*. Lancaster, Pa., 1952.

———. *The History of the Eastern Synod of the Reformed Church in the United States*. Lancaster, Pa.: Rudisill and Smith Co., 1943.

Klein, H.M.J., and Richard D. Altick. *Professor Koeppen*. Franklin and Marshall College Studies, no. 1. Lancaster, Pa., 1938.

Loose, John W. *Heritage of Lancaster*. Woodland Hills, Calif.: Windsor Publications, 1978.

Mays, Cyrus. "A Gymnasium or a University?" *Mercersburg Review* 19 (January 1872): 32–49.

Mercersburg Review. Vols. 1–25 (1849–78).

Mull, George. "The Study of English Literature." *Reformed Quarterly Review* 38 (October 1889): 516–32.

Nichols, James H. *Romanticism in American Theology: Nevin and Schaff at Mercersburg*. Chicago: University of Chicago Press, 1961.

Ranck, Samuel. "The Literary Societies. . . ." *Reformed Church Review* 7 (1903): 243–54.

———. "The Oxford Idea in Education." *Reformed Church Review* 7 (1903): 24–30.

Reformed Church in the United States. *Acts and Proceedings of the Eastern Synod* (1889–1916).

———. *Acts and Proceedings of the Synod* (1867–88).

Reformed Church Messenger (1870–1917).

Reformed Church Review. Vols. 1–20 (1897–1916).

Reformed Quarterly Review. Vols. 26–43 (1879–96).

Richards, George W. "The Mercersburg Theology—Its Purpose and Principles." *Church History* 20 (September 1951): 42–55.

Schaeffer, Rev. N. C. Letter to President T. G. Apple, 9 June 1886. Franklin and Marshall Archives.

Schiedt, Richard. "The Attitude of Present-Day Scientists toward Religion." *Reformed Church Review* 16 (January 1912): 46–70.

———. "College-Need and College Needs." *Reformed Quarterly Review* 41 (January 1894): 117–28.

———. "Germany and the Formative Forces of the War." *Reformed Church Review* 19 (1915): 19–48.

———. "The Natural Sciences Then and Now." *Reformed Church Review* 7 (April 1903): 196–213.

Stahr, John. "Evolutionary Theories and Theology." *Mercersburg Review* 19 (July 1872): 439–50.

———. "Remarks." In College Association of the Middle States and Maryland, *Proceedings* 22 (1908): 9–10.

Steiner, Lewis. "The American College on the Defensive." *Mercersburg Review* 18 (April 1871): 182–95.

The Student Weekly (1915–20).

Unsigned [probably Theodore Appel]. "The Vocation and Responsibilities of the American College." *Mercersburg Review* 24 (October 1877): 614–38.

Weaver, Glenn. "The German Reformed Church and the Home Missionary Movement Before 1863: A Study in Cultural and Religious Isolation." *Church History* 22 (December 1953): 298–313.

Winpenny, Thomas R. *Industrial Progress and Human Welfare: The Rise of the Factory System in Nineteenth-Century Lancaster*. Washington, D.C.: University Press of America, 1982.

Young, Henry J. *Historical Account of the Goethean Literary Society, 1835–1940*. Franklin and Marshall College Studies, no. 3. Lancaster, Pa., 1941.

Princeton University

Alexander, James W. "Undergraduate Life at Princeton—Old and New." *Scribner's Magazine* 21 (June 1897): 663–91.

Alexander, Stephen. *Address at the Laying of the Cornerstone of the Astronomical Observatory*. Newark, N.J., 1867.

Atwater, Lyman H. Lecture Notes on Political Economy. Recorded by William Barricklo, 1877–78. Princeton University Manuscript Collection.

———. "Proposed Reforms in Collegiate Education." *Princeton Review*, n.s., 10 (July 1882): 100–120.

Baker, Ray Stannard. *Woodrow Wilson: Life and Letters*. Vol. 1, *Youth, 1856–1890*; Vol. 2, *Princeton, 1890–1910*. Garden City, N.Y.: Doubleday, Page, 1927.

Beam, Jacob N. *American Whig Society*. Princeton: Privately printed, 1933.

Bragdon, Henry Wilkinson. *Woodrow Wilson: The Academic Years*. Cambridge: Belknap Press of Harvard University Press, 1967.

Brown, Coleman P. *A Social Plan of Undergraduate Life*. Princeton, 1923.

Collins, Varnum L. *Princeton*. American College and University Series. New York: Oxford University Press, 1914.

Condit, Kenneth W. *History of the Engineering School of Princeton University, 1875–1955*. Princeton: Princeton University Press, 1962.

Conklin, Edwin G. Papers. Princeton University Archives.

———. "The Place of the Physical and Natural Sciences in the College Curriculum." In *The American Colleges*, edited by William H. Crawford, 59–116. New York: Henry Holt, 1915.

Craig, Hardin. *Woodrow Wilson at Princeton*. Norman: University of Oklahoma Press, 1960.

Daily Princetonian (1877–1917).

Duffield, John T. *Historical Discourse on the Second Presbyterian Church of Princeton*. Princeton, 1897.

Garfield, Harry. Collection. Library of Congress.

Goldman, Eric F. *John Bach McMaster*. Philadelphia: University of Pennsylvania Press, 1943.

———. "The Princeton Period of John Bach McMaster." *Proceedings of the New Jersey Historical Society* 57 (January 1939): 214–30.

Guyot, Arnold. Lecture Notes on Geology. Recorded by William Barricklo, 1877–88. Princeton University Manuscript Collection.

Hibben, John G. *Essentials of a Liberal Education*. Princeton, 1912.

———. Papers. Princeton University Manuscript Collection.

Hoeveler, J. David. *James McCosh and the Scottish Intellectual Tradition: From Glasgow to Princeton*. Princeton: Princeton University Press, 1981.

Hopkins, E. M. "Social Life at Princeton." *Lippincott's Monthly Magazine* 39 (1887): 677–87.

Illick, Joseph E. "The Reception of Darwinism at the Theological Seminary and the College at Princeton, N.J." *Journal of the Presbyterian Historical Society* 38 (September and October 1960): 152–65, 234–43.

Irwin, Wallace. *Shame of the Colleges*. New York: Outing Publishing Co., 1906.

Journal of Presbyterian History (formerly *Journal of the Presbyterian Historical Society*, until 1962). Vols. 1–48. Philadelphia: Department of History of the Presbyterian Church, 1900–1970.

Kerr, Hugh T., ed. *Sons of the Prophets*. Princeton: Princeton University Press, 1963.

Landsman, Ned C. *Scotland and Its First American Colony, 1683–1765*. Princeton: Princeton University Press, 1985.

Lane, Wheaton J. *Pictorial History of Princeton*. Princeton: Princeton University Press, 1947.

Leslie, W. Bruce. "James McCosh in Scotland." *Princeton University Library Chronicle* 36 (Autumn 1974): 47–60.

Link, Arthur S., ed. *The Papers of Woodrow Wilson*. Vols. 1, 4–20. Princeton: Princeton University Press, 1966–.

———. "That Cobb Interview." *Journal of American History* 72 (June 1985): 13.
———. *Wilson: The Road to the White House*. Princeton: Princeton University Press, 1947.
Loetscher, Frederick. "A Century of New Jersey Presbyterianism." Typescript of address, 16 October 1922. Presbyterian Historical Society.
Loetscher, Lefferts A. *The Broadening Church*. Philadelphia: University of Pennsylvania Press, 1954.
Marsden, Donald. *The Long Kickline: A History of the Princeton Triangle Club*. Princeton, 1968.
Maxwell, Howard B. "The Formative Years of the University Alumni Movement as Illustrated by Studies of the University of Michigan and Columbia, Princeton, and Yale Universities." Ph.D. diss., University of Michigan, 1965.
McCosh, James. Letter to Daniel C. Gilman, 11 December 1876. Johns Hopkins University Manuscript Collection.
———. Papers. Princeton University Archives.
———. Papers. Princeton University Manuscript Collection.
Miller, Howard. *The Revolutionary College: American Presbyterian Higher Education, 1707–1837*. New York: New York University Press, 1976.
Mizener, Arthur. *The Far Side of Paradise*. Boston: Houghton Mifflin, 1949.
Mulder, John M. *Woodrow Wilson: The Years of Preparation*. Princeton: Princeton University Press, 1978.
Murray, James O. Lecture Notes on English Literature. Recorded by William Barricklo, 1877–88. Princeton University Manuscript Collection.
Myers, William S., ed. *Woodrow Wilson: Some Princeton Memories*. Princeton: Princeton University Press, 1946.
Nassau Literary Magazine (1842–1920).
New Princeton Review. Vols. 1–6 (1886–88).
Noll, Mark A. *Princeton and the Republic, 1768–1822*. Princeton: Princeton University Press, 1989.
Ormond, Alexander T. "The Aim of Philosophy Teaching in American Colleges." *Proceedings of the Middle States Association of Colleges and Secondary Schools* 13 (1899): 23–29.
———. "University Ideals at Princeton." *Journal of the Proceedings and Addresses of the National Education Association* 36 (1897): 355–57.
Osborn, Henry Fairfield. "The Seven Factors of Education." *Educational Review* 32 (June 1906): 56–82.
Osborne, Frederick S. "Two Hundred Years of Princeton University." *Journal of the Presbyterian Historical Society* 24 (June 1946): 90–96.
Patton, Francis Landey. Papers. Princeton University Archives.
———. *Speech: March 1, 1888*. New York: Princeton Club of New York, 1888.
Perry, Bliss. *And Gladly Teach*. Cambridge, Mass.: Riverside Press, 1935.
———. "The Life of a College President." *Scribner's Magazine* 22 (1897): 512–18.
Philadelphian. Vols. 1–2. Princeton: Philadelphian Society, 1887–88.
Philadelphian. New series, vol. 1 (1902).
Philadelphian Bulletin. Vols. 1–2 (1891–92).
Philadelphian Society. *Constitution and By-Laws*. Princeton, 1874.
———. *One Hundred Years, 1825–1925*. Princeton, 1925.
———. *Report of the General Secretary, 1915–1916*.
Presbyterian and Reformed Review. Vols. 1–13 (1890–1902).

Presbytery of New Brunswick. Minutes, 1876–1902. Presbyterian Historical Society, Philadelphia.
Princeton Alumni Weekly (1900–1919).
Princeton College. *Alumni Directory*. Princeton, 1888.
———. *Catalogue of the College of New Jersey*. Princeton, 1844/45–1895/96.
———. *Inauguration of James McCosh*. New York: Carter and Bros., 1868.
———. *Inauguration of Rev. F. L. Patton*. New York: Gray Bros., 1888.
———. *Opening Exercises of the Gymnasium*. Princeton, 1870.
———. *Plan for a Partial Endowment of the College of New Jersey* (1853).
———. *Replies of the Professors and Tutors of Princeton College to the Questions Addressed to Them by the Board of Trustees*. Elizabeth, N.J.: Journal Publishing House, 1881.
Princeton College Bulletin. Vols. 1–16 (1889–1904).
Princeton College, Class of 1891. *Triennial Report of the Class of 1891*. New York: E. Scott Co., 1894.
Princeton University. *Annual Report of the President* (1904–16).
———. *Catalogue*. Princeton, 1896/97–1921/22.
———. *Catalogue of the American Whig Society* (1865, 1872, 1883, 1893, 1914).
———. *Charters and By-Laws of the Trustees*. Princeton: Princeton University Press, 1883 and 1906.
———. *General Catalogue, 1746–1896*. Princeton: Princeton University Press, 1896.
———. *General Catalogue, 1746–1906*. Princeton: Princeton University Press, 1908.
———. *Nassau Herald* (1885–1915).
———. *Report of the Librarian*. Princeton, 1921.
———. *Undergraduate Announcement* (1913/14, 1921/22).
Princeton University, Academic Faculty. Minutes, 21 September 1898–12 December 1904. Princeton University Archives.
Princeton University, Class of 1884. *Fifty Year Record*. Princeton: Princeton University Press, 1937.
Princeton University, Class of 1899. *Record*. Privately printed, 1909.
Princeton University, Class of 1912. *The Twenty-Five Year Record*. Princeton: Princeton University Press, 1937.
Princeton University, Departments of English and Modern Languages. *Announcement* (1913/14).
Princeton University, Faculty. Minutes, 1870–1916. Princeton University Archives.
Princeton University, School of Science Faculty. Minutes, 21 September 1898–28 November 1904. Princeton University Archives.
Princeton University, Trustees. Minutes, 1870–1916. Princeton University Archives.
Robson, David W. *Educating Republicans: The College in the Era of the American Revolution*. Westport, Conn.: Greenwood Press, 1985.
Savage, Henry Littleton. *Nassau Hall, 1756–1956*. Princeton: Princeton University Press, 1956.
Scott, William B. Collection. Princeton University Manuscript Collection.
———. Papers. Princeton University Archives.
———. Some Memoirs of a Paleontologist. Ca. 1930. Princeton University Manuscript Collection. Typescript.

Segal, Howard. "The Patton-Wilson Succession." *Princeton Alumni Weekly* (6 November 1978): 20–24.

Shields, Charles W. Lecture Notes on History. Recorded by William Barricklo, 1877–78. Princeton University Manuscript Collection.

Sloan, Douglas. *The Scottish Enlightenment and the American College Ideal.* New York: Teachers College Press, 1971.

Sloane, William M., ed. *The Life of James McCosh.* New York: Charles Scribner's Sons, 1896.

Smith, Gary S. "Calvinists and Evolution, 1870–1920." *Journal of Presbyterian History* 61 (Fall 1983): 335–52.

Thompson, Robert Ellis. *A History of the Presbyterian Churches in the United States.* The American Church History Series, vol. 6. New York: Christian Literature Co., 1895.

Thorp, Willard. "The Cleveland-West Correspondence." *Princeton University Library Chronicle* 31 (Winter 1970): 69–102.

———, ed. *Lives of Eighteen from Princeton.* Princeton: Princeton University Press, 1946.

———, et al. *The Princeton Graduate School.* Princeton: Princeton University Press, 1978.

Van Dyke, Paul. "Are We Spoiling Our Boys Who Have the Best Chances in Life?" *Scribner's Magazine* 46 (1909): 501–4.

Veysey, Laurence. "The Academic Mind of Woodrow Wilson." *Mississippi Valley Historical Review* 49 (March 1963): 613–34.

Vreeland, William. "Modern Languages in Secondary Schools and Colleges." *Proceedings of the Middle States Association of Colleges and Secondary Schools* 17 (1904): 30–40.

Wertenbaker, Thomas J. "The College of New Jersey and the Presbyterians." *Journal of the Presbyterian Historical Society* 36 (December 1958): 209–16.

———. *Princeton, 1746–1896.* Princeton: Princeton University Press, 1946.

West, Andrew F. *American Liberal Education.* New York: Charles Scribner's Sons, 1907.

———. *The Graduate College of Princeton.* Princeton: Princeton University Press, 1913.

———. "Must the Classics Go?" *North American Review* 138 (February 1884): 151–62.

———. Papers. Princeton University Archives.

———. "The Tutorial System in College." *Educational Review* 32 (December 1906): 500–514.

———. "What Should Be the Length of the College Course?" In Middle States Association of Colleges and Secondary Schools, *Proceedings* 17 (1903): 53–60.

Williamson, Wallace J. *The Halls.* Princeton, 1947.

Wilson, Woodrow. *College and State.* Vols. 1 and 2. New York: Harper Bros., 1925.

———. Papers. Library of Congress Manuscript Division.

———. "Should an Antecedent Liberal Education Be Required of Students in Law, Medicine, and Theology?" *Proceedings of the National Education Association* 32 (1893): 112–17.

———. "What Is College For?" *Scribner's Magazine* 46 (November 1909): 570–77.

Swarthmore College

An Adventure in Education: Swarthmore College under Frank Aydelotte. New York: Macmillan, 1941.

Appleton, William Hyde. Presidential Papers. Friends Historical Library.

Aydelotte, Frank. *Breaking the Academic Lock Step*. New York: Harper Bros., 1944.

Babbidge, Homer D., Jr. "Swarthmore College in the Nineteenth Century: A Quaker Experience in Education." Ph.D. diss., Yale University, 1953.

Benjamin, Philip S. *The Philadelphia Quakers in the Industrial Age, 1865–1920*. Philadelphia: Temple University Press, 1976.

Birdsall, William W. Presidential Papers. Friends Historical Library.

Clark, Burton. *The Distinctive College: Antioch, Reed, and Swarthmore*. Chicago: Adams Publishing Co., 1970.

DeGarmo, Charles. Presidential Papers. Friends Historical Library.

Doherty, Robert W. *The Hicksite Separation*. New Brunswick, N.J.: Rutgers University Press, 1967.

Enion, Ruth C. "The Intellectual Incubation of a Quaker College, 1869–1903." Master's thesis, Swarthmore College, 1944.

Friends Intelligencer. Vols. 26–72 (1869–1915).

Hull, William I. "History of Swarthmore College." Ca. 1940. Friends Historical Library. Typescript.

James, Sydney V. *A People Among Peoples*. Cambridge: Harvard University Press, 1963.

Johnson, Emily Cooper. *Dean Bond of Swarthmore*. Philadelphia: J. B. Lippincott & Co., n.d.

Jones, Rufus M. *Haverford College: A History and an Interpretation*. New York: Macmillan, 1933.

Kannerstein, Gregory, ed. *The Spirit and the Intellect: Haverford College, 1833–1983*. Haverford, Pa.: Haverford College, 1983.

Magill, Edward. Letters to Daniel C. Gilman, 12, 14, and 17 December 1894. Johns Hopkins University Manuscript Collection.

———. Papers. Friends Historical Library.

———. Presidential Papers. Friends Historical Library.

———. "The Proper Relation of Colleges to the Educational Institutions of the State." In Association of Pennsylvania Colleges, *Proceedings* 1 (1887): 10–12.

———. *Sixty-Five Years in the Life of a Teacher, 1841–1906*. Boston: Houghton Mifflin, 1907.

Moore, John M., ed. *Friends in the Delaware Valley: Philadelphia Yearly Meeting, 1681–1981*. Haverford, Pa.: Friends Historical Association, 1981.

Parrish, Edward. *An Essay on Education in the Society of Friends*. Philadelphia: J. B. Lippincott & Co., 1866.

Parrish, Edward. Presidential Papers. Friends Historical Society.

The Phoenix. Vols. 1–36 (1881–1917).

Russell, Elbert. *The History of Quakerism*. New York: Macmillan, 1942.

Society of Friends. *Proceedings of the Friends General Conference* (1904, 1906).

Swain, Joseph. Presidential Papers. Friends Historical Library.

———. "Remarks." *Proceedings of the Middle States Association of Colleges and Secondary Schools* 16 (1902): 42.

———. "Remarks." *Friends Intelligencer* 60 (20 June 1903): 393.

———. "University Ideals at Stanford." *Proceedings of the NEA* (1897).
———. "Utilization of the College Fraternity in Student Life." *Proceedings of the Middle States Association of Colleges and Secondary Schools* 23 (1909): 32–34.
Swarthmore College. *Annual Catalogue* (1870/71–1919/20).
———. Deans Papers. Friends Historical Library.
———. Faculty Papers. Friends Historical Library.
———. *Papers on the Bequest of the Late Anna T. Jeanes*. Philadelphia: Franklin Printing Co., 1907.
———. *Proceedings of the Inauguration of Swarthmore College*. Philadelphia, 1869.
———. *The Register of Swarthmore College, 1862–1914*. Swarthmore, Pa., 1914.
Swarthmore College, Advisory Athletic Council. Papers. Friends Historical Library.
Swarthmore College, Athletic Advisory Board. Minutes, 1913–17. Friends Historical Library.
Swarthmore College, Athletic Committee. Minutes and Correspondence, 1911–13. Friends Historical Library.
Swarthmore College, Board of Managers. Minutes, 1862–1918. Friends Historical Library.
Swarthmore College Bulletin. Vols. 1–17 (1903–20).
Swarthmore College, Committee on Instruction. Minutes, 1885–1916. Friends Historical Library.
Swarthmore College, Eunomian Literary Society. *Constitution and By-Laws* (1900).
———. Minutes, 1891–1910. Friends Historical Library.
Swarthmore College, Executive Committee. Minutes, 1869–1918. Friends Historical Library.
Swarthmore College, Faculty. Minutes, 1877–1917. Friends Historical Library.
———. Papers. Friends Historical Library.
Swarthmore College, Household Committee. Minutes and Correspondence, 1911–18. Friends Historical Library.
Swarthmore College, Stockholders. *Minutes of the Annual Meeting of the Stockholders* (1869–1911).
Swarthmore Monthly Meeting. Membership, 1893–1930. Friends Historical Library.
Thomas, Allen C., and Richard Henry Thomas. *A History of the Society of Friends*. The American Church History Series, vol. 12. New York: Christian Literature Co., 1894.
Walton, Richard J. *Swarthmore College: An Informal History*. Swarthmore, Pa.: Swarthmore College, 1986.

Index